Yale Historical Publications

Lynn Berat

Walvis Bay

Decolonization and International Law

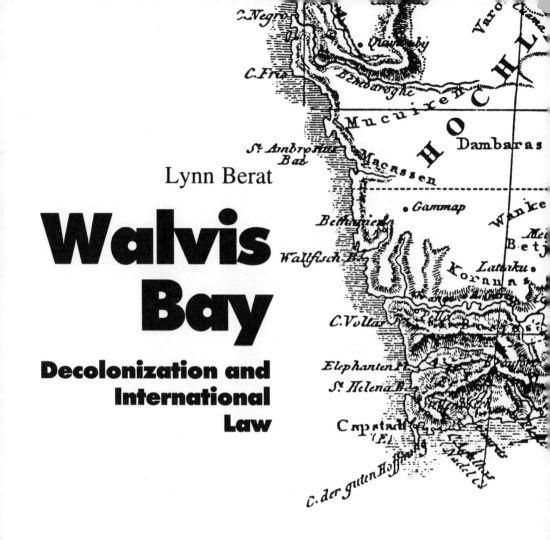

YALE
UNIVERSITY
PRESS
New Haven & London

Published with assistance from the
Kingsley Trust Association Publication Fund
established by the Scroll and Key Society of
Yale College.

Designed by James J. Johnson
Set in Times Roman and Futura types by
The Composing Room of Michigan, Inc.
Printed in the United States of America.

Library of Congress Cataloging-in-Publication Data
Berat, Lynn, (DATE)
    Walvis Bay : decolonization and international
law / Lynn Berat.
        p.   cm. — (Yale historical publications)
    ISBN 0–300–04549–2
    1. Walvis Bay (South Africa)—International
status.   2. South Africa—Foreign relations—
Namibia.   3. Namibia—Foreign relations—South
Africa.   I. Title.   II. Series.
JX4084.W34B47   1990
341.2'9'096881—dc20   89–27311
                                            CIP

*The paper in this book meets the guidelines of
permanence and durability of the Committee on
Production Guidelines for Book Longevity of the
Council on Library Resources.*

10   9   8   7   6   5   4   3   2   1

Contents

Maps

Preface

When I was a first-year law student, some of my professors impressed me with the legal maxim, "When the facts are against you, argue the law, and when the law is against you, argue the facts." Although that seemed easy enough for narrow problems, restricted both in time and in legal scope, I wondered whether such a pronouncement was adaptable to the resolution of major international questions with deep historical components. Even a summary look at the literature on such problems by historians and lawyers revealed that it was not. These problems demand a nuanced understanding of the relevant historical events that most lawyers do not have and an appreciation of the evolution of applicable concepts of law that most historians and an appalling number of lawyers do not possess. The failure of scholars from both disciplines to comprehend the dimensions of historico-legal problems prevents them from arguing the facts or the law with the sophistication that serious scholarship demands. In any event, because the equitable resolution of such international disputes is intimately bound up with peace and stability in international affairs, it is not enough to rely upon facts or law alone; rather, the applicable history and law should be understood as fully as possible.

The challenge to scholars is to illuminate internationally sensitive issues in a way that avoids polemics. Interdisciplinary studies may contribute to the resolution of disputes in the most equitable manner, thereby helping to preserve international faith in the rule of law. This study of Walvis Bay is an attempt to do just that, in the hope that others will take the same approach to similarly troublesome international questions.

In completing this work, I owe a debt of gratitude to many persons and organizations. Above all, Professor Leonard Thompson of Yale University provided excellent advice and guidance throughout. At Yale, thanks also go to Professors Leonard Doob, Robert Harms, and Burgess Carr; the members of the Yale Southern African Research Program; J. M. D. Crossey, African Curator, who was never too busy to find materials I required; and Pamela Baldwin, who drew the maps. Professor Hans Baade of the University of Texas School of Law was unfailing in his support.

In New York, valuable assistance was provided by Under-Secretary General of the United Nations Abdul Rahim A. Farah, Theo-Ben Gurirab and the SWAPO Observer Mission to the United Nations, and Third Secretary of the South African Mission to the United Nations Chris Kamp, as well as the staffs of the Office of the United Nations Commissioner for Namibia, the United Nations Library (especially Michael Dulka, Map Librarian), the South African Consulate, and the American Committee on Africa. In Washington, D.C., the staff of the Library of Congress and in Palo Alto the staff of the Hoover Institution, Stanford University, also rendered aid.

In London, the staffs of the Public Record Office, Kew; the British Library; the Institute for Advanced Legal Studies; the School of Oriental and African Studies; the Royal Institute of Foreign Affairs (Chatham House); and the International Defence and Aid Fund for Southern Africa (especially Gavin Cawthra) were most helpful. Thanks, too, to my lawyer colleague Sacky Akweenda.

In South Africa, I received aid from the staffs of the Cape Archives; the Library of Parliament; the libraries of the Universities of Cape Town and the Witwatersrand; the Central Archives Depot, Pretoria (especially G. Reynecke); the Department of Sea Fisheries, Cape Town; and the Department of Foreign Affairs, Pretoria (especially Albert Hoffmann). Special thanks go to Professor John Dugard and the Centre for Applied Legal Studies, University of the Witwatersrand, where I was a Visiting Associate, and to Professors Tim Couzens, Chris Saunders, and Rob Shell for their generous hospitality.

In Namibia, the staff of the Windhoek Archives (especially Christel Stern and Brigitte Lau); Advocate David Smuts of Lorentz and Bone; Jill and John Kinahan of the State Museum; David Pieters of Reuters; Anita Schmid of *Namibia Nachrichten;* and Jan Wilken, Walvis Bay Town Clerk, were particularly helpful.

Finally, I am most grateful for the generous financial support for my research and writing that came from the Fulbright-Hays Doctoral Dissertation Research Abroad Program, a Ford Foundation Doctoral Dissertation Fellowship, and a Yale Southern African Research Program Summer Research Grant.

CHAPTER ONE

Introduction

There are people in South West Africa, and in the outside world in particular, who adopt the standpoint that Walvis Bay belongs to South West Africa. I do not want there to be any misunderstanding whatsoever about this. Walvis Bay belongs to South Africa.
—*Prime Minister John Vorster of South Africa*

SWAPO fights to liberate each and every inch of Namibia, including Walvis Bay.
—*President Sam Nujoma of the*
South West Africa People's Organisation (SWAPO)

Halfway up the barren Namibian coast, where the icy Benguela current rushes up from the Antarctic and the giant golden sand dunes of the Namib Desert reach down to the sea, lies the port of Walvis Bay. Alternately scorched by the sun and enveloped in the cold mists from the nightly fog, it is a rather unexceptional looking little place of simply laid out streets lined with nondescript matchbox houses. The sulfurous air is notorious for corroding metal at an astonishing rate, and when the wind blows it brings with it the ever-encroaching sands and the smell of fish from the local processing plants. That the port and its environs, a mere 434 square miles with a population of eighteen thousand, and the twelve tiny, uninhabited Penguin Islands lying off the coast to the south could be the subject of an international controversy seems incredible. Yet appearance belies reality, for the Bay and the Penguin Islands hold the key to the economic, political, and military independence of a free Namibia.[1]

1. This study uses the terms Walvis Bay and the Walvis Bay territory to refer to the 434-square-mile disputed area. Walvis Bay also indicates the port and town in situations where the meaning of the appellation is clear. The names South West Africa and Namibia are both employed. For historical reasons, South West Africa is used for pre-1968 events. It is also used for post-1968 events depending upon the context, as, for example, with regard to events involving acts by the South African–sponsored authorities. The Penguin Islands are treated in the Appendix.

Epigraphs: Republic of South Africa, House of Assembly Debates, Apr. 23, 1976, col. 5278; Namibian, July 31, 1987, at 12.

To a great degree, control of Walvis Bay is synonymous with control of Namibia. This view is not new. In the late nineteenth and early twentieth centuries, the British and the Germans recognized that as long as one power dominated the Bay and the other the vast hinterland that became known as South West Africa, that hinterland could never be developed. The South Africans continue to be aware of the strategic value of the port. Walvis Bay is the terminus of Namibia's main railway line and is the only significant port in Namibia. With eight deep-water berths, it is the fifth largest port in southern Africa.[2] International shipping lines traveling to and from South Africa, Europe, North America, and Asia call there regularly. The port handles more than 90 percent of Namibia's export trade and ships all of Namibia's mineral production except for diamonds.[3] Walvis Bay is also the center of Namibia's fishing industry, its second largest industry after mining. South Africa has a growing air force base at Rooikop near the port. It uses the Bay as a forward staging post for South African naval units. The marines, a counterinsurgency section of the navy, are stationed at the Bay as part of the South African government's strategy to defend all South African ports. The only combined infantry/armor unit of the South African Defence Force (SADF), the elite 2 SA Infantry Battalion group, is also based in the area. With so much at stake, it is not surprising that the status of the Bay under international law is hotly contested.

South Africa claims that Walvis Bay is a South African possession. The South West Africa People's Organisation (SWAPO), which the United Nations has recognized as the authentic representative of the Namibian people and which will undoubtedly be a major force in any independent Namibian government, claims that the Bay is an integral part of Namibia and should be under Namibian sovereignty. In order to assess the validity of each side's claims, this book examines the issue of sovereignty from a historical perspective, thereby providing insights into the past, present, and future status of the Bay, as well as into the changing nature of international law. First, however, because the dispute over Walvis Bay forms part of the larger problem of Namibian independence, the nature of that problem must be understood.

Namibian Independence

In 1878, the captain of a British warship took possession of the port of Walvis Bay and its hinterland for the Crown.[4] Six years later, after trying in vain to

2. United Nations Office of Public Information, Objective: Justice, Special Supp. No. 2, at 3 (June 1978).
3. *Id.*
4. British Proclamation, taking possession of the Port and Settlement of Walfisch Bay, Mar. 12, 1878, 69 BRITISH AND FOREIGN STATE PAPERS 1178.

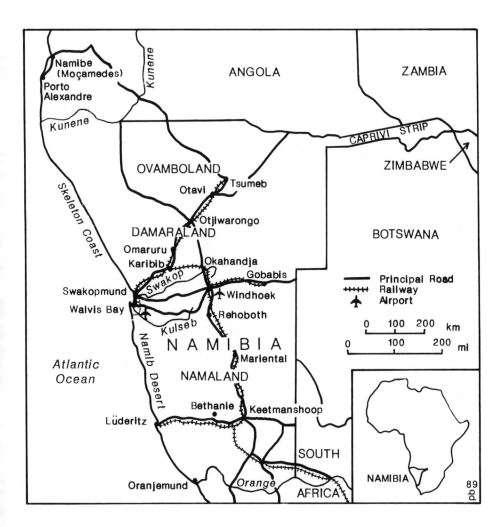

Map 1. Modern Namibia

persuade the British government to claim all of what is today Namibia, the Cape Colony, acting under letters patent issued by Queen Victoria, annexed the port and settlement of Walvis Bay as well as the surrounding area.[5] It did so only after Germany in the same year had claimed the rest of South West Africa as a protectorate.

South African forces occupied South West Africa during the First World War. After the war, according to the terms of Article 119 of the Treaty of Versailles, Germany renounced its sovereignty over its South West African protectorate in favor of the Allied and Associated Powers, which placed the territory under the mandate system of the League of Nations. The Union of South Africa administered the territory on behalf of the British Empire as a class C mandate. The mandate agreement permitted South Africa to administer the territory as an "integral portion" of the Union, subject to a trust obligation to advance "to the utmost the material and moral well-being and the social progress" of its indigenous inhabitants.[6] South Africa was also to submit an annual report to the League describing its administration in detail. The mandate agreement did not include Walvis Bay in the mandated territory, however.

South Africa treated the mandate as a veiled annexation, implicitly asserting South African sovereignty over the territory. Whenever the Permanent Mandates Commission challenged the Union, Pretoria either explained its actions away or backed down. The League also took South Africa to task for bombing civilians in the Bondelswart Massacre (1922) and for the high mortality rate among diamond miners, the territorial debt structure, and various aspects of the mandatory's native policy.

The Permanent Mandates Commission had ineffectual supervisory powers. By the time the League discussed them, actions were often faits accomplis. Africans could voice their complaints neither in person nor through an agent, whereas South Africa had a representative present at all discussions of the mandate's affairs. Yet, even though the League was captive to Western ethnocentrism, the Permanent Mandates Commission repeatedly rejected South Africa's requests for permission to annex the territory.

At the end of the Second World War, the United Nations replaced the League of Nations. All mandated territories were to come under the United Nations trusteeship system. At the first session of the U.N. General Assembly, South Africa sought to incorporate the territory. The General Assembly rejected this suggestion and decided that South Africa should place the man-

---

5. Proc. No. 184 of 1884.

6. South West Africa Mandate Agreement, Dec. 17, 1920, at art. 2, *reprinted in* J. DUGARD (ed.), THE SOUTH WEST AFRICA/NAMIBIA DISPUTE 72 (1973).

date under trusteeship.[7] At the time, there was much international pressure against South Africa's incorporation of the territory. The fifth Pan-African Congress, held in Manchester in 1945, demanded that the territory be submitted to trusteeship and called for an investigation into the civil and political rights of its indigenous inhabitants.

In spite of international pressure, South Africa refused to comply with the General Assembly's request to submit the territory to trusteeship. Its representative promised, however, that pending a settlement South Africa would continue to administer the territory "in the spirit of" the mandate.[8] Yet when South Africa submitted an annual report on its administration of the territory, the U.N. analysis of the report was unfavorable to South Africa. In response, in 1948, the newly elected National Party government refused to submit any more reports. The government also imposed South African citizenship upon all persons born in the territory but gave only white residents representation in the Union Parliament.

The General Assembly and the Union Parliament reached no accord. In 1949, the General Assembly asked the International Court of Justice (ICJ) for an advisory opinion on the legal status of the territory.[9] The court wrote that although there was no legal means of compelling South Africa to submit the territory to trusteeship, the Union could not alter the status of the territory without the General Assembly's concurrence. Thus, the mandate principles continued to apply to the territory while the supervision of its administration devolved upon the United Nations as the successor to the League of Nations.[10]

Various General Assembly resolutions urging submission to trusteeship proved ineffective. In 1954[11] and 1955[12] the General Assembly again called

7. U.N. GAOR Res. 65 (I), Dec. 14, 1946. The best treatment of the international controversy over Namibia until 1971 is J. DUGARD, *supra* note 6.

8. U.N. Doc. A/334 (1946).

9. U.N. GAOR Res. 338 (IV), Dec. 4, 1949.

10. International Status of South West Africa, Advisory Opinion, (1950) I.C.J. Reports 128. *See generally* Kahn, *The International Court's Advisory Opinion on the International Status of South West Africa*, 4 INT'L & COMP. L.Q. 78 (1951). For criticism, see Hudson, *The Twenty-ninth Year of the World Court*, 45 AM. J. INT'L L. 12 (1951); Nisot, *The Advisory Opinion of the International Court of Justice on the International Status of South West Africa*, 68 S. AFR. L.J. 274 (1951).

11. South West Africa Voting Procedure Case (Advisory Opinion), (1955) I.C.J. Reports 67. In 1954, the General Assembly adopted a special rule on the voting procedure to be used by the Assembly in deciding questions relating to reports and petitions that concerned South West Africa. According to this rule, the Assembly's decisions on the questions referred to were to be regarded as important questions within the meaning of art. 18(2) of the U.N. Charter, i.e., as being subject to a requirement for a two-thirds majority, whereas for the mandates system the Council of the League of Nations was governed by a requirement for unanimity. By Resolution 904 (IX) of November 23, 1954, the General Assembly asked whether the rule corresponded to a

upon the ICJ for guidance in exercising its supervisory powers. South Africa refused to accept any of the court's opinions insofar as they restricted its administration of the territory. The General Assembly established a committee to negotiate with South Africa on the matter, but South Africa refused to cooperate.

In 1957, the General Assembly established another committee to consider possible legal actions available to its members. The committee issued a report that was highly critical of the South African administration of the territory. The report recommended that member states invoke Article 7 of the mandate agreement to enforce South Africa's obligation to promote the well-being and development of the territory's indigenous inhabitants. According to the terms of Article 7, South Africa had agreed in advance to litigate in the ICJ any unresolvable dispute referred to the court involving the interpretation or application of the mandate agreement.[13]

In 1960, two former League members, Liberia and Ethiopia, responded to a request from the General Assembly for a qualified state to bring suit against South Africa under Article 7. They argued that South Africa had not complied with its obligation under the mandate agreement and called upon the

---

correct interpretation of the advisory opinion given in 1950. The ICJ advised unanimously in the affirmative because the rule comported with the court's statement in the 1950 opinion that "the degree of supervision to be exercised by the General Assembly should not . . . exceed that which applied under the Mandates system, and should conform as far as possible to the procedure followed in this respect by the Council of the League of Nations." *Id.* at 68. *See generally* Jennings, *The International Court's Advisory Opinion on the Voting Procedure on Questions Concerning South West Africa,* 42 TRANSACTIONS OF THE GROTIUS SOCIETY 85 (1957); Hudson, *The Thirty-fourth Year of the World Court,* 50 AM. J. INT'L L. 5 (1956); J. VERZIJL, 2 THE JURISPRUDENCE OF THE WORLD COURT 218 (1966).

12. Admissibility of Hearings of Petitioners by the Committee on South West Africa (Advisory Opinion), (1956) I.C.J. Reports 23. In 1955, the General Assembly, which in 1953 had established a Committee for South West Africa, requested an advisory opinion on the question of whether it was consistent with the advisory opinion given by the ICJ in 1950 for the committee to grant oral hearings to petitioners on matters relating to South West Africa. The court advised (8–5) that it would not be inconsistent with the 1950 opinion for the General Assembly to authorize a procedure for the granting of oral hearings by the committee to petitioners who had already submitted written petitions, provided that the Assembly was satisfied that such a course was necessary to maintain effective international supervision of the administration of South West Africa. Although oral hearings had not been granted to the petitioners during the League period, the League Council could have authorized that course had it wished, and the General Assembly in performing its supervisory functions in respect to the mandate had the same authority as the council. *See generally* Hudson, *The Thirty-fifth Year of the World Court,* 51 AM. J. INT'L L. 1 (1957); J. VERZIJL, *supra* note 11, at 231; Verloren Van Themaat, *Kan die Komitee oor Suidwes-Afrika van die Algemene Vergadering van die Vereinigde Volke mondelinge vertoë en getuienis aanhoor?* 21 TYDSKRIF VIR HEDENDAAGSE ROMEINS-HOLLANDSE REG 176 (1958).

13. Report of the Committee on South West Africa, U.N. GAOR, 12th Sess., Supp. No. A (A/3625).

ICJ to grant appropriate relief.[14] In 1962, the court ruled that the plaintiffs were legally entitled to pursue their claim.[15] Some of the judges, including Spender of Australia and Fitzmaurice of Britain, dissented, however. These two issued a joint opinion.

Four years later, instead of deciding the case on its merits, the court issued a decision on what it termed an "antecedent matter."[16] It held that the plaintiffs had no standing to bring suit. The 1962 joint dissenting opinion of the conservative Australian and British judges became the 1966 majority opinion by the tie-breaking vote of the Australian, who as judge president voted twice. The need for Spender's second vote arose because of the absence of three liberal judges from so-called Third World countries. These were Judge Bustamante y Rivero of Peru and the recently deceased Judge Badawi of Egypt—both of whom had voted in favor of the plaintiffs in 1962—and Judge Khan of Pakistan, who was disqualified by Judge Spender in the 1966 case without the consent of the rest of the court on the ground that the plaintiffs had asked him to be their judge ad hoc even though he had not accepted the invitation.[17]

South Africa greeted the decision with jubilation. Indeed, celebrations began in that country even before the court had delivered its judgment. The United Nations responded to the decision by revoking the mandate in General Assembly Resolution 2145 (XXI), having determined that South Africa's conduct amounted to a repudiation of the mandate agreement. The General Assembly directed South Africa to end its occupation of the territory and

14. South West Africa Cases, Preliminary Objections, (1962) I.C.J. Reports 319 at 322.

15. *Id.* at 328 et seq. Academic comment was largely favorable. *See generally* Ballinger, *The International Court of Justice and the South West Africa Cases*, 81 S. AFR. L.J. 35 (1964); Gross, *The South West African Cases: On the Threshold of Decision*, 3 COL. J. TRANSNT'L L. 19 (1964); Verzijl, *International Court of Justice: South West Africa and Northern Cameroons Cases (Preliminary Objections)*, 11 NETH. INT'L L. REV. 1 (1964); *Symposium on the South West Africa Cases*, 4 COL. J. TRANSNT'L L. 47 (1965).

16. South West Africa Cases, Second Phase, (1966) I.C.J. Reports 6. *See generally* M. KATZ, THE RELEVANCE OF INTERNATIONAL ADJUDICATION 87–99 (1968); Green, *South West Africa and the World Court*, 22 INT'L J. 39 (1966–67); Verzijl, *The Stone West Africa Cases (Second Phase)*, 3 INT'L RELS. 87, 95–96 (1966); Falk, *The South West Africa Cases: An Appraisal*, 21 INT'L ORGANIZATION 1, 11–13 (1967).

17. Article 24 of the Statute of the Court required the ICJ to meet to decide upon the disqualification of Judge Khan. However, no public record of such a meeting exists. Consequently, legal scholars have queried whether the proper procedure was followed and whether the reason given for Khan's disqualification was valid. *See* Reisman, *Revision of the South West Africa Cases*, 7 VA. J. INT'L L. 1, 55–58 (1966); Higgins, *The International Court and South West Africa: The Implications of the Judgment*, 42 INT'L AFFAIRS 573, 587–88 (1966); Cheng, *The 1966 South-West Africa Judgment of the World Court*, CURR. LEG. PROBS. 181, 196–99 (1967).

appointed an ad hoc committee to recommend measures for its administration. In the spring of 1967, the United Nations set up an eleven-member Council for Namibia under a commissioner for Namibia to administer the territory while preparing it for independence under a new constitution, which was to be drafted with popular participation.[18]

South Africa made it impossible, however, for the council to assume its duties in the territory. Instead of withdrawing from the territory, South Africa intensified efforts to annex it, following the recommendations of its Odendaal Plan.[19] Drafted in 1962–63 while the South West Africa cases were pending before the ICJ, the plan was designed to turn the territory into a fifth province of South Africa. Under the plan, South Africa rescinded the limited home rule it had granted to South West African whites in 1925; extended to the area its homeland policy, according to which Africans were divided into ethnic groups designated by the state ethnographer and relegated to lands that were supposedly their tribal domains; and increased its police and military forces in the territory in an attempt to crush opposition to its rule from SWAPO, which had been founded in 1960 to oppose South African domination.[20]

At SWAPO's request, in 1968 the General Assembly changed the name of the territory from South West Africa to Namibia. In 1969, the U.N. Security Council issued an ultimatum to South Africa demanding its withdrawal from the territory that October 4. The resolution noted that South Africa had committed "aggressive encroachment on the authority of the United Nations, a violation of the territorial integrity and a denial of the political sovereignty of the people of Namibia."[21] Still South Africa remained.

In 1970, the Security Council asked the ICJ for an advisory opinion on the proper conduct of states in regard to the territory.[22] In its fourth advisory opinion relating to South West Africa/Namibia, the court, whose composition had changed since 1966, wrote that South Africa should withdraw its administration from the territory and that other states—members and nonmembers of the United Nations—should treat South Africa's administration of the territory as illegal and refuse to recognize any actions taken by South Africa for the territory. The court noted, moreover, that to "establish . . . and enforce distinctions, exclusions, restrictions, and limitations exclusively based on grounds of race, colour, descent or national or ethnic origin which con-

18. U.N. GAOR Res. 2248 [AS–V] (1967).

19. Report of the Commission of Enquiry into South West African Affairs, 1962–63, RP 12/1964.

20. There is no adequate history of SWAPO. *See generally* M. Horrell, South-West Africa 81 (South African Institute of Race Relations, 1967); J. Dugard, *supra* note 6, at 216.

21. U.N. SCOR Res. 264 (1969).

22. U.N. SCOR Res. 284 (1970).

stitute a denial of fundamental human rights is a flagrant violation of the purposes and principles of the [U.N.] Charter."[23]

The United Nations tried yet again to end South Africa's illegal occupation of the territory. Between 1971 and 1973 the Security Council passed several resolutions calling upon states and their nationals, especially companies, to bring pressure on South Africa. The Security Council sent the secretary-general on a mission to the territory in 1972, but this brought Namibia no closer to independence.

Meanwhile, the General Assembly concerned itself with actions it could take outside the territory. It established the Fund for Namibia to assist refugees from the territory in 1971. In 1973 it recognized SWAPO as the "authentic" representative of the Namibian people[24] and in the following year authorized a yearly sum to maintain a SWAPO office in New York. In 1976, it called SWAPO "the sole and authentic representative of the Namibian people" and gave it observer status at the United Nations.[25] This recognition of the legal status of a liberation movement reflected developments in the new international legal order of the second half of the twentieth century.

When Portuguese rule in Mozambique and Angola collapsed in 1974, SWAPO's struggle against South African domination was transformed. In addition to raising hopes of independence among Namibians, the defeat enabled SWAPO's military wing, the People's Liberation Army of Namibia (PLAN), which had commenced the armed struggle after the ICJ rendered its opinion of 1966, to operate along Namibia's northern border with Angola. As SWAPO's military fortunes grew, so did its political standing both within and without the territory.

The U.N. General Assembly, which had just appointed its first full-time commissioner for Namibia, took various actions. It created the United Nations Institute for Namibia to give young Namibians the skills to enable them to administer their country after independence. The General Assembly also issued a decree to protect Namibia's interests by making it unlawful for companies to exploit or export any of Namibia's natural resources without authorization from the Council for Namibia. The decree also provided for the seizure of the resources involved if its terms were violated and empowered the government of a future independent Namibia to sue offenders for damages.[26]

23. Legal Consequences for States of the Continued Presence of South Africa in Namibia (South West Africa) notwithstanding Security Council Resolution 276 (1970), 1971 I.C.J. Reports 16. *See generally* Dugard, *The Opinion on South West Africa ("Namibia"): The Teleologists Triumph,* 88 S. AFR. L.J. 463 (1971).

24. U.N. GAOR Res. 3111 (XXVIII) (1973).

25. U.N. GAOR Res. A/31/146 (1976).

26. United Nations Council for Namibia, Decree No. 1 (1974). The General Assembly subsequently adopted the decree.

In 1974, the Security Council also passed Resolution 366, which demanded that South Africa leave Namibia and threatened economic sanctions if that country did not comply. However, because the sanctions clause had been weakened by revisions made in exchange for the agreement of the Western nations, it failed to conform to the formula required under Chapter VII of the U.N. Charter. South Africa thus ignored the resolution. In response, the majority of the Security Council voted for an arms embargo against South Africa. The three permanent Western members of the Council—the United States, the United Kingdom, and France—vetoed the measure. This was the first time these states exercised what became known as the triple veto on Namibian issues.

South Africa sent troops to seize the Calueque power station on the Cunene River, which forms the border between Namibia and Angola, as well as strategic areas in the vicinity, in mid-1975. Within a few months it was negotiating with U.S. Secretary of State Henry Kissinger to send troops north in collaboration with the pro–South African UNITA (National Union for the Total Independence of Angola) movement, led by Jonas Savimbi. At the same time, another Angolan faction, the FNLA (National Front for the Liberation of Angola), aided by the CIA, was to attack yet another Angolan faction, the MPLA (Popular Movement for the Liberation of Angola), from the Zairean border. The invading South Africans reached just south of the Angolan capital, Luanda, but MPLA forces backed by Cuban troops sent in at the MPLA's request drove the South Africans back into Namibia.[27]

The Security Council meanwhile drafted a plan to remove South Africa from Namibia and to install a representative Namibian government. Lengthy negotiations ensued. In January 1976, the Security Council adopted Resolution 385, which provided that (1) South Africa should abandon Namibia at once and the United Nations should temporarily administer the area; (2) the United Nations should have ample time to prepare Namibia for an election in which all Namibians would freely determine their own future; (3) an election should be held on a Namibia-wide basis "under United Nations supervision and control"; and (4) in the period before South Africa transferred power to the United Nations it should abolish homelands and all discriminatory and repressive laws in Namibia, release all political prisoners, permit all exiles to return safely, and grant full human rights to all. The resolution assumed that those Namibians elected in the U.N.-controlled election would draft a con-

27. On Angola, see generally J. MARCUM, THE ANGOLAN REVOLUTION (2 vols.) (1969, 1978); W. MINTER, KING SOLOMON'S MINES REVISITED: WESTERN INTERESTS AND THE BURDENED HISTORY OF SOUTHERN AFRICA (1987).

stitution under which Namibia would become independent. The resolution set August 31 as the deadline for South Africa's compliance.[28]

South Africa did not acquiesce, and only another triple veto saved it from a comprehensive arms embargo. Indeed, after Portuguese rule ended in Angola, South Africa increased repression in Namibia. It stringently enforced and expanded upon its homeland policy while offering to negotiate with U.N. officials. As the strength of the MPLA grew in Angola, South Africa resurrected a plan to create a greater Ovamboland, which would include Ovambos from both sides of Namibia's northern border with Angola and function, with a pro–South African leader, as a buffer state between Namibia and Angola. The plan failed.

Amid the rising international expectations generated by Security Council Resolution 385 that Namibia would become independent, South Africa determined to retain its influence over Namibia through control of Walvis Bay. In 1976, Prime Minister John Vorster of South Africa stated in Parliament that Walvis Bay was South African. The following year, the self-declared pro-African administration of President Jimmy Carter formed the Western Contact Group, which consisted of the three permanent Western members of the Security Council as well as Canada and West Germany, then newly elected nonpermanent members of the Council. Reacting to the failure of South Africa's Turnhalle Conference in Windhoek, which was to have established a pro–South African government in Namibia made up of members of South African–backed "internal parties," the five countries took it upon themselves to devise an "internationally acceptable solution" to the Namibian problem.

While negotiating with the Western Contact Group about a possible settlement of the Namibian issue and an agreement for elections in the territory, the South African regime, anticipating the establishment of an independent Namibia, endeavored to solidify its position in the area. It appointed an administrator-general for Namibia with plenary legislative and administrative powers, thus installing a "local" official whose status equaled that of any United Nations official who might oversee U.N.-sponsored elections in Namibia.[29] South Africa also issued a proclamation that took effect on September 1, 1977, the day the administrator-general assumed his duties, transferring the administration of Walvis Bay from Windhoek to Cape Town.[30] The South African government followed this proclamation with another one

28. U.N. SCOR Res. 385 (1976).
29. Proc. R180 (1977).
30. Proc. R202 (1977).

extending South African territorial waters to twelve nautical miles and its fishery zone to two hundred nautical miles.[31]

The publication of the first proclamation resulted in instant dispute. SWAPO reacted immediately. It rejected what it termed South Africa's annexation of the Bay and condemned the decision as illegal and void, an act of aggression against the Namibian people and a flagrant violation of the territorial integrity of Namibia. In addition, Sam Nujoma, the president of SWAPO, in a statement to the U.N. Security Council on July 27, 1978, requested that the Council ensure the immediate withdrawal of all "enemy troops and administrative machinery from Walvis Bay"—a reference to South Africa's use of the Bay for military purposes—and "its speedy and unconditional restoration to Namibia."[32]

Before 1977, U.N. General Assembly and Security Council resolutions on Namibia did not refer explicitly to Walvis Bay. Works by leading jurists did not question South African sovereignty.[33] In 1977, however, the General Assembly passed a resolution condemning the South African government and its attitude toward Walvis Bay.[34] The following year, it declared Walvis Bay an integral part of Namibia.[35] That same year, the Security Council called for the early reintegration of Walvis Bay into an independent Namibia.[36]

Both South Africa and SWAPO have appealed to international law in advancing their positions.

The Arguments of the Parties

South Africa bases its claims to Walvis Bay upon its chain of title, citing three factors to support the contention that, under the principles of international law, Walvis Bay is part of the Republic of South Africa. These are (1) the formal annexation of Walvis Bay at a time when it was *terra nullius,* (2) the effective and unchallenged occupation of the territory after annexation by the relevant lawful authorities, and (3) its formal incorporation into South Africa by due constitutional processes.

31. Proc. 234 (1977). A fishery zone is a zone adjacent to the coast in which a coastal state claims the exclusive right to control the activities of its own fishing vessels and foreign ones. *See generally* D. JOHNSTON, THE INTERNATIONAL LAW OF FISHERIES (1965); F. GARCIA AMADOR, THE EXPLOITATION AND CONSERVATION OF THE RESOURCES OF THE SEA (1959).

32. Statement of Nujoma to U.N. Security Council, July 27, 1978, *reprinted in* Namibia Bulletin, No. 1, at 22 (1978) (erroneously dated May 28).

33. *See, e.g.,* J. DUGARD, *supra* note 6, at 533.

34. G.A. Res. 32/9 (D), 32 U.N. GAOR Supp. (No. 45) at 16, U.N. Doc. A/32/45 (1978).

35. G.A. Res. S9/2, 9th Special Session, U.N. GAOR Supp. (No. 2) at 3, U.N. Doc. A/S–9/13 (1978).

36. Security Council Res. 432 (1978), 33 U.N. SCOR, U.N. Doc. S/INF/34.

These factors derive their significance from the following events. In 1878, Britain annexed the Bay, which at that time belonged to no state.[37] The Colony of the Cape of Good Hope annexed it in 1884,[38] and title passed to South Africa at the time of Union in 1910.[39] The Bay became part of the Republic in 1961 through the Republic of South Africa Act.[40] Earlier, on July 1, 1890, Britain and Germany had entered into an agreement at Berlin that regulated the position inter se regarding Africa and Heligoland, a North Sea island off the German coast valued for naval purposes.[41] The agreement recognized British authority over the Bay and German authority over the South West Africa protectorate.

During World War I, South Africa occupied South West Africa. After the war, South Africa administered the former German protectorate as a League of Nations class C mandate. The mandate agreement permitted South Africa to administer the territory as an integral portion of the Union. Although Walvis Bay was not part of the mandated territory, in 1922, for reasons of convenience, South Africa began to administer it as part of South West Africa from the territory's capital, Windhoek. It did so pursuant to the passage of the South West Africa Affairs Act of 1922 by the Parliament in Cape Town.[42] South African administration of the Bay continued in this manner until 1977, when the South African government issued a proclamation on August 31, transferring the administration from Windhoek back to Cape Town.[43]

SWAPO's claim that South Africa no longer has title to Walvis Bay and that it is an integral part of Namibia rests on various complementary and complex arguments of international law. First, SWAPO argues that the original British title, which had no consensual element, was invalid or at least will no longer support a colonialist claim. Second, the South African government voluntarily relinquished its sovereignty over Walvis Bay by transferring it to South West African administration and leaving it under that administration for more than half a century. Third, Walvis Bay is geographically, economically, and historically a part of Namibia. At best, South Africa exercised colonial jurisdiction over the Bay before transferring it to South West African administration. Modern international law recognizes that every colonial people is

37. British Proclamation, taking possession of the Port and Settlement of Walfisch Bay–Walfish Bay, Mar. 12, 1878, 69 BRITISH AND FOREIGN STATE PAPERS 1178.

38. Proc. No. 184 of 1884.

39. The central piece of legislation in the unification process was the South Africa Act of 1909, 9 Edward VII c9. *See infra* chapter 6, note 3 and accompanying text.

40. Republic of South Africa Constitution Act, No. 32 of 1961.

41. Agreement, *reprinted in* M. HURST, 2 KEY TREATIES FOR GREAT POWERS 873 (1972).

42. South West Africa Affairs Act, No. 24 of 1922.

43. Proc. R202 (1977).

entitled to self-administration and independence and denies the right to re-colonize any territory or people. This is particularly true when recolonization would involve reimposing apartheid—abandoned in Namibia—which the ICJ has held, in its June 21, 1971, advisory opinion on Namibia, is contrary to the purposes and principles of the U.N. Charter. Fourth, the United Nations has insisted that Namibia achieve its independence with territorial integrity. History, economics, and political and military considerations all indicate that this cannot be achieved if Walvis Bay remains excised from Namibia.

Some scholars suggest that the chain of title events give South Africa valid title to Walvis Bay. Others argue that the transfer of the administration of Walvis Bay to South West Africa and its apparent legal integration into the territory are sufficient to indicate that Walvis Bay became part of Namibia and that South Africa relinquished title to it.[44] Neither approach is adequate. Both are ahistorical and fail to appreciate the evolution of international law from the time Walvis Bay first attracted Western attention to the modern era.

Changes in the legal order reflect shifts in the nature of the world community and the international balance of power. Three international legal orders are discernible in this transformation: first, a colonialist legal order in which Western states denied sovereignty to non-Christian, and later non-civilized, peoples; second, a transitional legal order of the early twentieth century in which Western states employed the rhetoric of self-determination of peoples without translating these pronouncements into practice; and third, the modern legal order since World War II in which the law of decolonization based upon self-determination and equal rights has become entrenched in the jurisprudential corpus. Understanding these changes and their applicability to such historical problems as that of Walvis Bay will reveal the differing political visions that underlie the parties' claims and their implications for the future of a world governed by law.

44. The writings of scholars on this subject are examined in chapter 5 *infra*.

CHAPTER TWO

The Path of Conquest

For thousands of years, Nama-speaking peoples inhabited what is today southern Namibia, including the area around Walvis Bay. Then, in the seventeenth and eighteenth centuries, the advent of colonialism at the Cape of Good Hope unleashed a number of economic and social processes that ultimately destroyed the way of life of these peoples and made possible the late nineteenth-century British conquest of Walvis Bay.

Beginnings

Little archaeological work has been done in the southwest African region. Nevertheless, archaeologists have found evidence of human occupation in various parts of Namibia that dates to more than ten thousand years ago. The earliest evidence of human occupation discovered in the Walvis Bay area is dated between A.D. 1460 and 1635. It includes ostrich eggshell beads, bone points, potsherds, quartz scrapers, and schist grindstones, as well as remains of large and small bovids, fish, and birds.[1] These finds are located in middens in the Kuiseb River Delta, floods and shifting sands having probably destroyed or obscured older sites.

1. Sandelowsky, *Mirabib—An Archaeological Study in the Namib,* 10(4) MADOQUA 221, 226 (1977). *See also* Kinahan & Vogel, *Recent Copper-Working Sites in Khuiseb Drainage Area, Namibia,* 37 S. AFR. ARCH. BULL. 44, 45 (1982). For discussions of archaeological dating and its problems, see Beaumont & Vogel,

The archaeologist John Kinahan calls the Kuiseb Delta "part of the regional mosaic of settlement that stretched from the coast to the escarpment [the area where Windhoek is now located]."[2] Transhumant pastoralists, with their herds of cattle and flocks of sheep, probably moved along the Kuiseb River Valley in and out of Walvis Bay from early in the Christian era, but they left few traces for archaeologists to discover. There is, however, archaeological evidence of bartering between the inhabitants of the coast and inland peoples. Seashells have been discovered in the Mirabib cave some 25 miles inland;[3] seeds of the !nara melon, a local gourd that because of moisture from the nightly fog grows between the coast and about 19 miles inland, have been found 119 miles from the sea.[4] Conversely, beads produced more than 150 miles from the coast and dated well before the European conquest have been found in a midden in the !nara fields.[5]

Portuguese mariners began to put an end to the isolation of the region from the rest of the world in the fifteenth century. Prince Henry the Navigator sent a series of expeditions down the western coast of Africa, and after Henry's death in 1460, João II continued his uncle's policy of exploration. In 1483, Diego Cão reached the mouth of the Zaire River. Two years later, Cão erected a cross to commemorate his landing at what is still known as Cape Cross, about one hundred miles north of Walvis Bay. Outward bound on his epic voyage twelve years later, Bartholomeu Dias bypassed Walvis Bay and landed about 260 miles farther south at Angra Pequeña (now Lüderitz); then, standing far out to sea in a storm, he managed to round the southern end of the continent and make a landfall near Mossel Bay. On his return journey, Dias sighted what he called the Cape of Storms (subsequently named the Cape of Good Hope), and on December 8, 1487, he entered Walvis Bay in his ship *São Cristoforo* and named it Golfo de Santa Maria de Conceição. Eleven years later, Vasco da Gama followed Dias's route around the Cape and then sailed along the East African coast as far as Malindi, near Mombasa, where he engaged an Arab pilot to steer him across the Indian Ocean to Calicut. European trade with the East increasingly linked the Cape route after the

---

On a New Radiocarbon Chronology for Africa South of the Equator, 31 AFR. STUD. 65 (1972); Hall & Vogel, *Some Recent Radiocarbon Dates from Southern Africa,* 21 J. AFR. HIST. 431 (1980); MacCalman, *Carbon 14 Dates from South West Africa,* 20 S. AFR. ARCH. BULL. 215 (1965).

2. Kinahan, *Archaeology and the Image of the Khoe in Early Historic Contact on the Namib Desert Coast,* SOUTH WEST AFRICA ANNUAL 55, 57 (1984).

3. Sandelowsky, *supra* note 1, at 221.

4. Kinahan & Vogel, *supra* note 1, at 45.

5. *Id.*

Portuguese had opened it up to European shipping, but not until after the Dutch took possession of the Cape in the mid-seventeenth century did the modern history of Walvis Bay begin.

In 1652, the Dutch East India Company established a refreshment station at the Cape for vessels traveling to and from the Far East. In due course, the company sent exploratory expeditions from the Cape up the west coast to ascertain who inhabited the region and whether the Dutch could establish trading relations with them. Commanders of the vessels gave unfavorable reports of fighting between their men and the local inhabitants, whom they called Hottentots.[6]

Perhaps as a result of these accounts, the Dutch showed no further interest in the west coast for over a century. Whalers from other countries were not deterred, however. The Bay, which abounded in marine life, became known as Bahia de Baleas (Bay of Whales) or Walvis Bay, and by the end of the eighteenth century, American, British, and French seamen were all engaged in whaling operations along the coast. Once at the Bay, they encountered the indigenous inhabitants of its shores.[7]

By that time, rumors were proliferating of vast herds of game and cattle, as well as of huge copper deposits, in the area north of the Orange River. The British had already sent expeditions to explore the west coast in 1784 and 1786. Fearing that Britain might claim the west coast, including Walvis Bay, the Dutch sent the *Meermin* under Captain François Duminy to the west coast. On February 24, 1793, Duminy arrived at Walvis Bay, where the local Nama-speaking people were exploiting the marine life, herding cattle, and using the !nara melon.

On the morning of February 26, Duminy claimed possession of the Bay. He reported, "I sent the ship's boat with everything that would be required for erecting the 'Stone of Possession' in the Bay which we were taking in the name of the States General and the Noble Company and kept the name Walfish Bay."[8] Neither Duminy's diary nor the journal of Simon van Reenen,

6. Sydow, *Contributions to the History and Protohistory of the Topnaar Strandloper Settlement at the Kuiseb River Mouth near Walvis Bay,* 28 S. AFR. ARCH. BULL. 73 (1973). The term Hottentots, which has taken on a derogatory connotation, referred to indigenous pastoral peoples. In modern scholarship the term Khoikhoi is used instead. The term Bushmen referred to indigenous hunter-gatherers. In modern scholarship, the term San has replaced it. Both groups are often referred to in the literature as Khoisan.

7. *See, e.g.*, Cécille, *Bericht über die Fahrt der Korvette L'Héroïne,* 31 MITTEILUNGEN AUS DEN DEUTSCHEN SCHUTZGEBIETEN: DIE ÄLTESTEN REISEBERICHTE DEUTSCH-SUDWEST AFRIKAS 138 (1918); J. ALEXANDER, AN EXPEDITION OF DISCOVERY INTO THE INTERIOR OF AFRICA (1838).

8. DUMINY-DAGBOEKE (J. Franken ed. 1938).

one of the crew members, suggests that any local inhabitants were consulted.[9] This marked the first time a European power attempted to annex Walvis Bay. According to the international law of the period, however, this symbolic act was insufficient to effect a valid annexation.

Even nominal Dutch authority over the Bay was short-lived. In 1795, France invaded Holland. Believing that France might gain control of the sea route to India, the British government sent a naval force to the Cape. The Dutch capitulated, and the British took control of the Cape. The following year, the Cape government sent Captain Alexander in the frigate *Star* up the west coast to inspect its bays, including Walvis Bay, and to take possession of them for Britain.

Alexander purported to annex Walvis Bay by raising the British flag, firing three volleys, and turning over some soil. This annexation, like that by the Dutch before, failed to comply with prevailing standards of international law and was thus ineffective. Nevertheless, the British claimed that the whaling and sealing grounds off the coast were under their exclusive domain and commissioned a cruiser to protect those industries from exploitation by foreign nationals. Alexander's annexation was neither proclaimed nor confirmed, and in 1825 HMS *Leven* surveyed the Bay but made no attempt to annex it.

Early in the nineteenth century, European and American explorers, traders, and missionaries, as well as naval vessels, began to arrive in the Walvis Bay area. Written accounts they left behind gave often ethnocentric and unflattering descriptions of the local inhabitants, whom they called Topnaar and whose numbers they estimated in the hundreds. Whereas earlier visitors reported that the Topnaar did not know hunger, by the end of the century observers indicated that they had become impoverished and that they formed the base of the labor force used to load and unload boats that put into the Bay.[10] The Topnaar were in this condition because of decades of social upheavals that led to the eventual British annexation of Walvis Bay.

The Nama

It is not known when the first Nama-speaking people arrived in what is today Namibia. The historian Richard Elphick suggests, however, and anthropolog-

9. *English Translation of Parts of Sebastian Valentyn van Reenen's Journal of the Expedition to Walfish Bay, 1793,* in *id.* at 304; S. van Reenen, *Report,* 28 MITTEILUNGEN AUS DEN DEUTSCHEN SCHUTZGEBIETEN (1915).

10. *Compare* Cécille and J. ALEXANDER, *supra* note 7, *with* W. PALGRAVE, REPORT OF THE SPECIAL COMMISSIONER TO THE TRIBES NORTH OF THE ORANGE RIVER OF HIS MISSION TO DAMARALAND AND GREAT NAMAQUALAND IN 1876, 6 (1877); B. TINDALL (ed.), THE JOURNAL OF JOSEPH TINDALL 70 (1959).

ical linguists support the proposition, that they originated somewhere in present-day Botswana and gradually moved south and west.[11] The Nama were hunter-gatherers; some of them also became pastoralists at about the time of Christ.

Apart from the few archaeological data available and information furnished by ethnocentric missionaries, travelers, and traders, little is known about the life of the Nama-speakers of southern and central Namibia, including Walvis Bay, before their first contact with Europeans. Various ethnographic works written after World War I about the peoples of Namibia claim to reveal information on precontact social structure,[12] but their conclusions are unreliable. Written from a structural-functionalist perspective, which regarded ethnic groups as discrete entities for analytical purposes, these studies are ahistorical. In addition, they accept oral information gathered in this century as sufficiently accurate evidence for the reconstruction of social and political formations that flourished more than a century earlier, even though the destruction of the old order was complete long before any of these ethnographic materials were collected.

Nevertheless, it appears that the people in southern Namibia did identify themselves as members of specific groups. This continued long after colonization occurred; indeed, some of these group names are still used today. A Nama myth of origin repeated by twentieth-century ethnographers seems accurate at least in describing how the Nama at some point grouped themselves.

According to this myth of origin, there were once five brothers, each of whom became the founder of a Nama group. The eldest was the ancestor of the Gai-//khaun, or Rooi Nasie (Red Nation). The other brothers founded the !Gami-=nûn, or Bondelswarts (Black Bundles); the //Haboben, or Veldskoendraers (Fieldshoe Wearers); the Khara-khoen, or Fransmann Hottentots or Simon Kopper Hottentots; and the //Khau-/gân, or Swartboois (Black Boys), who are said to have descended from the youngest brother. The =Aonin, or Topnaar, of the Walvis Bay area and the Gomen, or Groote Doode

11. R. ELPHICK, KRAAL AND CASTLE: KHOIKHOI AND THE FOUNDING OF WHITE SOUTH AFRICA (1977); A. Pfouts, Economy and Society in Pre-Colonial Namibia: A Linguistic Approach (c. 1500–1800 A.D.), Paper for African Studies Conference, Boston (Dec. 6–10, 1983), and reproduced as Paper No. 30, International Conference on Namibia, City University, London (Sept. 10–13, 1984); Ehret, *Patterns of Bantu and Central Sudanic Settlement in Central and Southern Africa (c. 1000 B.C.–500 A.D.)*, 3 TRANSAFRICAN J. HIST. 64 (1973); Ehret, *The Spread of Food Production in Southern Africa*, in THE ARCHAEOLOGICAL AND LINGUISTIC RECONSTRUCTION OF AFRICAN HISTORY 158–81 (C. EHRET & M. POSNANSKY eds. 1982). The Nama languages belong to the northern and central branches of the Khoisan families.

12. *See, e.g.*, Hoernlé, *The Social Organisation of the Nama Hottentots of South West Africa*, AMERICAN ANTHROPOLOGIST 6 (1925); I. SCHAPERA, THE KHOISAN PEOPLES OF SOUTH AFRICA (1930).

(Great Dead), were not part of this tale but themselves claimed to be offshoots of the Gai-//khaun. In the 1850s a new Nama group, also related to lineages of the Gai-//khaun, established itself at Keetmanshoop and became known as Karo-ôan, or Tseibschen Hottentots.[13]

The Dutch names appear to be literal translations of the Nama names. Some, like Veldskoendraers and Bondelswarts, were known at least from the beginning of the nineteenth century. The word Topnaar, which early visitors applied to the people of the Walvis Bay area, seems to be a Dutch translation of the Nama name the people use for themselves, =Aonin, which means "the people of the point," the point presumably being the northern- or westernmost point inhabited by Nama-speaking peoples.[14] Although this is a useful term for referring to the Nama-speaking people of Walvis Bay, it smacks of structural-functionalism to accept Topnaar as a fixed category.[15] In the case of the Topnaar and all other indigenous peoples referred to in this book, groups were flexible conglomerations of constantly shifting patterns of allegiance.

At the turn of the nineteenth century these Nama-speaking groups shared structures of sociopolitical and economic organization, language, myths, and rites. They also had a consciousness of being related to one another that they expressed in genealogical terms real or fictitious. They did not live in rigidly defined territorial groupings. Although they all had their own water holes, these were not limited to a specific territory but were widely dispersed. An analysis of water holes and cattle posts based on early sources clearly indicates that until the 1840s certain groups did claim specific places for themselves. This concerned rights to water holes, however, and did not extend to territorial claims.[16]

In the context of settlement patterns, people were not separated into strictly defined territories but lived in an intermixed or checkerboard fashion. It is not possible to delineate even an approximate area occupied exclusively by groups of, for example, Topnaar or Swartboois. Notions of territoriality appear to have been vague; they were generally characterized by incorporation rather than by mutual exclusion. The Gai-//khaun, for example, lived scattered over a wide area in settlements that were interspersed with those of other groups, which held first claims to the water holes.

Precontact Nama social organization was based on kinship ties and the

---

13. Hoernlé, *supra* note 12, at 6.

14. *Id.* at 5–16; Budack, *A Harvesting People on the South Atlantic Coast,* 6 S. Afr. J. Ethnology 1 (1983) (translating Topnaar as "people of a marginal area").

15. In this study, Topnaar, like other ethnic terms, is used for convenience and assumes fluidity in the composition of groups. As employed here, Topnaar designates the indigenous people of Walvis Bay at any particular time.

16. Hoernlé, *supra* note 12, at 72.

acquisition of cattle and clients to enhance one's status rather than on capitalist means of gaining wealth, such as commodity exchange. From early visitors' accounts, it appears that there was a strict sexual division of labor.[17] Women made mats and built huts with them. Married women were the main producers because they milked the cattle and thus provided the staple food, sour milk. This was supplemented by veldkos—edible wild plants, plants with medicinal qualities, herbs, honey, and fruit—which they collected. Among the coastal peoples, such as those in the Walvis Bay area, the women also gathered the !nara melon and processed the kernels for food, ᵢ coastal peoples of southwestern Africa seem to have done for some eight ꞌusand years.[18] In addition, they collected marine life from the beaches.[19] Uninitiated young males performed tasks related to the tending of livestock, such as herding and watering. Hunting and the conduct of political affairs was the domain of adult males. Men from coastal groups also speared fish and sealed but did not use boats, nets, hooks, or lines.[20]

Among the Nama-speaking groups, decision-making processes, the distribution of cattle posts, and the distribution of power were determined by kinship relations. Each group seems to have been ruled by a chief who controlled a system of reciprocity, surplus extraction, and accumulation that was characteristic of many precapitalist African societies and that encouraged followers to become dependent upon their chiefs and buttressed chiefly power.[21] Its purpose was to increase not the number of commodities of exchange but the number of followers or dependents. In this system, it appears that the labor of uninitiated young men was directed toward the strenuous task of cattle raising. The chief's authority to allocate the labor of these young men seems to have derived from control over matrimony. To withhold a wife from a young man meant that he had to do more years of cattle tending for an adult male owner. This system seems to have obtained throughout Namibia south of the Swakop River, in the vast area inhabited by these Nama-speaking people that came to be known to Europeans as Namaland or Great Namaqualand.[22]

17. London Missionary Society Journals [hereinafter cited as LMS Journals], Albrecht, May 25, 1808 (Cape Archives, Cape Town) [hereinafter cited as KAB].

18. Sandelowsky, *supra* note 1, at 22.

19. For Namibia there is evidence dating to 10,000 years ago that shellfish were collected for food, and there is similar evidence dating to 30,000 years ago for other parts of southern Africa. Speed, *Prehistoric Shell Collectors*, 24 S. AFR. ARCH. BULL., parts 3, 4 (1969).

20. Budack, *The =Aonin or Topnaar of the Lower !Kuiseb Valley and the Sea,* in 3 KHOISAN LINGUISTIC STUDIES 15–17 (A. Traill ed. 1977).

21. Wesleyan Missionary Notices (1821), Shaw, Account, 120 (Cory Library, Grahamstown) [hereinafter cited as WMN].

22. Transactions of the London Missionary Society, III, 212 (KAB) [hereinafter cited as TLMS]; LMS Letters, A. Albrecht, *Observations,* n.d. (KAB).

When in the eighteenth century white Afrikaner pastoralists called trek-boers crossed the northern border of the Cape Colony and settled just beyond its bounds, fugitive slaves and other emigrants joined them. This area became known as Little Namaqualand. By the time the name was established, all the people dwelling in those parts had become part of a trade network originating in the Cape. Without goods obtained from the Cape, their very existence would be threatened. Through the exchange of goods, the colonial frontier was gradually extended north and east. The change to British rule in the Cape sparked new impulses and created pressures for a further extension of the network of social relationships based at the Cape. Thus the action once taken by a mere handful of pioneers—namely, to cross the Orange River and settle on the other side—came to be considered necessary by whole groups of people.

It is not clear when the term Great Namaqualand came into use. Contacts across the Orange River seem to be much older than is suggested by the earliest written records of Europeans living on the northern side.[23] As early as 1805, missionaries of the London Missionary Society wrote of the people residing on the northern side as Great Namaquas.[24] By that time it was also known that north of the Great Namaquas lived the Tamaras, or Damaras. After groups of people known as Orlam moved from Little Namaqualand and the Cape Colony into Namaland at the end of the eighteenth and the beginning of the nineteenth centuries and the Afrikaner Orlam established themselves under Jonker Afrikaner at what is now Windhoek, a rough borderline was drawn in the north along the Swakop River. Thus Great Namaqualand, which included what is today the Walvis Bay territory, became a fairly well defined area, bounded by the Atlantic in the west, the Kalahari Desert in the east, the Swakop River in the north, and the Orange River in the south.

North of the Swakop boundary line was Damaraland, also called Here-roland—roughly the area north of Windhoek up to Otavi, though during the 1870s it also included Windhoek.[25] From the mid-eighteenth century on, this

23. By 1820, the head of the Gai-//khaun was well acquainted with the authority of the Cape governor. LMS Journals, Kitchingman 16 (1820) (KAB).

24. LMS Journals, Albrecht, Aug. 30, 1905 (KAB). As early as 1796 these people were referred to as Greater Nimiquas. K. Budack, Die traditionelle politische Struktur der Khoe-Khoen in SüdwestAfrika 22, Ph.D. dissertation, University of Pretoria (1972).

25. In the far north was Ovamboland, populated by people speaking the Ovambo language. With nearly 700,000 people, the Ovambo comprise almost 55 percent of modern Namibia's population of 1,252,500. U.N. Institute for Namibia 1970 census figures quoted in SWAPO, To BE BORN A NATION 3 (1981) (670,000 Ovambo constitute 53.5 percent of the population, whereas whites account for 8 percent). *See generally* Moorsom and Clarence-Smith, *Underdevelopment and Class Formation in Ovamboland,* in THE ROOTS OF RURAL POVERTY (R. PALMER & N. PARSONS eds. 1977).

area was populated mainly by diverse and largely unconnected groups of pastoral nomads who spoke the Herero language.[26] Like Great Namaqualand, the area was ultimately incorporated into a larger system of economic and social relationships dominated by merchant capital that destroyed the old order. The first agents of this profound change were the Orlam.

The Orlam

By the end of the eighteenth century, people who became known as Orlam were moving north across the Orange River.[27] A combination of Nama-speaking hunting-and-gathering and pastoral peoples whose societies had been destroyed by expanding merchant capitalism at the Cape, people of mixed descent, and fugitive slaves, the Orlam were Westernized dependents of white farmers, traders, and hunters. They knew how to use guns, wore Western clothing, were Christian, and had a knowledge of Dutch.[28] They depended for survival upon European trade goods, and because their knowledge of pastoral techniques had decayed or long since disappeared, they procured cattle to pay for desired commodities by raiding the stock of Nama- and Herero-speakers. They carried out their raiding through the institution of the commando.[29]

Typically composed of between ten and fifty armed men on horseback, the commando was the main means of appropriating wealth used by Orlam groups. It also structured social relations within the groups. The leader of the

26. A Pfouts, *supra* note 11, at 5. The Herero language falls into the Bantu sub-branch of the Benue-Congo branch of the Niger-Congo family. Like the word Topnaar, the term Herero is used for convenience to indicate these diverse peoples. As a result of the paucity of archaelogical evidence, it is not clear when the first Herero-speakers entered Namibia. One theory is that they arrived from the east in the mid-sixteenth century and began to push south in the second half of the eighteenth century. *See* T. SUNDERMEIER, DIE MBANDERU 11–17 (1977). In 1876, William Coates Palgrave estimated their population to be 85,000. G. 50–'77 at 83.

27. The origin of this word is disputed. One scholar argues that it comes from the phrase "over land." Kienetz, *The Key Role of the Orlam Migrations in the Early Europeanisation of South West Africa (Namibia),* 10 INT'L J. AFR. HIST. STUD. 554 (1977).

28. Legassick, *The Northern Frontier to 1820: The Emergence of the Griqua People,* in THE SHAPING OF SOUTH AFRICAN SOCIETY, 1652–1820 (R. Elphick & H. Gilliomee eds. 1979); J. Du Bruyn, The Oorlam Afrikaners: From Dependence to Dominance, c. 1760–1823, 6, University of South Africa (1981) (unpublished paper); Bradlow, *The Significance of Arms and Ammunition on the Cape's Northern Frontier at the Turn of the Eighteenth Century,* 26(1) HISTORIA (1981).

29. *See generally* B. Lau, The Emergence of Kommando Politics in Namaland, Southern Namibia, 1800–1870, 84–103, M.A. Thesis, University of Cape Town (1982) [hereinafter cited as B. Lau, M.A. Thesis]; Lau, *The Kommando in Southern Namibia, 1800–1870,* in NAMIBIA: PAST AND PRESENT (C. Saunders, ed., University of Cape Town, Centre for African Studies, Occasional Papers No. 4, 1983).

commando was the *kaptein* (captain), and its other members were his *raad,* or council. This small group of men often controlled thousands of people.

Although the leadership of the commando operated outside the scope of Western democratic institutions, those institutions had a profound influence upon Orlam groups. Various groups adopted *ryksboeke,* or constitutions, which showed strong Western influence and are good examples of how Orlam and indigenous Nama societies differed. According to the ryksboeke, the members of the governing raad were to be elected. Sessions of the raad had to be public, with decisions based upon the will of the majority of raadsmen. Whole sections of the ryksboeke were devoted to church laws. Included was a prohibition on polygamy.[30] This stricture in particular demonstrates a shift away from a precapitalist order, in which the accumulation of followers was central to wealth accumulation, toward one in which the acquisition of commodities was paramount.

As Orlam groups moved across the Orange River, they established dominance first over Nama- and then over Herero-speakers. Their success was a result of the commando's military superiority, which was largely due to the use of guns and horses. The fact that the Nama- and Herero-speakers possessed large herds may also have made them easy victims, because the herds could not be moved readily and quickly.

In contrast to the indigenous Nama groups, the Orlam had strict notions of territoriality.[31] Although at some point the Orlam groups may have had Nama names for themselves, such names soon disappeared and groups came to be known by the name of their principal place of settlement. Thus, there were the Bethanie people, or Bethaniens, the Berseba people, and the Gobabis people. Orlam groups might also be known by the family name of their captain. The Witboois, for example, were followers of the Witbooi family; the Afrikaners, or Afrikaner Orlam, under Jonker Afrikaner—not to be confused with the white Afrikaners—played a central role in the history of Namaland.

The Afrikaners were the first Orlam group to cross the Orange River in the 1790s. Before that time, they, like other Orlam groups, had raided across the Orange into Namaland against both indigenous peoples and white farmers who had moved there early in the eighteenth century.[32] As Orlam groups

---

30. *See, e.g., Ryksboek, bevattende alle wetten en regten van het kapteinskap te Bethanie, bestaande uit drie boeken: 1. Het boek der ryks-geskiedenis, 2. Het boek der wetten en 3. Het boek van aanmerkingen.* A.8 Rust Collection (typed copy), State Archives, Windhoek [hereinafter referred to as WA].

31. Hahn Papers 9, Apr. 22, 1858 (KAB). *See* B. TINDALL, *supra* note 10, at 35–36.

32. Legassick, *supra* note 28, at 271. *See* J. Du Bruyn, *supra* note 28; Bradlow, *Petrus Pienaar: Ruffian or Courageous Pioneer,* 34 Q. BULL. S. AFR. LIBRARY 3 (1980).

moved farther and farther into Namaland at the beginning of the nineteenth century, the conflict between these groups and the indigenous Nama-speakers intensified. The first four decades of the century were a time of great struggle for water holes, territorial rights, and people, in which indigenous Nama-speaking groups lost claims to water holes, pastures, and many thousand head of cattle.[33]

During these years of turmoil, the Afrikaners emerged as the dominant group in Namaland. By the mid-1820s, Jonker Afrikaner had become the most successful commando leader and had established himself along the border between Namaland and Damaraland.[34] Between 1825 and 1835, he moved to the area around Rehoboth and Windhoek and formed an alliance with the head of the senior indigenous Nama-speaking group, the Gai-//khaun. By 1835, Jonker had established headquarters at Windhoek.[35] Jonker's alliance with the Gai-//khaun gave his people political legitimacy in Namaland and confirmed their ascendant position in the area until the 1860s.

It appears that the Afrikaners did not conquer the Gai-//khaun, because there is no evidence of tributary or exploitive relations between them. Instead, in exchange for ensuring that Herero chiefs would not use land south of the Swakop River for grazing, the Afrikaners seem to have obtained hegemony over the land and people between the Swakop and Kuiseb rivers, including the land and people of Walvis Bay.

From his headquarters at Windhoek, Jonker carried out raids on the herds of neighboring groups and collected taxes and tribute. Commando operations often involved traveling over such great distances as that from Windhoek to Walvis Bay, which is at least 187 miles.

Jonker increasingly exerted his influence over the region, especially the Walvis Bay area. By the mid-nineteenth century, a growing number of vessels were calling at the Bay to supply the missionaries in the interior with provisions. Jonker, who because of his people's dependence on European commodities was keen to control the trade, built a road from Walvis Bay along the Kuiseb River and linked it with the Bai Weg (Bay Road), the existing road

33. The evidence on the size of the indigenous Nama-speaking and Orlam populations is contradictory. The historian and archivist Brigitte Lau argues that the Nama were numerically superior to the Orlam. B. Lau, M.A. Thesis, *supra* note 29, at 74. However, the Rev. C. Hugo Hahn, for example, estimated for the early 1850s that there were 12,300 Nama out of 25,000 Namaland inhabitants. Hahn Papers, Diary 3, last page (KAB). Such estimates must be treated with caution because, by the 1850s, the incoming Orlam had severely disrupted indigenous Nama societies and intermarriage had occurred.

34. Schmelen 222 (1832) in AFRIKANISCHER HEIMATKALENDER.

35. In 1842, there seem to have been 1,000 people living in Windhoek and another 1,000 dependents living on its outskirts. Kleinschmidt 256 (1942) in AFRIKANISCHER HEIMATKA-LENDER.

from Otjimbingwe.[36] The road facilitated trade and further consolidated Jonker's control over the Bay.

In addition to furnishing taxes and tribute, dependents of the Afrikaner Orlam looked after Afrikaner cattle. By 1845, the people of Walvis Bay were employed by Jonker and had placed themselves under his protection.[37] Dependents also collected veldkos, which together with cattle products was the basis of subsistence in Orlam groups; grew tobacco and dagga; made copper ornaments; served in commandos as carriers, guides, and combatants; built and repaired roads; collected taxes; served as messengers; and guarded the women and children of the settlement when most adult males were absent on raids or hunting expeditions.[38]

The effects of the Orlam presence on the indigenous Nama-speaking inhabitants of Namaland were so profound that by mid-century they had taken on Orlam economic and social structures, with their emphasis on trade with the Cape and cattle raiding. Indigenous Nama-speaking groups adopted guns and horses for their raids on the herds of Herero-speakers, which were generally on a massive scale. From the 1840s, the decline or disappearance of skills in animal husbandry noticeable among Orlam groups began to occur among Nama groups. They ceased to dig wells for their cattle, relying instead upon surface water, which was rapidly depleted; they were therefore constantly searching for sources of water. The Topnaar of Walvis Bay suffered particularly, because all the cattle that went to Cape Town via Walvis Bay used the Kuiseb pastures and eventually destroyed them.[39] With the cattle they obtained through raiding, the indigenous Nama-speakers bought guns, ammunition, and horses, as well as wagons and European clothing and furniture. What once were discretionary or luxury items, such as European clothing, became necessities. By the 1850s, non-Western dress had disappeared.[40]

The old kinship structures and sanctions of chiefly power lost their importance. Whereas polygamy was a central institution of precapitalist sur-

---

36. B. TINDALL, *supra* note 10, at 36.

37. *Id.* at 79.

38. *Id.* at 90–143; Hahn Papers 9, July 26, 1846; Aug. 1, 1846 (KAB); Knudsen, *Nachrichten über die Damara und Nama,* AFRIKANISCHER HEIMATKALENDER 109 (1963); Berichte der Rheinischen Missionsgesellschaft 201 (1849) [hereinafter cited as BRMG]; BRMG 212 (1852); BRMG 51 (1855); BRMG 214 (1860); BRMG 263, 270 (1869); T. BAINES, EXPLORATIONS IN SOUTH WEST AFRICA 73–74 (1864).

39. Hahn Papers 9, Jan. 8, 1858 (KAB).

40. B. RIDSDALE, SCENES AND ADVENTURES IN GREAT NAMAQUALAND 82–83 (London: 1838). When the mother of the leader of the Veldskoendraers donned full "traditional" dress on one occasion in the 1840s, it created a sensation. *Id.* at 166.

plus appropriation, by the late 1840s it had all but vanished from indigenous Nama-speaking groups. Power was no longer intertwined with control over kinship structures but with access to commodities. By mid-century, there were many instances of intermarriage between Nama and Orlam groups.[41] No longer were patterns of conflict and allegiance understandable in terms of genealogical or kinship notions. The Nama also began to accept the leadership of captains who did not necessarily rule because of genealogical connections, and like Orlam groups, Nama groups came to be known by the names of leading families.[42]

From the 1840s on, travelers, traders, and missionaries ceased to distinguish between the Nama and Orlam except when mentioning a former state of affairs; they referred to all collectively as Namaquas.[43] Old concepts of territoriality disappeared. There was a shift to settlement patterns characterized by exclusivity and a more definite delineation of group boundaries. Christianity was adopted also, and missionaries—the first mission station in Namaland had been founded in the south at Bethanie in 1806—became a major political force.

The War of the Missionaries and Traders

By the 1850s, missionaries who represented a number of denominations, among which the Rhenish Mission Society was most powerful, had a central role in the politics of Namaland and Damaraland. The reasons for this were strategic and economic rather than religious. As the Nama/Orlam groups were entirely dependent upon trade with the Cape for their survival, the missionaries' ties to that network were of great value to them. Missionaries often acted as traders.[44] Until 1840 they were the main suppliers of arms and ammunition, and throughout the century churches served as munitions depots.[45] Missionaries also attracted itinerant traders, acted as informants about prices, and taught such useful skills as the reading and writing of Dutch, the language of trade.

Jonker was keenly aware of the threat that missionaries posed to his

41. BRMG 19, 34 (1855); BRMG 334 (1856); BRMG 26 (1859); 20 QUELLEN ZUR GESCHICHTE SÜDWESTAFRIKA (H. Vedder & E. Meier eds.) Sept. 18, 1842 (WA).

42. *See, e.g.,* BRMG 344 (1856).

43. Andersson Papers 10, x (WA); Knudsen, *Nachrichten über die Damara und Nama: Tagebuchaufzeichnungen,* AFRIKANISCHER HEIMATKALENDER 109 (1963).

44. H. LOTH, DIE CHRISTLICHE MISSION IN SÜDWEST-AFRIKA. ZUR DESTRUKTIVEN ROLLE DER RHEINISCHEN MISSION BEIM PROZESS DER STAATSBILDUNG IN SWA 31–34 (1963).

45. *See, e.g.,* BRMG 1862 at 22; BRMG 1865 at 179.

hegemony because of their links to the Cape trade network. Even though he allowed the Rhenish missionaries Carl Hugo Hahn and Johann Rath to station themselves at Neu-Barmen and Otjimbingwe, respectively, he wished to prevent Europeans from exploring Damaraland and Ovamboland in the far north for fear that they would supply the Herero with guns. He also wanted to prevent the missionaries from establishing any contact with Herero chiefs who were independent of his control.

Already in the 1840s, Jonker had made several alliances with Herero leaders, including Kamaherero.[46] Through these Jonker sought to maintain control over the access of the Herero chiefs to guns and thereby over his own access to Herero labor and cattle and the northern hunting veld, which provided the ostrich feathers and ivory so important in trade with the Cape.[47]

If missionaries were to operate among the Herero, their activities would lessen Herero dependence on the Afrikaners and threaten the dominant position of the Afrikaners in Namaland and Damaraland. New lines of struggle were being drawn. There were those who sought to maintain the Afrikaners' hegemony over Herero labor and cattle and the northern hunting veld. Others sided with the missionaries in seeking to break the Afrikaners' power. Competition for access to commodities from the Cape rather than historical ties determined these divisions. The Topnaar of Walvis Bay were, for example, deeply divided in their loyalties. Although some supported the Afrikaners, in the early 1850s, instead of following Jonker's orders, many deserted to other Nama/Orlam leaders and others simply returned to the Bay.[48]

In their struggle against the Afrikaner Orlam, the missionaries found willing partners in the numerous traders of diverse nationalities in the area. Although little research has been done on these traders, it is known that by the 1870s they numbered in the hundreds.[49] The traders wished to undermine Jonker's hegemony because of the great profits to be made through free access to the Namaland trade. For this trade, Walvis Bay was the major point of entry and exit. Traders brought in vast quantities of ammunition, which they bartered with the local inhabitants for cattle, sheep, goats, ivory, and ostrich feathers. By 1854, eight to ten thousand cattle a year were being sent to the Cape from Namaland.[50] By 1865, the amount of ivory exported from Walvis Bay per year had reached fifteen to twenty thousand pounds.[51] Consequently,

46. *See, e.g.,* Hahn Papers 9, July 29, 1849 (KAB).

47. Hahn Papers 9, Feb. 10, 1847 (KAB).

48. BRMG 1854 at 15; BRMG 1855 at 24–29.

49. Interview with B. Lau, Whk. Archives, Jan. 1986. *See also infra* notes 54–56 and accompanying text (Andersson at Otjimbingwe).

50. C. ANDERSSON, LAKE NGAMI 37 (1856).

51. G.H. 19/10, J. Chapman, Memo., Feb. 1865 (KAB).

in the 1860s, the traders joined with the missionaries to usurp the power of the Afrikaner Orlam.

Together the traders and missionaries began and were the driving force behind what is usually referred to as the Orlam-Herero War or the Herero War of Liberation,[52] terms developed by the missionaries and traders in the belief that they would make it easier to enlist the support of the German and Cape governments.[53] In fact, the Herero played only a minor role as mercenaries, and the war was instead one in which the missionaries and traders and, regardless of ethnicity, groups with missionaries among them—the southern Orlam captains in particular—worked together against the Afrikaner Orlam.

In 1860, at the Rhenish Mission Society headquarters at Otjimbingwe, a trader named Charles John Andersson founded a large permanent trading center.[54] There he armed and trained some Cape Coloured volunteers and some Herero target shooters.[55] With them and with the help of the missionaries and seventy-five white traders, he asserted his supremacy in the area. The Afrikaner Orlam retaliated, and war began on June 15, 1863.[56]

During the war, loyalties were continually realigned, and the level of violence rose. The Afrikaners were gradually weakened. Throughout, however, they and their allies attacked only traders and missionaries out of the conviction that it was they who wished to take the country away. Kamaherero never offered the missionaries and traders more than halfhearted support, and even that only after the missionaries and traders appealed to his desire to lessen his dependence on the Afrikaners.[57] By the end of 1867, after significant Herero losses, there arose an antimission movement among the Herero, all of whom left Otjimbingwe.[58] Feeling their position threatened, the missionaries called upon the Cape government to end the war between the villainous Afrikaners and the peace-loving Herero and southern captains, to protect Walvis Bay, and to safeguard the route between the Bay and Otjimbingwe.[59]

52. *See, e.g.,* H. VEDDER, SOUTH WEST AFRICA IN EARLY TIMES 325–91 (1966); I. GOLDBLATT, HISTORY OF SOUTH WEST AFRICA FROM THE BEGINNING OF THE NINETEENTH CENTURY 31–34 (1971).

53. *See, e.g.,* Andersson Papers 5, Oct. 25, 1864 (Andersson refers to "the war of independence of the Damaras") (WA). *But see* G.H. 19/10, J. Chapman, Memo., Feb. 1865 (urging Cape government not to see conflict as Herero War of Liberation) (KAB).

54. I. GOLDBLATT, *supra* note 52, at 31.

55. *See* BRMG 1862; Andersson Papers 4 (1862) (WA).

56. BRMG 1863 at 340–50; BRMG 1864 at 245–46. For a detailed discussion of the war, see B. Lau, M.A. thesis, *supra* note 29, at chapter 9.

57. Andersson Papers 5 (WA), Green to Andersson, May 12, 1865; Hahn to Andersson.

58. BRMG 1868 at 243. T. SUNDERMEIER, *supra* note 26, at 51.

59. G.H. 34/19. Enclosure to Despatch No. 14 to Secretary of State, 1868 (KAB).

The Road to Annexation

This was not the first time the Cape Colony had been urged to take an active role in South West African affairs. In the 1860s, the Colony had acquired various islands off the west coast, known collectively as the Penguin Islands.[60] In 1867, rumors proliferated of vast mineral deposits, especially silver, along the coast opposite the islands.[61] Although Cape Governor Sir Philip Wodehouse first wished to annex the coast and then most of what is today Namibia out of fear of foreign intervention,[62] the home government rejected his scheme when it discovered the size of the area he proposed to annex.[63]

Wodehouse then turned his energies to ending the war, exerting pressure on both sides. In May 1870, the missionary Carl Hugo Hahn went to Okahandja, Kamaherero's headquarters, and negotiated a peace treaty that put the Afrikaners' diminished status in writing. It prohibited Jan Jonker, now their leader, from interfering with the Herero and their land. By the terms of the treaty, Kamaherero lent Windhoek to Jan Jonker as grazing ground. The treaty did not affect Orlam ascendancy in the rest of Namaland, including Walvis Bay.[64]

An uneasy peace prevailed during the 1870s. In 1872, Kamaherero sent a letter to Henry Barkly, Wodehouse's successor, requesting that he arbitrate between the Orlam and the Herero so that another war might be prevented. The request went unheeded. Kamaherero asked "that the excellent British Government will give us a hint how to govern our poor country, and extend a helping hand to our poor people in giving us good advice as to what we are to do to retain our country because the Namaquas will not live in peace."[65] In 1874, Kamaherero sent another request.[66] He feared that the Dorsland Trekkers, a group of white trekboers from the Transvaal—a Boer republic established by Dutch-speaking emigrants from the Cape Colony and recognized by Britain in 1852—who had entered Damaraland from the east would take his land and cattle.

By this time, the Cape had been granted responsible government, and

60. *See infra* Appendix.
61. E. LEWIN, THE GERMANS AND AFRICA 71 (1915); G.H. 31/10, No. 20, Nov. 3, 1867 (KAB).
62. G.H. 31/10, No. 20, Nov. 3, 1867; G.H. 31/10, No. 51, June 14, 1867 (KAB).
63. G.H. 1/14, No. 43, Aug. 23, 1867 (KAB).
64. G. 50-'77 at ii–iv. The treaty, which did not define the boundaries between Namaland and Damaraland, presumably left the lands as they had been before the years of war, i.e., divided by the Swakop River.
65. *Id.* at 20. G. THEAL, 5 HISTORY OF SOUTH AFRICA FROM 1795 TO 1872, 104–05 (1920).
66. G. 50-'77, Annexure 2, at iii.

Prime Minister Sir John Molteno and his cabinet took an interest in Ka-maherero's appeal. Curiosity about the area was high because rumors of great mineral wealth once again abounded. Gold and silver had been discovered in Damaraland. The belief arose that Great Namaqualand was also laden with minerals. The possibility of acquiring the area also intrigued Molteno because control of it meant control over trade, especially in guns and gunpowder, with the interior.[67]

The British government meanwhile feared Portuguese involvement in the area, because Portuguese territory already extended to the eighteenth degree of south latitude, and Portugal excluded other Europeans from its colonies. The British government worried that if the Portuguese annexed the area, Portugal would monopolize trade with the interior. Moreover, the De-lagoa Bay Arbitral Award, rendered in July 1875, increased British distrust of the Portuguese.[68] In that case, the arbitrator, the president of France, found that Portugal and not Britain had sovereignty over the southern portion of Delagoa Bay, on the southeastern coast of Africa. Portugal already had title to the northern portion.

The British government was also concerned by the presence of the Dorsland Trekkers, fearing that if the Trekkers created a new state with an outlet to the sea, it would be tremendously popular among white Afrikaners and perhaps attract many of them from the Cape.[69] Moreover, such a republic would presumably strengthen the positions of the Transvaal and the Orange Free State, another Boer republic, recognized as independent by Britain in 1854.[70] The new state might be sympathetic to other Afrikaner polities, or it might even be incorporated into the Transvaal. Whatever happened, a Boer republic with access to the sea would threaten British hegemony in the area. Germany did not figure in British fears of foreign intervention at that time.

It was in this political environment that the Cape House of Assembly first raised the annexation issue in June 1874.[71] On June 23, 1875, the Legislative Assembly adopted a resolution favoring extension of the Cape Colony's boundaries to include Walvis Bay and "such tract of Country inland as may be found necessary, with due regard to the rights of the Native Chiefs and

67. In 1871 the Cape government had endeavored to restrict the trade in guns and gun-powder by forbidding their shipment to any area beyond the Cape Colony's boundary without special permission. Cape Argus, March 7, 1874.

68. Delagoa Bay Arbitration (Great Britain v. Portugal) (1875) 149 CONSOLIDATED TREA-TY SERIES 363; MOORE, INT. ARB. 4984.

69. G. 50–'77 at 88.

70. On the Boer republics, see generally Thompson, *Co-operation and Conflict: The High Veld*, in 2 THE OXFORD HISTORY OF SOUTH AFRICA 391 (M. Wilson & L. Thompson eds. 1969).

71. Cape Argus, June 20, 1874.

others."[72] The task of carrying this out fell to William Coates Palgrave, whom the government appointed in March 1876 as special commissioner to the tribes north of the Orange River. Palgrave had been in southwestern Africa as a hunter, traveler, and explorer during the 1860s and had been employed in the civil service since 1869.

The British home government was not as sanguine about annexation as the Cape. Lord Carnarvon, the secretary of state for the colonies, feared that the Cape's acquisition of territory would interfere with his confederation scheme, a plan for a union of the British colonies and the Boer republics of southern Africa, which the Legislative Assembly had already rejected in 1875.[73] Nevertheless, on April 10, 1876, the Cape government sent an expedition from Cape Town to Walvis Bay in the schooner *Themis*. The group, which comprised Palgrave and three assistants, arrived fifteen days later. Palgrave was to act as "a Commissioner of Enquiry into the resources of the country, and the disposition of the various Tribes towards Colonial Rule."[74] He was also "to ascertain the character and capabilities of the country lying North of the Orange River known as Great Namaqualand and Damaraland, and the rights of Native Chiefs and others to territory therein with the view of paving the way for annexation of British dominion over them."[75]

After the expedition arrived at Walvis Bay, the handful of white residents and traders in the area gave Palgrave a petition with twenty-three signatures that favored British annexation of the Bay.[76] From there, Palgrave proceeded to Okahandja, where he hoped to extract a request from the Herero for colonial protection. He arrived on May 26 to encounter much opposition from Kamaherero, who had by then been strongly influenced by the German missionaries in the vicinity.[77] Those missionaries, in light of the rise of the Colonial Party in Germany, wished to see the country become a German possession.

In the face of Kamaherero's hostility toward the Cape government, Palgrave had to devise another means of forcing him to seek Cape protection.

---

72. Cape Colony, Votes and Proceedings of the House of Assembly, 1875, No. 45, at 443.

73. G.H. 1/22, Despatches Received, Confidential: No. 147, Nov. 24, 1875; G.H. 1/23, Despatches Received, No. 9, Jan. 24, 1876 (KAB). On confederation, see generally Thompson, *Great Britain and the Afrikaner Republics, 1870–1899,* in 2 THE OXFORD HISTORY OF SOUTH AFRICA 292–300 (M. Wilson & L. Thompson eds. 1971).

74. G.H. 31/13, No. 35 of Apr. 4, 1876, at 208.

75. *Id.*

76. G.50-'77 at 7. According to Palgrave, the white population of Walvis Bay, "consisting usually of not more than five or six persons, was at the time of my arrival augmented by the presence of some hunters and upcountry traders who had come down for supplies." *Id.*

77. N.A. 1139, Palgrave's Letter Book, at 42 (KAB).

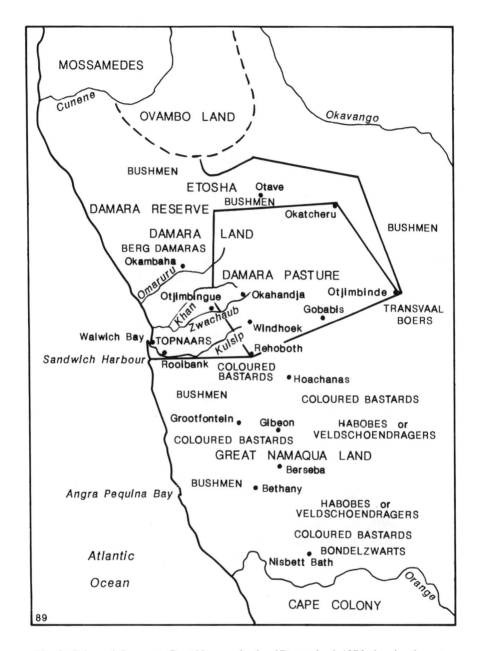

Map 2. Palgrave's journey to Great Namaqualand and Damaraland, 1876, showing the route of the special commission

Source: W. PALGRAVE, REPORT OF THE SPECIAL COMMISSIONER TO THE TRIBES NORTH OF THE ORANGE RIVER, OF HIS MISSION TO DAMARALAND AND GREAT NAMAQUALAND IN 1876 (1877).
G50-'77, Cape Archives, Cape Town.

He did this by exploiting the rivalries between Kamaherero and those lesser chiefs who sought to unseat him. Palgrave did much politicking among those chiefs. In a July 1876 meeting with Kamaherero and other chiefs who owed him allegiance, including some of those opposed to his rule with whom Palgrave had spoken, Palgrave claimed that the Cape had sent him to the country in response to Kamaherero's letters of 1872 and 1874.[78] He stated that it was entirely up to the Herero whether they accepted Cape rule but added that it was the sole means of preserving their independence from foreign invaders. Refusing to allow any action to be taken without the presence of the chiefs Kamoretti and Kambathembe, Kamaherero adjourned the meeting until August 31.

Palgrave spent the time between the two meetings lobbying Kamaherero's adversaries for annexation and settling disputes between Kamaherero and the whites in the country. So successful was he that at a meeting on September 4, Kamaherero, perhaps fearful of losing his leadership if he continued to object to annexation, threw his support behind those favoring Cape intervention. Palgrave reported that Kamaherero, with the support of the other chiefs, said that he wished to have Cape protection because "the Portuguese are our enemies, the Boers are our enemies" and asked that a resident, namely, Palgrave, be sent to the country.[79]

Palgrave then proposed through Robert Lewis of Barmen, a trader and member of Kamaherero's council, that Kamaherero cede a piece of land (later known as the Reserve) to the Cape and that the revenue from it be used for administrative purposes. At a meeting on September 9, various Herero chiefs agreed to grant a reserve and ceded those parts of the coast that the government desired. The Reserve, which included Walvis Bay, was forty-five thousand square miles of land, from Rehoboth in the south to the Cunene River in the north. The land retained by the Herero, including Windhoek, covered thirty-five thousand square miles in the east of the country.[80]

According to Palgrave, Kamaherero agreed to these definitions of the boundaries after they were read aloud by Lewis, saying, "These are the boundaries. Mr. Lewis has described them correctly, as well as those of the part we wish to keep for our own occupation and uses."[81] Palgrave then sent a letter to the governor signed with Xs by Kamaherero and the majority of the Herero chiefs, headmen, and councillors present, informing him of the proceedings. The letter indicated that the parties had the following rights

78. G.50–'77 at 31.

79. N.A. 1137, Palgrave's Journal, Sept. 4, 1876 (KAB). He also castigated the Griquas, a people of mixed descent. On the Griquas, see R. Ross, ADAM KOK'S GRIQUAS (1976).

80. G.50–'77 at 40–41.

81. *Id.*

and duties. The British were to (1) appoint a resident to rule the country and establish administrative machinery required under the institution of protectorate and (2) protect the Herero against attack. The Herero chiefs were to (1) acknowledge the authority of the British representative sent to their country, including his right to punish foreigners for crimes committed on their land; (2) cede such portions of their territory as were necessary for the resident's performance of his tasks under the agreement; and (3) give financial contributions, if necessary, for the maintenance of British administration over the land.[82]

After achieving what from his point of view was a great success with the Herero, Palgrave turned his attention to the Afrikaner Orlam. He went to Windhoek but failed to extract a similar agreement from Jan Jonker. Then, at a November 29, 1876, meeting of Nama/Orlam captains that the northern captains, including Jan Jonker, did not attend, Palgrave told those present that they were in great danger from the Portuguese and the trekboers. He also claimed that the Cape had no interest in Namaland though it might consider protecting the land from invasion were it to receive a request to do so from the captains.[83] In the end, Jan Jonker and the other captains were not to be persuaded. Palgrave did, however, induce the Bondelswart leader Willem Christian and his raad to accept Cape domination, because on December 22 they allegedly requested protection.[84] His mission ended, Palgrave crossed the Orange River and returned to the Cape.

In his official report, Palgrave extolled Walvis Bay as the economic lifeline of an area that would figure prominently in expanding the country's trade.[85] Much of this expansion would result from the cattle-raising efforts of four hundred white farming families with whom Palgrave wished to people the Reserve. Palgrave thus urged the Cape to comply with the Herero request and annex the coast.

The Cape Parliament and public opinion supported Palgrave's views, and he was sent to Damaraland to prepare the land for annexation.[86] Although the government did not receive the letters patent during the parliamentary session and was consequently unable to introduce the bill for the annexation of the land in the Walvis Bay area, it still sent the second commission on its journey.

Palgrave was to prepare the land for annexation and put into effect the

82. *Id.* at 41–43.
83. N.A. 1137, Palgrave's Journal, Nov. 27, 1876 (KAB).
84. G.50–'77 at 100.
85. *Id.* at 10–11.
86. G.H. 32/2, Confidential Despatches Sent, at 20. Confidential Despatch of Nov. 13, 1877 (KAB).

measures he had recommended. He arrived at Walvis Bay on October 3, 1877, and proceeded to Okahandja, where he delayed his meeting with Kamaherero for a week because he was unable to find an interpreter. When they did meet, Palgrave informed Kamaherero of his purpose in returning to Damaraland; Kamaherero purportedly voiced disappointment at Palgrave's failure to bring a magistrate with him and at the Cape government's failure to annex the coast.[87] In a series of despatches, Palgrave then urged the Cape to send a magistrate who would facilitate the settlement of five hundred trekboers in the area.[88] The response was dilatory because of political developments occurring in the Cape Colony. When war broke out in 1877 between the Colony and the Xhosa chief Sarhili, Governor Sir Bartle Frere, Barkly's successor, was summoned to the eastern frontier. He was there when he received details of the plans for the second commission. As he was preoccupied with events of the war, it was not until November 13, 1877, that he wrote from King William's Town to Lord Carnarvon telling him of the Colonial Parliament's decisions and actions regarding annexation.[89] Fearing that independent Boer republics would be founded, he urged that Walvis Bay be annexed as quickly as possible and that a protectorate be established over that area bounded on the north by the border of the Portuguese colony later called Angola, on the south by the Orange River, on the east by the Transvaal border, and on the west by the Atlantic Ocean.

In his response to Frere, Carnarvon again rejected the idea of establishing an extensive protectorate because of the instability in the region and because the conflicts between whites and indigenous peoples on the Cape Colony's eastern frontier demanded much of the government's energies. His position was different regarding Walvis Bay, which he recognized as the key to strategic and economic control of the region. With its considerable trade and good harbor, "the only safe one within a long distance," it was "the only door of entrance to very large regions in which the Colony is materially interested."[90] Thus, Britain should exercise jurisdiction over the Bay but no more.

When Frere received this despatch, he immediately made plans for annexing Walvis Bay. On March 1, 1878, Commander Richard Cossantine Dyer, R.N., left Simon's Town for Walvis Bay in HMS *Industry* with orders "to hoist the British flag, to take possession of, and to declare and proclaim the port, the settlement of Walfisch bay, and the country immediately sur-

---

87. N.A. 844 at 345, No. 820 of Sept. 19, 1877 (KAB).

88. N.A. 1140, Palgrave's Letter Book, No. 11 of Jan. 31, 1878 (KAB).

89. G.H. 32/2, Confidential Despatches Sent, Confidential Despatch of Nov. 13, 1877 (KAB).

90. A.14–'81 at 20–21.

rounding the same for a distance inland to be determined by him [Dyer] to be British territory."[91] Before acting he was to consult Palgrave.

Dyer reached Walvis Bay on March 6 while Palgrave was away in the interior. Dyer thus had to decide for himself how much territory to annex. In this regard, he consulted the Bay's white inhabitants about their desires and the likely needs of the port. They informed him that because neither fresh water nor produce was available at the Bay or in its immediate vicinity, the annexed territory should incorporate land that yielded both. They also told him that virtually the only place from which they could be obtained was the Rooibank, estimated to lie some thirteen to eighteen miles inland. After viewing the place—he called it "the plateau"—which was an oasis, he decided to include it within the territory.

Having so concluded, Dyer issued a proclamation annexing Walvis Bay to Her Majesty's dominions. It fixed the boundaries of the territory as follows: "On the south by a line from a point on the coast fifteen miles south of Pelican Point to Scheppmansdorf; on the east by a line from Scheppmansdorf to the Rooibank, including the plateau, and thence to ten miles inland from the mouth of the Swakop River; on the north by the last ten miles of the course of the said Swakop River and on the west by the Atlantic Ocean."[92]

On March 12, 1878, Dyer hoisted the Union Jack and took formal possession of the territory in the name of the queen. He reported that the proclamation was read to all the white inhabitants of the Bay and "some of the neighboring Hottentot and Damara tribes."[93] An interpreter explained the annexation to those blacks who were present, and Dyer claimed that they "appeared to be well-pleased with the Imperial Government's action."[94]

The British government approved of Dyer's annexation, and on December 14, 1878, letters patent issued under the great seal at Westminster.[95] They ratified and confirmed Dyer's proclamation and authorized the governor of the Cape Colony acting with the consent of the Colonial Legislature to declare that the Walvis Bay territory was part of the Cape of Good Hope and subject to its laws. Although Walvis Bay was now annexed to Her Majesty's dominions, six years elapsed before the territory was formally annexed to the Cape.[96]

91. *Id.* at 122.
92. *Id.* at 25; C. 2144 at 8, Enclosure No. 5; 69 BRITISH AND FOREIGN STATE PAPERS 1177.
93. C. 2144 at 6, Further Correspondence Respecting the Affairs of South Africa, Dyer to Secretary of the Admiralty, Mar. 28, 1878.
94. *Id.* It is not clear exactly who was present at the annexation. The number of people present is also unclear.
95. 70 BRITISH AND FOREIGN STATE PAPERS 495–96.
96. 75 BRITISH AND FOREIGN STATE PAPERS 407.

Annexation

After Dyer annexed the Bay, Frere continued to lobby for the annexation of the coast between the Bay and the Portuguese boundary.[97] In this he was rebuffed by Carnarvon, who felt that because Walvis Bay was the only viable harbor, no European power would have designs on the surrounding area.[98] The Portuguese consul in Cape Town meanwhile expressed displeasure with Dyer's proclamation because of a mistaken belief that it included all the land in Palgrave's Reserve, some of which, under the Anglo-Portuguese Treaty of 1815 and the Supplementary Convention of 1817, Britain had acknowledged as Portuguese.[99]

The British government eventually persuaded Portugal that it had not intentionally encroached upon Portuguese territory. Rather, Palgrave's instructions charged him with respecting the "rights of civilized powers."[100] The Herero had made such an agreement with Palgrave, the government said, because they had "no idea" that the Portuguese had any claims of sovereignty.[101]

After Dyer's annexation, the Colonial government took over the administration of Walvis Bay. On June 1, 1878, Major D. Erskine, former colonial secretary of Natal, became the first resident magistrate of Walvis Bay. Palgrave, who was still in the country, turned his attention to two tasks: completing his mission to the Orlam and peopling the Reserve. In both he failed.

The Orlam received news of the annexation of Walvis Bay "with indifference" and set themselves against foreign intervention.[102] Some groups also contacted Kamaherero and suggested that they stand together "for our country."[103] Even Kamaherero questioned the government's control, saying, "Why should white people be taxed? The country does not belong to them. They are only here to hunt and trade. But now they have a bit of paper and will go about saying 'the country is ours, we have bought it with this.' "[104] Palgrave thus concluded that his mission to the Orlam could not succeed.

97. G.H. 32/2, Confidential Despatches Sent, at 164. Confidential Despatch, Sept. 17, 1878 (KAB).

98. G.H. 2/2, Confidential Despatches Received, Confidential Despatch No. 73 of Oct. 15, 1878, Enclosure 3 (KAB).

99. G.H. 2/2, Confidential Despatches Received, Confidential Despatch No. 88, Nov. 14, 1878, Enclosure 2; Confidential Despatch No. 73, Oct. 15, 1878, Enclosure 2 (KAB).

100. G.H. 2/2, Confidential Despatches Received, No. 73, Oct. 15, 1878, Enclosure 3 (KAB).

101. *Id.*

102. N.A. 1140, Palgrave's Letter Book, No. 20, June 25, 1878 (KAB).

103. G.33–'79 at 147 (Native Affairs Blue Book for 1879).

104. *Id.* at 157.

Palgrave also faced resistance in peopling the Reserve. The Herero, many of whom lived in the Reserve, resented Palgrave's plans to settle trekboers there. In 1879, fever broke out among whites in the area, leaving the trekboers destitute and starving. The Cape sent a relief expedition that included Palgrave—he had returned to Cape Town at the beginning of the year—to aid those who were in the northern part of the Reserve and at Fort Rock on the coast near the border with the Portuguese territory. The reasons for the expedition were not, however, humanitarian but strategic. The Cape was concerned that the Portuguese might attempt to extend the southern boundary of their territory to Fort Rock or that the trekboers themselves might assert a claim to the area. In the end, the Boers left northern Damaraland and established themselves in Portuguese territory.

In spite of his failures, Palgrave continued to press for annexation because it was solicited by the Herero, "the dominant race" in the area.[105] Fearing German intervention, Frere also urged the annexation of the coast.[106] Britain still refused to grant any of these requests, because it did not believe that other states had designs on the area. Since it controlled Walvis Bay, the only viable harbor, it was adamant that no foreign power could use the coast to advance a claim on the territory.[107] Periodically, the government had received reports of harbors between Walvis Bay and the border of the Portuguese territory. Such harbors would have decreased Walvis Bay's strategic significance—both economic and military. In 1879, when HMS *Swallow* traveled to Fort Rock on the trekboer relief expedition, its captain was given orders to examine the coast between Walvis Bay and Fort Rock and to evaluate the suitability of Ogden's Harbor, north of Walvis Bay, and Fort Rock. The captain reported that it was impossible to land at Fort Rock, which was not a harbor at all, and that he found no trace of Ogden's Harbor, while observation revealed no harbor along the entire coast between Walvis Bay and Fort Rock.[108]

In 1880, Palgrave replaced Erskine as resident magistrate of Walvis Bay; he also became the commissioner for Damaraland, using Walvis Bay as his base. He was to seek "no fresh annexation of territory."[109] Upon his arrival in Walvis Bay, Palgrave learned that many disputes had arisen there between

---

105. N.A. 1140, Palgrave's Letter Book, No. 117, Aug. 14, 1878 (KAB).
106. G.H. 32/2, Confidential Despatches Sent, at 273, Confidential Despatch, Oct. 28, 1879; Confidential Despatch, Jan. 12, 1880, at 333 (KAB).
107. G.H. 2/3, Confidential Despatch Received, No. 59, Dec. 25, 1879 (KAB).
108. A.40–'80 at 48, 56–58.
109. G.H. 1/32, Despatches Received, No. 39, Feb. 17, 1880 (KAB).

white traders and the local chiefs, who charged for the privilege of passing through their land or drawing water.

In October, after conflicts over grazing land, war broke out between Kamaherero and Jan Jonker and their respective allies. When news of the war reached the Colonial government Palgrave was recalled to Cape Town and Major Benjamin D'Urban Musgrave, who had been at Okahandja, was transferred to Walvis Bay, where he was to be resident magistrate. The Cape then abandoned its interest in Namaland and Damaraland. The Earl of Kimberley, secretary of state for the colonies, in instructions to Cape Governor Sir Hercules Robinson, emphasized Britain's unwillingness to become involved with the land north of the Orange River, except for Walvis Bay. In his view, the Bay should be retained because of "the importance of controlling the only port along a great extent of coast through which arms and trade can pass into the interior."[110]

After the Cape government prohibited the importation of arms and munitions through Walvis Bay in March 1881, Musgrave began to receive petitions for assistance from the white inhabitants. By that time there had been a collapse of trade, which had grown steadily after the 1870 Peace of Okahandja to reach its highest level in 1878, when combined imports and exports totaled £178,864.[111] Transporting items inland from the Bay became dangerous. The stores of Eriksson and Company, the main traders at the Bay, were due to close; Musgrave believed that the only other store at the Bay would follow suit and that traders would abandon the port for the haven of Portuguese territory.[112]

Meanwhile, on February 16, 1881, several German missionaries and traders sent a letter to the imperial German commissioner, W. A. Lippert, complaining that Palgrave was hostile to them and that, by favoring the Orlam in the war, he was endangering their lives as well as those of other white residents in Damaraland.[113] Lippert in turn wrote to the Cape secretary for native affairs, complaining that Musgrave had encouraged the Topnaar, British subjects, to join forces with Abraham Swartbooi, who sought to remove whites from Damaraland.[114] In fact, the Topnaar entered the war as allies of Abraham Swartbooi out of fear that he would kill them if they did not.[115]

110. C. 2754 (1881) at 8, Instructions Addressed to Governor Sir Hercules Robinson, Kimberley to Robinson, Dec. 30, 1880.
111. J. ESTERHUYSE, SOUTH WEST AFRICA 31 (1961).
112. A.71–'82 at 1–4.
113. C. 3113 at 25–26. Enclosure 3 in No. 16.
114. *Id.*
115. *Id.* at 13–15. Enclosure 4 in No. 6.

Toward the end of 1881 Musgrave was again under pressure from the whites of the Bay and the adjacent areas, who had heard a report that the Herero chiefs planned to send to the Bay a thousand-man commando opposed to Musgrave. As a precautionary measure, the high commissioner agreed to send twenty-five men to the Bay in the gunboat *Wrangler* under the command of Captain E. J. Whindus. The Reverend Hahn, who led the expedition as special commissioner for the Walvis Bay territory, decided upon arrival to leave Whindus and ten constables at the Bay to keep order.[116] He then departed for the interior, and the *Wrangler* set sail for Cape Town on February 25, 1882.

In June 1882, the Herero and most of the Nama/Orlam groups, with the exception of the Witboois and Jan Jonker's people, concluded the Peace of Rehoboth. Since Jan Jonker was not a party, however, the fighting continued. Destitute blacks came to the Bay; Whindus reported that there was much misery in the Walvis Bay territory and that these blacks often appealed to him and the other white residents for food.[117]

Kimberley expressed dismay at the retention of Walvis Bay, especially because it was still not incorporated into the Cape Colony but was merely annexed to Her Majesty's dominions as a direct imperial responsibility. Neither its white population nor its trade had increased since Dyer's proclamation of 1878, and arms and ammunition were still reaching the interior via the Portuguese possession in the north and Angra Pequeña in the south.[118]

At that time there arose the feeling in the Colony that Walvis Bay was a useless possession.[119] As public debate over the Bay raged, its anomalous status received much attention. Although Dyer's proclamation had annexed the territory to Her Majesty's dominions, it was not joined to any colony and no governor had been appointed for it. The territory thus had no apparatus for administering justice.[120]

Although this situation had never caused difficulties before, it became a problem in 1883 when an African named Frederick allegedly committed an unprovoked murder in the Walvis Bay settlement. At the time, Captain

116. Whindus served as acting resident magistrate. A.71–'82 at 23, 24.

117. In this work, the term *blacks* is used to indicate Africans, Indians, and people of mixed descent classified as Coloured (e.g., the Nama/Orlam) under South African and South West African racial legislation.

118. C. 3113 at 38, No. 25, Feb. 7, 1882, Kimberley to Robinson.

119. *See, e.g.,* A.82–'82. Annexures to the Votes and Proceedings of the House of Assembly, Cape of Good Hope, 4th Sess., 6th Parl. 1882, Petition of the Inhabitants of the Division of Albert.

120. C. 4190 at 21 (1884). Correspondence Respecting the Settlement at Angra Penqueña on the South West Coast of Africa. No. 26, Smyth to Derby, Oct. 30, 1883.

Whindus, who as acting resident magistrate was an officer appointed and remunerated by the Cape Colonial government, managed the internal affairs of the Walvis Bay territory. There was, however, no legal code for the Bay, no court in the territory capable of adjudicating the matter, and, because of the peculiar status of the territory, no Cape Colony court that had jurisdiction over its affairs. Although the Cape government could not legally detain Frederick, to release him would indicate to the black residents of Namaland and Damaraland that the Cape authorities lacked power.[121] The solution it offered was annexation of the Walvis Bay territory to the Cape Colony.

The growth of German interest in southwestern Africa in the 1880s was another, more important factor in the debate over the annexation of not only the Walvis Bay territory but also all Namaland and Damaraland. As early as 1868, groups were forming in Germany to promote German colonization. In 1879, Frere had pointed to Germany as having designs on the area. At that time, however, it was widely known in British and German diplomatic circles that Bismarck's policy disfavored colonialism. In 1875 he had declined to establish a colony in the Transvaal. Two years later he had responded mildly to Britain's annexation of the Transvaal, and he had not exploited British difficulties during the Anglo-Boer War of 1881, when the Transvaal Boers rose in revolt against British rule.[122]

Fearing that failure to establish an overseas empire would have serious economic repercussions for Germany, Bismarck began to change his mind. German trade with Africa and Asia, though still only a fraction of the country's total trade, grew steadily in the 1870s. As long as there was free trade in the colonial world, Germany was content with access to the markets. In the 1880s, however, there were signs that free trade was ending as the colonial powers began to favor their own nationals through the use of differential tariffs and other restrictive legislation.[123]

Bismarck's fear of losing access to these markets was heightened by various developments that ended in the 1885 colonial partition of Africa. Not least among these was the much-publicized race between Pierre Savorgnan De Brazza and John Morton Stanley to claim territory along the Congo (Zaire) River in the early 1880s. While parts of Africa and Asia remained free of colonial rule, Germany would still have access to their markets and resources.

121. *Id.* at 22. Enclosure No. 26, Ministers to Administrator, Oct. 3, 1883.

122. Butler, *The German Factor in Anglo-Transvaal Relations*, in BRITAIN AND GERMANY IN AFRICA 178, 183 (P. Gifford & W. Louis eds. 1967) [hereinafter cited as Gifford & Louis].

123. Turner, *Bismarck's Imperialist Venture: Anti-British in Origin?*, in Gifford & Louis, *supra* note 122, at 47, 50–51.

If the European powers carved up those continents, a Germany without colonies would be at an economic disadvantage. With these concerns in mind, Bismarck changed his policy.[124]

At the end of 1883, the German threat in Namaland and Damaraland loomed large for the Cape Colony. The year before, F. A. E. Lüderitz, a German merchant from Bremen, had sought protection from the German government for any territory he might acquire on the southwest African coast. Lüderitz informed the German foreign office that he wished to trade and that he desired a port that would allow him to avoid the import duties at Walvis Bay. The foreign office replied that it would grant his request provided that his acquisitions did not interfere with the rights of any other person or company.

In May 1883, Lüderitz's agent purchased Angra Pequeña harbor and the land surrounding it in a five-mile radius from Captain Josef Frederiks, leader of the Bethanie people.[125] Three months later, Frederiks, in a treaty he signed with an X, purportedly sold Lüderitz the entire coast from the Orange River to the twenty-sixth degree of southern latitude, including all the harbors and bays as well as the hinterland to a distance of twenty miles.[126] Once more Lüderitz called for German protection. At the same time, a series of articles appeared in the German press praising Lüderitz's actions as part of the colonial enterprise.

The Cape ministers then called upon the British government to assert its rights to the coasts of Namaland and Damaraland. In a minute dated January 30, 1884, they declared that because of projected difficulties, the west coast should be under "the formal sovereignty of some recognized power."[127] These difficulties stemmed from the presence of rival traders of various nationalities who might incite rebellion among the blacks in the area. Hence, "the interests of order and civilisation" would best be served by the annexation of the remainder of the coast from the Orange River to the Portuguese territory and the appointment of a governor to administer the territory.[128]

Germany had meanwhile already taken the initiative for annexation. When hostilities began in 1880, the German foreign office had asked the British government to accord its missionaries and traders in Namaland and Damaraland the same protection it would give its own subjects. As Britain decided not to become involved in the conflict, the German authorities re-

124. *Id.*
125. G.H. 31/8 at 330, Despatches Sent, No. 230, Aug. 13, 1833; No. 235, Aug. 20, 1883, at 333 (KAB).
126. I. GOLDBLATT, *supra* note 52, at 81.
127. G.70–'84 at 11.
128. *Id.*

ceived official notice that Britain sought no responsibility for events outside of Walvis Bay.

The German government was also aware of a despatch of December 30, 1880, from the Earl of Kimberley to Sir Hercules Robinson, which stated: "It is the opinion of Her Majesty's Government that the Orange River is to be regarded as the north-western frontier of the Cape Colony, and the Government will not give its support to plans for extending British jurisdiction over Great Namaqualand and Damaraland."[129] Although aware of these British disavowals of sovereignty over Namaland and Damaraland, on February 7, September 10, and November 16, 1883, the German government inquired whether Britain claimed to own Angra Pequeña Bay. There was no definite answer. On December 31, 1883, Bismarck demanded a firm reply, but not until May 29, 1884, did the Cape government take charge of the territory in case the British government should decide to annex it.[130]

Meanwhile, on April 24, 1884, Bismarck had cabled the German consul at Cape Town with instructions to declare officially that Lüderitz and his establishment were under German protection. Bismarck then spoke with the British ambassador in Berlin and told him that Germany would extend protection to those commercial enterprises in which German subjects acquired territory and that he would grant a royal charter to such persons. Bismarck's object was "to obtain from England the official admission that those waste districts were . . . res nullius. I wanted to make sure by England's own admission that she had no demonstrable claims or titles of possession in those regions."[131]

At the end of June, Britain learned through diplomatic channels that "the German Government had . . . made up its mind to take its subjects in that region under its protection and, in effect, to adopt the grant to Mr. Lüderitz as a grant of sovereignty or supremacy to itself."[132] By then the Cape ministers had decided to ask the Cape Parliament to annex the coast from Walvis Bay to the Orange River. On July 14, Derby informed Robinson that Britain did not oppose the German claim. Therefore, the land surrounding Angra Pequeña, which Lüderitz acquired in a manner comporting with the legal norms of the day, should fall under German protection. Britain should instead place under its protection the coast north of the twenty-sixth degree of south latitude.[133]

129. C. Lowe, Prince Bismarck 217 (1886); W. Aydelotte, Bismarck and British Colonial Policy 34 (1935).

130. G.70–'84 at 13–14.

131. L. Lavers, Walfish Bay and Angra Pequeña 30, M.A. thesis, Columbia University (1924).

132. C. 4265 at 6.

133. *Id.*

The Cape Parliament had already passed a resolution favoring the annexation of the coast from Walvis Bay to the Orange River. Sentiment was that the Cape should send a gunboat to Angra Pequeña so that Germany could not predicate its actions upon the lack of British protection. On July 16, the House of Assembly passed a resolution favoring the annexation to the Cape Colony of the coast between the southern boundary of Portuguese territory and Walvis Bay and between Walvis Bay and the Orange River.[134] In light of these developments, the Cape annexed Walvis Bay. On July 24, 1884, the Cape Colonial Parliament passed the Walfish Bay and St. John's River Annexation Act (No. 35 of 1884),[135] and on August 7 the governor issued a formal Proclamation of Annexation (No. 184).[136] Its publication ended the six-year delay since the issuance on December 14, 1878, of the letters patent confirming Dyer's proclamation to the final act of incorporation into the Cape Colony.

With the exception of the Cape's annexation of the Bay, it was too late for British designs on Damaraland and Namaland. Germany had decided to act. On August 7, the same day that the governor's proclamation of annexation of Walvis Bay appeared, Captain Schering, commandant of a German warship, complying with orders from his government, put the territory Lüderitz had acquired under German protection and hoisted the German flag. That territory extended from the north bank of the Orange River to the twenty-sixth degree of south latitude, twenty miles inland; it also included all the islands belonging thereto by the law of nations, namely, those within gunshot distance of the coast. On August 16, 1884, Schering issued a proclamation announcing the establishment of a German protectorate over Namaland and Damaraland.[137]

The day before, the German consul at Cape Town had informed the governor of these actions. On September 5, he told Robinson that Germany had now also annexed the coast from Cape Frio to Walvis Bay and from Walvis Bay to the twenty-sixth degree of south latitude. The British government received official confirmation on October 15 that the area was a German protectorate.[138]

In spite of the Cape ministers' protestations, the British government accepted the German actions. It acknowledged that Germany had acquired, "by the recognized means," territory to which Britain had "no sufficient legal title" and in which Germany had the greater trading and missionary in-

---

134. *Id.* at 5.
135. Walfish Bay & St. John's River Territories Annexation Act (No. 35 of 1884).
136. Proc. No. 184 of 1884, Cape of Good Hope Government Gazette, Aug. 8, 1884, at 408.
137. C. 4262 at 12–13.
138. E. HERTSLETT, 2 MAP OF AFRICA BY TREATY 693 (1909).

terests.[139] Britain recognized the acquisition especially because it already possessed "large tracts of unoccupied territory."[140]

The Cape was not prepared, however, to abandon plans for the annexation of Namaland and Damaraland. It began discussions with various Orlam leaders and sent Palgrave to the area. He induced Kamaherero to request Colonial protection on February 23, 1885.[141] After much diplomatic correspondence, however, a July 30 minute from Robinson insisted that because Britain had recognized Germany's annexation and claims, it was not possible for the Colony to intervene in the area.[142] Upon receiving this communication, the Cape Colony abandoned all hope of annexing Namaland and Damaraland, which were now German, and contented itself with the Walvis Bay territory.

139. C. 4265 at 6–7.
140. *Id.*
141. A.5–'85 at 24–25.
142. N.A. 293, Letter Received from Resident Magistrate Walvis Bay, Governor's Minute No. 55, July 30, 1885 (KAB).

CHAPTER THREE

From the Annexation to the Proclamation, 1884–1977

uring the ninety-three years following the Cape's annexation of Walvis Bay, the Bay grew in economic and strategic importance. Legislative changes linked the Bay to the former German South West Africa territory, which South Africa began to administer after World War I as a League of Nations mandate.

Administrative Changes

As the economic and strategic significance of the Walvis Bay territory for controlling all of South West Africa was well known to Britain and Germany, in 1885 the precise delimitation of its southern boundary came under dispute.[1] At issue was the wording of Dyer's proclamation and the documents repeating it—the letters patent of 1878 and the Annexation Act of 1884—which Germany interpreted to exclude the water supply at Rooibank and the fertile land at Ururas from the Walvis Bay territory.[2] This would have

---

1. Discussions of the boundary dispute are found in I. BROWNLIE, AFRICAN BOUNDARIES 1273 (1979); Barnard, *Die Walfisbaai Grensgeskil,* 1 J. GEOG. (S. AFR.) (1962); Lansdown, *The Walfisch Bay Arbitration,* 6:6 THE STATE 566 (1911).

2. The British and German statements of their cases are found in C.O. 2292 and C.O. 2293 (KAB).

deprived the Bay of fresh water and made continued British control impossible.

After three Anglo-German commissions had failed to reach any agreement about the boundary,[3] the dispute was finally settled by arbitration in 1911.[4] The arbitrator, a Spanish jurist, found in favor of Britain and fixed the boundary in accordance with an 1885 survey conducted by a Cape government surveyor. Accordingly, Walvis Bay became bounded on the south by a line from a point on the coast fifteen nautical miles south of Pelican Point to Scheppmansdorf or Rooibank, including the Ururas tract; on the east by a line from Scheppmansdorf to Rooikop; from there to ten miles inland from the mouth of the Swakop River; and on the north by the last ten miles of the course of the Swakop.

Even as the boundary dispute raged, on July 1, 1890, Britain and Germany concluded an agreement regarding Africa and Heligoland that, though it left the boundary issue undecided, recognized British authority over the Bay and German supremacy over the South West Africa protectorate.[5] Then, in 1910 the four British colonies of the Cape Colony, Natal, the Transvaal, and the Orange River Colony joined to form the Union of South Africa.[6] As a Cape Colony possession, Walvis Bay passed to the Union. Until that time, the Cape Parliament and administration had treated Walvis Bay as they did the Transkeian territories. This meant that the Bay fell under the administration of the native affairs department and that Parliament authorized the governor to legislate for the territory by proclamation.[7] Consequently, the Bay's white population, which was thirty-one in 1891,[8] had no representation in the Cape

3. *See id.*

4. Award of Don Joaquin Fernandez Prida, Arbitration in the Matter of the Southern Boundary of the Territory of Walfisch Bay, Madrid, May 23, 1911, Parliamentary Paper, Africa, No. 1 (1911), Cd. 5857, 104 BRITISH AND FOREIGN STATE PAPERS 50.

5. Agreement, *reprinted in* M. HURST, 2 KEY TREATIES FOR GREAT POWERS 873 (1972).

6. The central piece of legislation in the unification process was the South Africa Act of 1909, 9 Edward VII c9. On the Union, see generally L. THOMPSON, THE UNIFICATION OF SOUTH AFRICA (1960).

7. Proc. of Governor of the Cape of Good Hope, Aug. 7, 1884, 75 BRITISH AND FOREIGN STATE PAPERS 407; Walfish Bay & St. John's River Territories Annexation Act, No. 35. of 1884, 75 BRITISH AND FOREIGN STATE PAPERS 408. Accordingly, Section 1 of Annexation Act No. 35 of 1884 provided that the Walvis Bay territory was "subject to the Laws of the Cape of Good Hope." Section 2 provided that those laws might, until otherwise provided by act of Parliament, be "repealed, altered, amended and modified; that the Governor might make, repeal, alter, amend, and modify new laws applicable to the territory; and that no Act thereafter passed by the Cape Colonial Parliament should extend or be deemed to extend to the territory unless expressly so stated."

8. Results of a Census of the Colony of the Cape of Good Hope as on the Night of Sunday, the 5th April, 1891, at 50, 64 (1892).

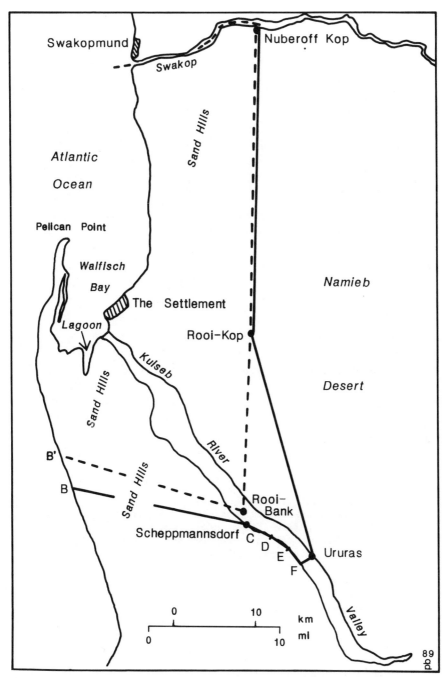

Map 3. Walvis Bay territory during Anglo-German boundary dispute, 1885–1911. The British line ran from B at the coast to C, then through D, E, and F to Ururas, and then to Rooikop. Germany contended that it should run from B' at the coast, then to the mission house at Rooibank, and then to Rooikop, as indicated by the dotted line.

Source: Landsdown, *The Walfisch Bay Arbitration,* 6:6 THE STATE (1911).

Parliament, and laws passed by that body applied to Walvis Bay only when the governor's proclamation so extended them. With the formation of the Union of South Africa, the governor's legislative power, which the South Africa Act did not affect, vested in the British governor-general.[9]

From 1910 to 1915, for legislative and administrative purposes, the Union government treated the Walvis Bay territory, which had a population of thirty-two whites and seven hundred blacks,[10] as part of the Union. In 1915, Union forces fighting in World War I on the side of the Allied and Associated Powers occupied German South West Africa. The South African military governor issued a proclamation on September 20, providing that "for the better administration of the said Territory and Port of Walvis Bay on account of its contiguity to the [German South West African] Protectorate," all proclamations and martial law regulations issued or to be issued in the protectorate would apply to Walvis Bay.[11]

After the war, the Union administered what had been German South West Africa on behalf of Britain as a League of Nations C mandate.[12] Less than two years after the Union accepted the mandate in 1920, it enacted three related laws that expanded upon the legislative relation between South West Africa and Walvis Bay established by the Martial Law Proclamation of 1915, creating legislative unity between the two territories.

The first law was the South West Africa Affairs Act of July 19, 1922, which granted the governor-general of South Africa the power to set a date after which "the port and settlement of Walvis Bay . . . shall be administered as if it were part of the mandated territory and as if inhabitants of the said port and settlement were inhabitants of the mandated territory."[13] It also permitted

9. South Africa Act of 1909, *supra* note 6.

10. Results of a Census of the Colony of the Cape of Good Hope as on the Night of Sunday, the 17th April, 1904, at xxvi, li, 60–61 (1905); Census of the Union of South Africa, 1911, at clxx (1913). The population was the same in the 1904 and 1911 censuses. The figures for the black population must be regarded with suspicion.

11. Proc. No. 12 of 1915.

12. *See infra* chapter 7.

13. Act No. 24 of 1922. The South West Africa Affairs Act provided that: "(1) From a date to be fixed [by the British Governor-General of the Union of South Africa] . . . the port and settlement of Walvis Bay which forms part of the Cape of Good Hope shall be administered as if it were part of the mandated territory and as if the inhabitants of the said port and settlement were inhabitants of the mandated territory; and the powers conferred upon the Governor-General . . . [to legislate for Walvis Bay] may be delegated by the Governor-General to the Administrator of the mandated territory to the intent that the said Administrator may, by the repeal, alteration, amendment or modification of laws and the making of new laws bring the laws in force in that port or settlement into conformity with the laws of the mandated territory . . . (4) No act of the Union Parliament passed after . . . [the date fixed by the Governor-General] shall apply to the said port and settlement unless by such Act it is specifically ex-

the governor-general to delegate his powers to make laws in Walvis Bay to the South African–appointed administrator of South West Africa. The act further provided that after the date set by the governor-general, no act of the Union Parliament should apply to Walvis Bay unless "it is specifically expressed so as to apply or unless it is declared to apply by proclamation of the Governor-General in the [official] Gazette [of the Union]."[14]

On September 15, the governor-general promulgated the second law. According to the terms of the South West Africa Affairs Act, he issued a proclamation that designated October 1 as the day when the administration of Walvis Bay would be transferred to the mandated territory and delegated all the governor-general's lawmaking powers for Walvis Bay to the administrator of South West Africa.[15]

On the day after the changes provided for in the governor-general's proclamation became effective, the administrator of South West Africa promulgated the third law.[16] Among other things, it (1) repealed the South African laws then in effect in Walvis Bay and substituted South West African laws for them and (2) made all territorial laws issued by the administrator automatically applicable to Walvis Bay unless such application was specifically excluded.[17]

The three laws thus placed Walvis Bay under South West African territorial administration, including territorial licensing authorities. Moreover,

---

pressed so to apply or unless it is declared to apply by proclamation of the Governor-General . . . (5) As from the date fixed as aforesaid the said port and settlement shall for all judicial purposes be regarded as forming part of the mandated territory and not as forming part of the province of the Cape of Good Hope."

The act also provided that South West African criminal law as well as civil law applied to Walvis Bay so that "any act or omission which would, if committed within the [mandated] territory constitute a crime, would, under the same law, likewise, constitute a crime if committed or omitted within the port and settlement of Walvis Bay."

14. Act No. 24 of 1922.
15. Proc. No. 145 of 1922.
16. Walvis Bay Administration Proc. No. 3 of 1922 (SWA).
17. *Id.* In accordance with the terms of the other two enactments, the proclamation: (1) made Walvis Bay part of the Swakopmund magisterial district; (2) repealed all legislation in force in Walvis Bay and substituted for it the legislation then "existing and applied" in the mandate; (3) made all legislation to be issued by the South West African administrator applicable in Walvis Bay unless the legislation expressly excluded its operation there; (4) provided that parties should regard suits and proceedings pending in the magistrate's court in Walvis Bay as removed to the court of the magistrate of the Swakopmund district and actions pending in the Cape Provincial Division of the South African Supreme Court as pending in the High Court of South West Africa; (5) provided that licenses previously issued by Walvis Bay (i.e., South African provincial) authorities would thereafter be issued (or renewed) by, and fees in connection therewith be payable to, the corresponding territorial authorities; and (6) stipulated that "all taxes, duties, dues and revenue of every kind and nature" payable within Walvis Bay to the Union or provincial government be payable to the South West African administration.

they subjected Walvis Bay to South West African legislation rather than South African and/or Cape provincial legislation. They also transferred Walvis Bay from Union to South West African judicial administration and provided that in the case of any difference of interpretation between South West African and Cape courts, the former would control in Walvis Bay. This legislative integration was complete except that throughout the mandate period, South African legislation applied to South West Africa only if by its terms a law was specifically applicable thereto. However, even if an act of the Union Parliament was specifically applicable to South West Africa, it did not apply to Walvis Bay unless by its terms it also applied to the Walvis Bay territory, because Section 1(4) of the South West Africa Affairs Act provided that no acts of the Union Parliament applied to Walvis Bay unless made specifically applicable thereto.[18] Thus, Section 1(4) required authors of parliamentary legislation to include separate provisions making the relevant laws applicable to Walvis Bay as well as to the mandated territory or to use another formulation, such as making a law applicable to South West Africa, "including Walvis Bay."[19]

That this was the effect of the laws was not apparent to members of various Union and South West African governmental departments. Confusion arose about the status of Walvis Bay and the laws that applied there. Consequently, in 1944, the Union government promulgated an act to change the anomalous legislative position of the Walvis Bay territory.[20] It made any Union legislation that obtained in the mandate automatically applicable to the Walvis Bay territory. Thereafter, all laws applicable to the mandate, and only those laws, obtained in Walvis Bay. In spite of this new enactment, however, the practice of making Union legislation expressly applicable to the Walvis Bay territory did not disappear completely. For more than ten years after the enactment of the 1944 provision, some acts that Parliament applied to the mandated territory, especially consolidation acts that reenacted verbatim long segments of existing legislation, contained provisions making them specifically applicable to Walvis Bay.

Meanwhile, the Union Parliament had promulgated a constitution for South West Africa in 1925 that granted the white population a measure of legislative and executive power.[21] In accordance with Section 1(4) of the

18. Act No. 24 of 1922.
19. *Id.*
20. Act No. 28 of 1944. It replaced Section 1(4) of the 1922 Act with a new provision stipulating that "any Act of Parliament or proclamation by the Governor-General . . . shall, as long as and to the extent to which it is in force in the mandated territory be in force also in the said port and settlement, unless the Act or Proclamation otherwise provides."
21. South West Africa Const. Act, No. 42 of 1925.

South West Africa Affairs Act, Section 43(a) of the constitution provided that "the port and settlement of Walvis Bay shall be deemed to form a part of the territory for purposes of this Act."[22] In 1968, another constitution replaced the 1925 constitution.[23] As amended a year later,[24] the constitution was to implement the Odendaal Plan, which aimed at turning South West Africa/Namibia, as it was known by then, into a fifth province of South Africa.[25] It included Section 43(a) of the 1925 document as new Section 36,[26] even though the 1944 act, which made all Union legislation automatically applicable to Walvis Bay, had rendered the section superfluous.[27]

The confusion engendered by the 1922 and 1944 legislation did not cause much litigation, however. One of only two exceptions was *Rex v. Offen*.[28] In that 1935 case, Offen received a conviction for contravening the South African Customs Tariff and Excise Amendment Act of 1925 while he was in Walvis Bay.[29] In the trial court, the defendant had argued that he could not be found guilty because the authorities had not properly enacted the law in Walvis Bay. On appeal, J. W. Wessels, chief justice of the Appellate Division of the Supreme Court, South Africa's highest court, upheld the conviction on the ground that publication of the act in the official Union *Gazette* constituted proper promulgation. He based his reasoning on the relation between the mandated territory and the Walvis Bay territory created by Section 1 of the South West Africa Affairs Act. He wrote that Section 1 "means that laws passed for the mandated territory shall be applicable to Walvis Bay, but not that it is to be a part of such territory."[30] Wessels then turned his attention to Section 38(1) of the Customs Act, which stated that South West Africa formed part of the Union for customs and excise purposes, and subsection (3), which provided that the act applied to Walvis Bay, "which for the purpose of this section shall be deemed to be a part of the mandated territory."[31] He wrote that promulgation in the Union *Gazette* made the act applicable to Walvis Bay "not as part of the Union territory only but as part of the Union territory which is deemed to be part of the mandated territory."[32]

22. *Id.* at §43(a).
23. South West Africa Const. Act, No. 39 of 1968.
24. *Id.* as amended by South West Africa Affairs Act, No. 25 of 1969.
25. Republic of South Africa, Report of the Commission of Enquiry into South West Africa Affairs, 1962–1963, R.P. No. 12/1964 [hereinafter cited as Odendaal Report].
26. South West Africa Const. Act, No. 39 of 1968, as amended by South West Africa Affairs Act, No. 25 of 1969, at §36.
27. Act No. 28 of 1944.
28. 1935 S.A. 4 [A.D.], *aff'g* 1934 SWA 73.
29. Act No. 35 of 1925.
30. 1935 S.A. 4, at 6–7 [A.D.].
31. *Id.* at 7.
32. *Id.*

Nineteen years after *Offen* and ten years after the enactment of the 1944 law, the High Court of South West Africa rendered its 1954 decision in *R. v. Akkermann,*[33] which contributed to the view that Walvis Bay had become part of the South West African territory. In that case, the accused was a Coloured man who had permission to travel throughout the Cape Province. When he arrived in Walvis Bay, the authorities charged him with wrongfully entering South West Africa on the ground that territorial legislation prohibited immigration by "non-whites" who did not have official permission. In the Magistrate's Court, Akkermann was acquitted because the magistrate did not think that Walvis Bay was part of South West Africa for purposes of immigration law. The High Court of South West Africa reversed the decision, however, and ruled that for the purpose of immigration law, "the word 'territory' must be interpreted to include the port and settlement of Walvis Bay."[34] Accordingly, by entering Walvis Bay without a permit, Akkermann had violated the law. Judge C. J. Claassen determined that the South West Africa administrator's proclamation of 1922 established that "for all practical . . . purposes . . . unless specifically excluded," Walvis Bay was to be regarded "as if it were an integral part of the Territory of South West Africa."[35]

The Judicial System

Although the changes wrought by the 1922 and 1944 laws were not the subject of much judicial decision making, the judicial system of South West Africa integrated Walvis Bay into itself pursuant to the legislation. Section 1(5) of the South West Africa Affairs Act had provided that after the date fixed by the governor-general, "the said port and settlement shall for all judicial purposes be regarded as forming part of the mandated territory and not as forming part of the province of the Cape of Good Hope."[36] Section 2 of the South West African administrator's 1922 proclamation refined this statement by providing for the removal of cases pending in the Walvis Bay Magistrate's Court or in the Cape of Good Hope Provincial Division of the Supreme Court to the Swakopmund Magistrate's Court or the High Court of South West Africa.[37]

In November 1922, the administrator decided that Walvis Bay "in the [magisterial] district of Swakopmund should be the site of a periodical court."[38] In 1929, the administrator established a justice of the peace district

33. 1954(1) S.A. 195 [SWA].
34. *Id.* at 196.
35. *Id.* (emphasis added).
36. Act No. 24 of 1922 at §1(5).
37. Walvis Bay Administration Proc., No. 3 of 1922 (SWA).
38. Proc. No. 31 of 1922 (SWA).

that had Walvis Bay as its seat and included parts of the Swakopmund and Lüderitz magisterial districts.[39] The High Court of South West Africa sitting in Walvis Bay served as an admiralty court, and at the time of the Second World War it became a prize court for the duration of hostilities.[40] Then, in 1958, the mandated territory added Walvis Bay as a separate magisterial district.[41] When a boom in the fishing industry caused the postwar population of Walvis Bay to grow from six hundred in 1946 to ten thousand in 1960,[42] Walvis Bay, which before 1958 had been part of the magisterial district of Swakopmund, became a separate district. Thus, from 1958 until 1977, the Walvis Bay territory was, in official parlance, "the magisterial district of Walvis Bay in the territory of South West Africa."[43]

Fiscal Affairs

The 1922 laws also effected the fiscal integration of the Bay into the mandated territory. The South West Africa administrator's 1922 proclamation provided that all taxes and revenue from Walvis Bay were to be due to the South West Africa administration.[44] The proclamation also provided for the transfer of licensing power from Cape or Union officials to South West African authorities.

As revenue laws, like all other laws enacted in South West Africa after 1922, applied to the Walvis Bay territory, Walvis Bay became linked to South West Africa and its fiscal structure. From 1922 to 1977, all South West African income tax laws applied to Walvis Bay.[45] South African and South West African authorities, seeking to separate their respective geographical regions in tax matters, entered into a February 13, 1959, agreement that defined the Union of South Africa as "South Africa, excluding the Port and Settlement of Walvis Bay,"[46] whereas South West Africa included the "Port and Settlement."[47] As a result, the residents of Walvis Bay paid the same taxes as all residents of South West Africa and were exempt from such South

39. G.N. 139 of 1929 (SWA).

40. Union of South Africa, Proc. No. 72 of 1940.

41. Proc. No. 43 of 1958 (SWA), *amending* Proc. No. 15 of 1950.

42. Union of South Africa, Census of Population 1946; Union of South Africa, Census of Population 1960; *see also* J. WELLINGTON, SOUTH WEST AFRICA AND ITS HUMAN ISSUES 120 (1967).

43. Proc. No. 43 of 1958 (SWA), preamble.

44. Proc. No. 3 of 1922 (SWA) at §5.

45. *See, e.g.,* South West Africa Income Tax Ordinance, No. 5 of 1974; Republic of South Africa, Income Tax Act, No. 58 of 1962, effective in Namibia, 1969.

46. Income Tax Ratification Ordinance, No. 13 of 1959, art. II, §1(a).

47. *Id.*

African taxes as the South African gift tax and death duties, which did not apply to the residents of South West Africa.[48]

The Franchise

Franchise laws also linked Walvis Bay to South West Africa. Prior to Union, the Bay's white male population had no representation in the Cape Parliament.[49] After 1910, white males voted in South African elections as part of the Cape Town Harbour electoral district.[50] When the government abolished the Cape Town Harbour constituency, Walvis Bay became part of the Cape Province's Sea Point electoral district. Before Walvis Bay residents had voted in the new district, however, the South West Africa Affairs Act transferred Walvis Bay to South West African administration, and Walvis Bay residents lost their South African franchise.[51] Then, the 1925 South West African constitution provided that white residents of the mandated territory could elect twelve members to a South West African Territorial Legislative Assembly, and for that purpose, Walvis Bay became part of the Swakopmund electoral district,[52] which included the Swakopmund magisterial district and portions of adjoining magisterial districts.[53]

The number of elected members of the South West African Legislative Assembly increased in 1949 from twelve to eighteen,[54] and South West Africa received six seats in the South African House of Assembly.[55] At that time Walvis Bay was still part of the South West African Legislative Assembly's electoral district of Swakopmund, and because of the small combined population of Walvis Bay and Swakopmund, whites from some adjoining rural areas were also part of the constituency. However, the population increase at Walvis Bay that ended in the establishment of a separate magisterial district for Walvis Bay also resulted in the creation of a separate electoral district for Walvis Bay.[56] By 1974, Walvis Bay no longer formed a single electoral division; rather, part of the white electorate was in the Walvis Bay electoral division, consisting of the southern part of the "port and settlement," and part, including some of the residents of the northern part of the Walvis Bay territory,[57] was in the Swakopmund division.

48. Windhoek Advertiser, Sept. 9, 1977.
49. *See supra* note 9 and accompanying text.
50. Namib Times, Oct. 17, 1980.
51. Act No. 24 of 1922.
52. Act No. 42 of 1925.
53. G.N. 41 of 1926 (SWA).
54. Act No. 23 of 1949 at §38.
55. *Id.* at §27.
56. Union of South Africa, Act No. 105 of 1950.
57. Namib Times, Oct. 17, 1980.

Treatment of Walvis Bay in Official Publications

Official South African publications from 1922 to 1977 treated Walvis Bay as part of South West Africa for statistical and analytical purposes. Information about Walvis Bay appeared in South African statistics only when South African and South West African data were added in order to yield a single composite figure that the publication attributed to South Africa. Thus, figures for Walvis Bay's population, area, rainfall, and economic activity appeared in South West African statistics and analyses.[58]

South African official yearbooks treated the Bay as part of South West Africa in spite of certain pro forma assertions that it was South African. Physical descriptions of the Union and, later, of the Republic did not include Walvis Bay. For example, the 1922 *Official Year Book of the Union* did not feature Walvis Bay in its physical description of the Union, though the historical section mentioned that Britain had annexed Walvis Bay in 1878.[59] There was no mention in the yearbook of Walvis Bay's status since the British annexation. The chapter on South West Africa also referred to the British annexation while the physical description of South West Africa defined its boundaries so as to include Walvis Bay.[60] Later Union yearbooks also mentioned Walvis Bay in the South West Africa chapter and indicated that it was "administered by the Administration of South West Africa, but the area remains nevertheless an integral part of the Cape Province."[61] Such chapters went on to include Walvis Bay in their discussions of South West African services, facilities, harbors, and economic performance.[62] Still later in the Union period, yearbook descriptions of South Africa noted that Walvis Bay was administered with South West Africa and continued to include Walvis

---

58. *Compare* REPUBLIC OF SOUTH AFRICA, BUREAU OF STATISTICS, STATISTICAL YEAR BOOK 1964 AT V–4, W–4 (South West African figures included in South African figures) *with* UNION OF SOUTH AFRICA, REPORTS OF THE ADMINISTRATOR OF SOUTH WEST AFRICA 1922–39, 1946 (Walvis Bay treated as part of South West Africa), UNION OF SOUTH AFRICA, OFFICIAL YEAR BOOKS OF THE UNION 1922–60 (Walvis Bay included in chapter on South West Africa); *compare also* REPUBLIC OF SOUTH AFRICA, BUREAU OF STATISTICS, STATISTICAL YEAR BOOK 1964 at T–6 (South West African figures included in South African figures) *with* 30 OFFICIAL YEAR BOOK OF THE UNION OF SOUTH AFRICA AND OF BASUTOLAND, BECHUANALAND PROTECTORATE AND SWAZILAND, Pocket Part, table 2 (1960) (First Results of the 1960 Population Census. Union of South Africa and South West Africa. Listing Walvis Bay under the population and principal urban centers of South West Africa. Giving Walvis Bay population figure as 4,765 whites, 2,051 Coloureds, 1 Asian, and 5,438 Bantu for a total of 12,165).

59. *Compare* UNION OF SOUTH AFRICA, 5 OFFICIAL YEAR BOOK 23 (1922) (Walvis Bay not included in physical description of Union) *with id.* at 931–32 (Walvis Bay annexed by Britain and statement implying Walvis Bay made part of South West Africa).

60. *Id.* at 932.

61. *See, e.g.,* UNION OF SOUTH AFRICA, 8 OFFICIAL YEAR BOOK 967 (1925).

62. *See, e.g., id.* at 966–1015.

Bay in the chapter on South West Africa.[63] Maps of southern Africa in Union yearbooks did not portray an international boundary around Walvis Bay.[64] Maps of the Union or of the Cape Province never showed Walvis Bay in an inset, but in the 1925 edition, for example, the chapter on South West Africa contained a map of Walvis Bay.[65]

From 1961 to 1973, no official yearbooks appeared. Once publication resumed, tables giving the length of the South African coastline excluded the Walvis Bay coastline[66] but included the coast of the "independent" Republic of the Transkei, a black South African homeland to which the South African government has granted an "independence" recognized by no other state.[67] Physical descriptions of the Republic in the yearbooks were at odds with the tables. In 1975, for example, descriptions of South Africa and South West Africa indicated that Walvis Bay was part of the Republic.[68] In 1976 and 1977, however, there was no mention of Walvis Bay in the description of the Republic, and a description of Walvis Bay appeared only in the chapter on South West Africa. This description, which was the same in all the 1970s editions, noted that "the total area of South West Africa is 824,269 km^2 (318,261 square miles). . . . This area includes that of Walvis Bay (1, 124 km^2) which is actually part of South Africa. It was proclaimed a British Crown territory in 1878 and annexed to the Cape of Good Hope."[69]

The treatment of Walvis Bay in maps in these 1970s yearbooks was inconsistent and contradictory. Endpaper maps and a "general orientation map" depicting southern Africa showed an international boundary around Walvis Bay.[70] However, the vast majority of maps of the Republic or the Cape Province had no inset for Walvis Bay, and maps of Namibia had no international boundary around Walvis Bay.[71]

63. *See, e.g.*, UNION OF SOUTH AFRICA, 28 OFFICIAL YEAR BOOK 723–72 (1954–55).

64. *See, e.g.*, UNION OF SOUTH AFRICA, OFFICIAL YEAR BOOKS vols. 5, 8, 23, 26, 28, 30.

65. UNION OF SOUTH AFRICA, 8 OFFICIAL YEAR BOOK (1925), S.P. 47 (map of Walvis Bay facing p. 1008).

66. *See, e.g.*, REPUBLIC OF SOUTH AFRICA, DEPARTMENT OF INFORMATION, SOUTH AFRICA 1974, OFFICIAL YEAR BOOK OF THE REPUBLIC OF SOUTH AFRICA 1974 at 39; SOUTH AFRICA 1975 at 1; SOUTH AFRICA 1976 at 3; SOUTH AFRICA 1977 at 1.

67. *See, e.g.*, SOUTH AFRICA 1974 at 39; SOUTH AFRICA 1975 at 1; SOUTH AFRICA 1976 at 1; SOUTH AFRICA 1977 at 1. The Transkei became independent in 1976. For a pro–South African view of Transkeian independence, see Booysen, Wiechers, Van Wyk, & Breytenbach, *Comments on the Independence and Constitution of the Transkei*, 2 S. AFR. Y.B. INT'L L. 1 (1976).

68. SOUTH AFRICA 1975 at 1, 933.

69. SOUTH AFRICA 1977 at 911; SOUTH AFRICA 1976 at 907.

70. *See, e.g.*, SOUTH AFRICA 1974 at 40 and endpapers; SOUTH AFRICA 1975 at 2 and endpapers; SOUTH AFRICA 1976 at 2 and endpapers; SOUTH AFRICA 1977 at 2 and endpapers.

71. *See, e.g.*, SOUTH AFRICA 1974, SOUTH AFRICA 1975, SOUTH AFRICA 1976, SOUTH AFRICA 1977. *Compare* maps in chapters on South Africa (no insets for Walvis Bay) *with* maps in chapter on South West Africa (no international boundary around Walvis Bay).

In addition to yearbooks, many official and quasi-official South African publications from 1922 to 1977 treated Walvis Bay as part of South West Africa. For example, a State Information Office book, *The Peoples of South Africa,* published in the late 1940s or early 1950s, did not mention Walvis Bay or its inhabitants, and maps in the book did not show the Bay.[72] Similarly, the *Atlas of the Union of South Africa,* published in 1959 by the University of Cape Town Department of Geography in conjunction with the South African Council for Educational, Sociological, and Humanistic Research, did not indicate Walvis Bay in any of its maps or tables[73] or include the Bay in its section on fishing and fish processing in the Union.[74]

Official South West African yearbooks, like the South African yearbooks, also contained pro forma assertions that Walvis Bay was part of South Africa. However, they, too, treated Walvis Bay as part of South West Africa in their discussions of South West African services, facilities, and economic performance. In the 1967 *South West Africa Survey,* for example, the figure for the area of South West Africa included Walvis Bay, "which, although part of the Republic of South Africa, is administered, for the sake of convenience, as part of South West Africa."[75] The *Survey* went on to include Walvis Bay in its examination of medical care and harbors.[76] By 1974, as the international controversy over South African control of Namibia grew, assertions of South African sovereignty had become more emphatic. A footnote in the *South West Africa Survey* of that year gave the figure for Namibia's total area as "including the area of Walvis Bay ($1,124$ km^2) which is part of the Republic of South Africa as a result of the area's proclamation as a British Crown Territory in 1878, and its subsequent annexation to the Cape of Good Hope in 1884."[77] Examining the state of Namibia's harbors, the same *Survey* reported that "Walvis Bay has become the Territory's gateway to the outside world" but stressed that it was South African.[78] As in earlier editions, however, maps in

72. REPUBLIC OF SOUTH AFRICA, STATE INFORMATION OFFICE, THE PEOPLES OF SOUTH AFRICA (n.d.).

73. UNIVERSITY OF CAPE TOWN, DEPARTMENT OF GEOGRAPHY & SOUTH AFRICAN COUNCIL FOR EDUCATION, SOCIOLOGICAL, AND HUMANISTIC RESEARCH, ATLAS OF THE UNION OF SOUTH AFRICA (1959).

74. *Id.* at 152.

75. REPUBLIC OF SOUTH AFRICA, DEPARTMENT OF FOREIGN AFFAIRS, SOUTH WEST AFRICA SURVEY 1967 at 7. This and many other official South West African publications were written and printed in South Africa by a branch of the South African government. The SOUTH WEST AFRICA SURVEY was prepared by the same department that was responsible for South African yearbooks.

76. *Id.* at 82, 127.

77. SOUTH WEST AFRICA SURVEY 1974 at 3.

78. *Id.* at 53.

that edition portrayed Walvis Bay inconsistently, some maps indicating an international boundary and others omitting one.[79]

Other Aspects

Beyond the legislative and administrative state of affairs confirmed in official and quasi-official documents and maps, Walvis Bay was physically integrated into South West Africa as early as the First World War, when South Africa occupied South West Africa. At that time there were no visible indications that the mandated and the Walvis Bay territories formed distinct political units.[80] The work of the postarbitration boundary delimitation commission came to nought,[81] and when Union forces occupied German South West Africa, the boundary dividing it from Walvis Bay, though depicted on various maps, was not distinguished by physical markers. Even the roads that led to the Bay had no signs or markers to indicate the boundary between the two territories. Neither were there any fences, guards, guardhouses, or changes in traffic markings. Moreover, although there were no immigration or customs posts or other immigration formalities to contend with when one entered or left the Bay from the South West African territory by road or rail, immigration controls did exist for individuals journeying between Walvis Bay and South Africa. In addition, government officials in Walvis Bay wore the uniforms and insignia of South West African officials. Residents of the Bay used South West African stamps for mail.[82] Walvis Bay motor vehicles had South West African license plates, with the letters sv indicating the district;[83] drivers had South West African permits that were valid in South Africa because South West African authorities had issued them. Walvis Bay schools were part of the South West African school system and governed by South West African law. Hospitals in Walvis Bay[84] fell under the South West African hospital system, established in the mandated territory in 1922.[85] Even canned fish, Walvis Bay's primary export, appeared in markets labeled as a "product of South

79. Compare *id.* at 1 and endpapers (maps showing international boundary) with *id.* at 2 (map showing no boundary). *See also* SOUTH WEST AFRICA SURVEY 1967 at 8 (map showing international boundary) and *id.* at 9–14 (maps showing no international boundary).

80. *See infra* chapter 4.

81. Cape and South African authorities originally estimated the area of the Walvis Bay territory at 374 square miles. In 1962, South African authorities reestimated the area at 434 square miles. Odendaal Report, *supra* note 25.

82. *See infra* chapter 4.

83. *See infra id.*

84. G.N. No. 27 of 1928 (SWA) (Walvis Bay becomes a district of the South West African hospital system).

85. Proc. No. 5 of 1922 (SWA) (establishing a South West African hospital system).

West Africa." Indeed, economically, Walvis Bay was well integrated into the rest of Namibia.

Economic Significance of Walvis Bay

From the middle of the nineteenth century, Walvis Bay served as the major outlet for the considerable trade in cattle, ivory, and ostrich feathers with northern and central Namibia. After Germany proclaimed its South West Africa protectorate, it attempted to free the territory from dependence upon Walvis Bay by using Swakopmund—which, shallow and unprotected, was inferior to Walvis Bay—as the protectorate's harbor and linking it to Windhoek by rail.[86]

Once South African forces gained control of the German protectorate in 1915, South Africa used Walvis Bay instead, and Swakopmund ceased to serve as a port. Almost immediately, the South African authorities linked Walvis Bay by rail with the terminus of the main railway line at Swakopmund.[87] In 1922, the South African Railways and Harbours (SAR&H) began administering the port and the railway. By the end of the decade, SAR&H, with a financial guarantee from the South West African administration, had completed three deep-water berths, a dredged channel, and a wharf.[88]

Before World War II, Walvis Bay was used extensively for exporting frozen meat, mainly to Europe.[89] Commercial production and consumption in South West Africa were small. As in the nineteenth century, South West Africa continued to have an export-oriented economy.

After the war, the South West African economy expanded, and Walvis Bay became central to the export trade in cattle, karakul, minerals, and fish, the last two being most important. By the late 1970s, some two-thirds of Namibia's gross domestic product was exported.[90] In contrast, the majority of its manufactured and capital goods, as well as all of its bulk foods and half of its basic foodstuffs, were imported.[91] In addition, some 40 percent of Namibia's total foreign trade (by weight) passed through Walvis Bay.[92]

86. University of Stellenbosch, Transport Research Centre, Report of an Investigation into the Potential Development at Walvis Bay 71–72 (1977) [hereinafter cited as Stellenbosch Report].

87. *Id*. at 72.

88. *Id*. at 63–64.

89. *See, e.g.*, Union of South Africa, Department of Customs, Annual Statements of Trade and Shipping (1925–39).

90. R. Green, Namibia: A Political Economic Survey, University of Sussex Institute of Development Studies, Discussion Paper No. 144, 30–31 (1979) (unpublished).

91. *Id*.

92. *See* R. MOORSOM, WALVIS BAY: NAMIBIA'S PORT 23 (1984).

During the postwar years, multinational corporations invested in mining, particularly in Tsumeb, and Walvis Bay became a major ore terminal, with exports averaging 270,000 tons a year between 1953 and 1970.[93] Exportation of fish products also rose in the postwar years, from almost nothing to 300,000 tons a year between 1964 and 1976.[94] The volume of goods handled at Walvis Bay rose from fewer than 200,000 tons a year in the mid-1940s to 1.5 million tons in the mid-1970s.[95]

This postwar growth in exports demanded an improvement in harbor facilities. In the 1950s a storage shed and conveyor belt for ore from Tsumeb, as well as fish oil tanks,[96] were completed. Facilities were expanded during the 1960s to include new and deeper berths, more feet of wharf, an offshore tanker berth, cargo sheds, increased bulk oil storage capacity, and a reconstructed railway station and stockyards.[97]

Although most of Namibia's products, especially ore, passed through the port, the fishing industry was most important to the local economy of the Walvis Bay territory.[98] For centuries the Bay's indigenous inhabitants had depended on fishing for survival. In the eighteenth and nineteenth centuries, the Bay became the center of the local whaling industry. Even in 1914, two whaling companies continued to operate from the Bay. During the two decades after World War I local whales disappeared, but Norway's Antarctic whaling fleet used the Bay as its center, operating there a shore-based factory and, later, factory ships. After World War II, whaling operations moved to Cape Town and the Bay ceased to be a whaling center, though it continued to flourish as a center for deep-water white fishing and coastal pelagic fishing.

Local handline fishing was already thriving in Walvis Bay before the First World War.[99] By the 1950s, there were some twenty to thirty small open-decked boats run by Coloured fishermen in the Bay.[100] These line fishermen were joined by trawlers and South African corporate inshore fishing interests.

93. *See, e.g.,* Union of South Africa, S.A.R.&H., Annual Reports 1953–60 [hereinafter cited as Union S.A.R.&H.]; Republic of South Africa, S.A.R.&H. (later SATS), Annual Reports 1961–77 [hereinafter cited as Republic S.A.R.&H.].

94. Republic S.A.R.&H., *supra* note 93, 1964–76.

95. Union S.A.R.&H., *supra* note 93, 1940–60; Republic S.A.R.&H., *supra* note 93, 1961–76.

96. *Id.* (to both sources cited above).

97. *Id.*

98. *See generally* R. Moorsom, *supra* note 92, at 27–35. On Namibia's fishing, see R. Moorsom, Exploiting the Sea (London: Catholic Institute for International Relations 1984) [hereinafter cited as R. Moorsom, Exploiting]; Pieters, *Restructuring Namibia's Fisheries,* 1 In Formation 39 (1987–88).

99. W. Macdonald, The Destiny of Walvis Bay 51 (1915).

100. Stellenbosch Report, *supra* note 86, at 29.

The trawling industry for sole, an inshore fish, sustained a small-scale fishery at the Bay from the 1960s on, but the South African deep-sea trawlers that operated in Namibian waters discharged their catches in South Africa. From the late 1950s to the late 1970s, there were only two small plants for shore-based freezing and processing at the Bay.

In the late 1940s, a group of South African companies began to take control of South West African fishing.[101] By 1954, there were six factories engaged in large-scale production of fishmeal, fish oil, and pilchards.[102] From the mid-1960s until 1976, nine factories operated at capacity.[103] By the late 1960s, these factories were responsible for over 25 percent of Namibia's gross domestic product.[104] The largest catch ever was in 1968. Canneries processed 829,000 tons of pilchards that year, and factory ships processed 558,000 tons.[105]

Companies were not concerned with the long-term conservation of fishing stocks, however, and the pilchard stock in particular was rapidly depleted because of the companies' profit motive. Initially the most common species in inshore waters, the pilchard was particularly attractive to the fishing companies because it brought greater financial gain and was easier to catch than the anchovy.

The South African and South West African governments made no attempt to enact conservation measures,[106] in spite of warnings by fisheries expert Jan Lochner that the fish stocks would soon be depleted.[107] By 1971, Lochner's predictions had come true, though from 1972 to 1975 fishing stocks enjoyed a brief recovery and the South West African authorities disregarded scientific warnings and abandoned scientific monitoring of hauls.[108] The government also spent R5 million to improve landing and repair facilities for the fishing fleet.[109] Eventually this plundering of Namibian marine resources

101. *See generally* R. MOORSOM, EXPLOITING, *supra* note 98, at 52; Pieters, *supra* note 98, at 69–80.

102. Odendaal Report, *supra* note 25, at 345–47.

103. Stellenbosch Report, *supra* note 86, at 34.

104. R. MOORSOM, *supra* note 92, at 28.

105. R. MOORSOM, EXPLOITING, *supra* note 98, at 23.

106. Pieters, *supra* note 98, at 62–63. The 1963 South African Territorial Waters Act had fixed South African territorial waters at six nautical miles and its fishing zone at twelve nautical miles. The act defined South African waters as including Namibian waters. *See infra* Appendix. The confusion engendered by conflicting exercises of jurisdiction in Namibian waters by South African and South West African authorities is discussed in Pieters, *supra* note 98, at 62–63.

107. Rand Daily Mail, Aug. 27, 1979; Star, Apr. 19, 1980; Cape Times, Apr. 16, 1981.

108. Windhoek Advertiser, Mar. 14, 1977; Financial Mail, May 19, 1978; Star, Apr. 19, 1980; Cape Times, Apr. 16, 1981.

109. Star, Mar. 28, 1981.

had grave consequences for the fishing industry and the economies of Walvis Bay and Namibia. In 1976, however, Walvis Bay was as prosperous as ever.

Like industries elsewhere in South Africa and Namibia, the fishing industry relied heavily upon black labor. After the Second World War, as Walvis Bay grew into an industrial town, the second largest in Namibia, its population grew from 800 in 1946 to 22,000 in 1970 and then to more than 27,000 in 1976.[110] By the mid-1970s, more than 90 percent of Walvis Bay's black population was born in Namibia, the rest having come from South Africa's Western Cape.[111]

In 1976, Walvis Bay's labor force was 16,000 strong.[112] Whites comprised 20 to 30 percent of the labor force and were found exclusively in professional, managerial, administrative, and skilled manual occupations; most blacks performed semiskilled or unskilled manual labor.[113] Of the blacks in the work force, 9,400 were migrant workers, the majority of these Ovambo contract workers from northern Namibia.[114] Since the apartheid legislation governing the contract labor system prohibited these workers from bringing their families with them, the number of those directly dependent upon the Walvis Bay economy was several times larger than the number of persons living in the Walvis Bay territory. The fishing industry was the major Walvis Bay employer;[115] in 1976, half of the labor force worked in the processing factories and fishing boats.[116] Thirty percent were employed in commerce, workshops, services, and administration; ten percent worked as domestics;[117] and ten percent worked in the railway and harbor complex.

Among blacks, the laws discriminated between Coloureds and Africans and between permanent and migrant workers. As opposed to Africans, Coloureds had more freedom of movement and some access to industrial training.

110. Union of South Africa, Census 1946, *supra* note 42; Republic of South Africa, Department of Statistics, Statistical News Release No. 64 (1971); Stellenbosch Report, *supra* note 87, at 18. In 1976 there were 10,100 whites, 4,200 Coloureds, 12,947 Africans, and 1 Asian in Walvis Bay.

111. R. MOORSOM, supra note 92, at 37.

112. *Id.*

113. P. WALLER, SEKTORSTUDIE MATERIELLE INFRASTRUKTUR 25 (Berlin: German Development Institute 1979); *see generally* G. CRONJE & S. CRONJE, THE WORKERS OF NAMIBIA (London: International Defence and Aid Fund for Southern Africa 1979).

114. R. MOORSOM, *supra* note 92, at 37. *See generally* P. Banghart, Migrant Labour in South West Africa and Its Effects on Ovambo Tribal Life, M.A. thesis, University of Stellenbosch (1969) (unpublished); J. KANE-BERMAN, CONTRACT LABOUR IN SOUTH WEST AFRICA (Johannesburg: South African Institute of Race Relations 1972); Gottschalk, *South African Labour Policy in Namibia, 1915–75*, 4 S. AFR. LAB. BULL. 1 (1978).

115. R. MOORSOM, *supra* note 94, at 37.

116. *Id.*

117. *Id.*

Although most were permanent residents of Walvis Bay, some migrated from the Cape yearly. In Walvis Bay, the Coloureds lived in the township of Narraville, built in the 1960s on the outskirts of the town.

Africans were subject to influx control, the pass laws, and the labor bureaus. The authorities divided Africans into permanent and migrant workers. Those classified as permanent, 15 to 20 percent of Walvis Bay's African workers, clustered in skilled jobs.[118] Migrant or contract workers served as unskilled laborers.

The fish factories at Walvis Bay had long relied heavily on contract workers. Numbering from 2,000 to 2,500 in the 1950s, contract workers in these factories eventually totaled some 15 percent of all Namibian contract workers.[119] The system, which excluded women, suited the needs of the factories because the factory owners were responsible for the workers only during the fishing season—nine months in the 1960s and six months in the 1970s.[120] Two other factors also contributed to the appeal of the system for the factories. First, since South African official dogma was that contract workers' wages only supplemented what their families produced in the homelands, these wages were the lowest paid to any workers, and even workers who returned regularly for many years received no pension.[121] Second, the contract system discouraged labor unrest because workers feared dismissal, which meant being sent back to their homelands and being barred from further employment.[122]

In Walvis Bay, Africans lived in the Kuisebmond township, which, like Narraville for the Coloureds, was built on the edge of town in the 1960s. Among the inhabitants were further legally created divisions. There were permanent residents with so-called Section 10 rights; they were permitted small houses.[123] There were short-term migrants from central and southern

118. Permanent residents were those Africans who qualified by birth or residence, or under influx control laws, especially §§10(1)a–c of the Natives (Urban Areas) Act No. 25 of 1945. Such persons could reside with their families as long as they wished in a particular urban area. By contrast, migrant workers were legally obliged to take short-term contracts, live in single-sex hostels, and return to their "homeland" when each contract ended.

119. U.S. Department of Commerce, Bureau of Foreign Commerce, Basic Data on the Economy of South West Africa 5 (1956); Stellenbosch Report, *supra* note 87, at 18.

120. P. Banghart, *supra* note 114, at 57; V. NDADI, BREAKING CONTRACT (1974); Financial Gazette, Aug. 22, 1975.

121. *See, e.g.,* Financial Mail, Dec. 13, 1974.

122. R. GORDON, MINES, MASTERS, AND MIGRANTS 19–20 (1977). *See* Gordon, *A Note on the History of Labour Action in Namibia,* 1 S. AFR. LAB. BULL. 14 (1975); INTERNATIONAL LABOUR ORGANIZATION, LABOUR AND DISCRIMINATION IN NAMIBIA 67–70 (1977); Gottschalk, *supra* note 114, at 90–91; *see also* Moorsom, *Worker Consciousness and the 1971–2 Contract Workers Strike,* 4 S. AFR. LAB. BULL. 130 (1978).

123. *See supra* text accompanying note 118.

Namibia who enjoyed some freedom of movement but had to live in single-sex hostels. Last there were contract workers from northern Namibia who were required to live in the municipal compound, which could house 7,400 workers.[124]

Other Industries

In spite of three decades of growth in the fishing industry, the South African companies that controlled fishing operations in Walvis Bay skimmed off the profits instead of reinvesting them in the Bay. Consequently, the economy did not become diversified. Local industry was able to exist only because of the fishing industry and the railway and harbor. There was a major can factory at the Bay, run by the British company Metal Box, which opened the plant in 1957. Less than two decades later, it was able to produce 750 million cans a year, and at one point in the mid-1970s, it produced one million cans a day.[125] There was a small paint factory, as well as engineering and ship-repair businesses. Hotels also made money by serving liquor, mostly to sailors from foreign vessels calling at the Bay but also to crews of South African naval vessels.

The economy showed some diversification in the small-scale production of casein, margarine, and jute bags in the town; a guano platform halfway between the town and Swakopmund; and a salt factory south of the town. The salt factory, a subsidiary of South West Africa Fishing Industries, Ltd., called Salt and Chemicals' Evaporation Works, was a major enterprise. By 1977, it was responsible for some 190,000 tons of salt per year, an amount equivalent to half of Namibia's output.[126] This factory also furnished South Africa with 55 percent of its salt, much of which was used in chemicals and weapons manufacturing.[127]

Strategic Importance

As Walvis Bay grew economically, it also gained strategic importance. During the Second World War, the harbor played a role in defending the southern Atlantic, and some convoys were assembled there. From the 1960s, the Walvis Bay territory began to figure prominently as a navy, army, and air force base, as well as an SADF training center. The South African government used it

---

124. J. KANE-BERMAN, *supra* note 114, at 15–17; Kane-Berman, *The View from the Shop Floor: Interviews with Black Workers in Namibia,* 4 S. AFR. LAB. BULL. 14–26 (1978).

125. R. MOORSOM, *supra* note 92, at 36.

126. *See infra* chapter 4 at 86.

127. *Id.*

to maintain military control over Namibia[128] and built up forces there.[129] By the mid-1960s, Walvis Bay was one of three SADF bases in the vast area from the Orange to the Cunene rivers, and it had a military airport.[130] This base, with its sophisticated equipment, appears to have been used mainly for training in desert warfare.[131] This desert warfare was the task of the 2 SA Infantry Battalion, the SADF's only combined infantry/armor unit, which had its home in the Walvis Bay territory and was a major force in the South African invasion of Angola in 1975–76.[132]

In 1974, the SADF assumed responsibility for Namibian counterinsurgency operations previously performed by the South African police.[133] Facilities at Rooikop were expanded as a result; it became the major military center in the Walvis Bay territory, complete with a military airfield,[134] at the same time that the SADF was enlarging all its facilities in Namibia.

This, then, was the position of the Walvis Bay territory in early 1977. The ensuing years brought myriad confusing and contradictory legislative changes, economic collapse, and an ever-increasing military presence.

128. R. FIRST, SOUTH WEST AFRICA 223 (1963).

129. *Id.*

130. INTERNATIONAL DEFENCE AND AID FUND FOR SOUTHERN AFRICA (IDAF), APARTHEID'S ARMY IN NAMIBIA 18 (1982) [hereinafter cited as APARTHEID'S ARMY]. On South Africa's military capabilities, see generally IDAF, THE APARTHEID WAR MACHINE (1980) [hereinafter cited as APARTHEID WAR MACHINE]; R. LEONARD, SOUTH AFRICA AT WAR (1984).

131. Star, Nov. 25, 1972; APARTHEID WAR MACHINE, *supra* note 130, at 64.

132. APARTHEID WAR MACHINE, *supra* note 130, at 84.

133. APARTHEID'S ARMY, *supra* note 130, at 10.

134. *Id.*

CHAPTER FOUR

The Next Decade, 1977–1987

When the South African state president issued the 1977 Walvis Bay Administration Proclamation (R202), transferring the administration of Walvis Bay from Windhoek to the Cape Province, most Walvis Bay inhabitants had no idea that the territory was South African. Instead, they saw themselves as Namibians or South Westers. Some time later even the mayor of Walvis Bay said, "I don't think anyone here had any idea Walvis Bay had a separate status."[1] Once the proclamation was implemented, no one could fail to notice that the South African government was treating Walvis Bay differently from Namibia. The legislative changes that ensued brought confusion, consternation, and often anger and resentment.

The Walvis Bay Administration Proclamation

The state president issued the Walvis Bay Administration Proclamation[2] in terms of Section 38(1) of the South West Africa Constitution Act of 1968,[3] as amended by Section 1(a) of the South

1. Washington Post, Dec. 10, 1980.
2. Proc. R202 (1977).
3. Act 39 of 1968.

West Africa Constitution Amendment Act of 1977.[4] Section 38 as amended gave the state president broad powers.[5] It entitled him to legislate for South West Africa and Walvis Bay or to repeal or amend any legal provision, including an act of the South African Parliament, insofar as it was directly related to South West Africa. The state president could also repeal or amend any act of the South African Parliament insofar as it was affected by the exercise of his powers in respect to South West Africa. Never before in the constitutional history of South West Africa had such extensive powers been granted to any such executive official.

Promulgated on August 31, 1977, the Walvis Bay Administration Proclamation (R202) took effect the following day. It provided first that "Walvis Bay shall cease to be administered as if it were part of the territory and as if inhabitants thereof were inhabitants of the territory and shall again be administered as part of the [Cape] province."[6] The succeeding paragraphs changed the entire legislative structure of Walvis Bay. All enactments of the South African Parliament and those ordinances of the South West African Legislative Assembly that had been in force in Walvis Bay prior to September 1, 1977, would remain in force, but any law in force or any that might in future become operative in the Cape Province would also apply to Walvis Bay. Although not specifically mentioned in the proclamation, the bylaws of the Walvis Bay municipality also remained in force. As a result, many conflicting and contrary applications of law occurred. The proclamation, as well as later laws that applied only to Walvis Bay, all derived their authority from Section 38(1) of the South West Africa Constitution Act as amended,[7] even though by the time the later laws were enacted, Walvis Bay was supposedly part of South Africa. This section as amended also permitted the state president to legislate by proclamation for the "eventual attainment of Namibian independence"[8] and permitted the issuance of the proclamation that installed an administrator-general in Windhoek on the same day the director for Walvis Bay took office.[9]

4. Act 95 of 1977. Immediately before their amendment, the provisions of Section 38(1) functioned as a general enabling clause; they restricted the state president's powers to legislate by proclamation to those matters that went beyond the competence of the Legislative Assembly but only to the extent that such a proclamation was not repugnant to an act of the South African Parliament. As amended, Section 38 gave the state president broad powers. These were even wider than those originally granted to the governor-general under the mandate and those contained in the South West Africa Constitution Act of 1925 before its amendment by the South West Africa Affairs Amendment Act of 1949.

5. Act 95 of 1977.

6. Proc. R202 (1977).

7. South West Africa Const. Act §38(1) as amended by §1(a) of the South West Africa Const. Act of 1977.

8. *Id.*

9. Proc. R180 (1977).

When the administration of Walvis Bay was transferred from Great Britian to the Cape Colony in 1884, there was no confusion about Walvis Bay.[10] At that time, the few British laws that may have applied in the Bay were superseded by the laws in force in the Cape Colony. Even after South West Africa began to administer Walvis Bay in 1922 and the South West African administrator was empowered to bring the laws in force in Walvis Bay into conformity with those in force in the mandated territory, there was only minor confusion.[11]

Once Walvis Bay had become linked legislatively and administratively with South West Africa/Namibia after 1922, a smooth transition was not possible even though a means, albeit complicated, of reconciling conflicting legislation was devised. This involved the exercise of authority by both the state president and the administrator of the Cape.[12] In terms of Section 38, the

10. *See supra* chapter 2 at 45–46.

11. *See id.*

12. For the purpose of reconciling any possible conflict of laws in force in Walvis Bay, the powers vested in the state president in terms of Section 38 of the South West Africa Constitution Act, as amended, were used, and, subject to certain limitations, legislative powers were granted to the administrator of the Cape Province.

Paragraph 2(2) of the 1977 proclamation also made provision for the reconciliation of any conflicting legislation already in force in Walvis Bay. It provided that all existing laws that applied to Walvis Bay would remain in force until repealed, amended, or modified, subject to the provisions of paragraph 4, which had an interpretive function. Paragraph 4 comprised several interpretive clauses whereby all official bodies or other administrative arrangements that related to the South West African legislative structure were replaced by their South African counterparts in parliamentary and provincial legislation. For example, depending upon the context, references in any law to the South West African Legislative Assembly were to be construed as references to the South African Parliament or to the Cape Provincial Council. Similarly, references to the South West African administrator were to be construed as references to the appropriate Department of State of the Republic or to the Cape Provincial administration.

As paragraph 2(2) dealt only with the laws that were already in force in Walvis Bay on the date of the transfer of its administration to the Cape Province, some provision had to be made for the existing and future laws of the Cape, of which Walvis Bay was to be a part. Paragraph 2(3), read together with paragraph 3, addressed the problem. The latter gave limited powers to the administrator of the Cape Province for the purpose of reconciling any conflict that might have arisen between the laws of the Cape Province and those of the Legislative Assembly of South West Africa. In terms of paragraph 2(3), any law in force in the Cape Province and not already in operation in Walvis Bay or any law coming into operation in the province would also apply in Walvis Bay, subject to the provisions of paragraph 3. Paragraph 3 gave the administrator of the Cape limited legislative powers and determined their scope. According to paragraph 3(1), by proclamation in the Official Gazette of the Cape Province, the administrator may: "(a) declare that any provision of any law contemplated in paragraph 2(3) and relating to any matter entrusted to the provincial council shall come into operation in Walvis Bay on a date and subject to such amendments, additions, modifications, exceptions or conditions, as may be specified in the proclamation; (b) repeal, amend or modify any provision of any law in force in Walvis Bay and relating to any matter entrusted to the provincial council." Any such proclamation could contain any transitory provisions the administration deemed fit. In addition, by proclamation in the

state president repealed, amended, or modified parliamentary legislation that was incompatible with the transfer of the administration of Walvis Bay to the Cape. The administrator of the Cape Province acted similarly regarding laws relating to provincial matters.[13]

The state president exercised his powers regarding numerous matters, including the application of industrial, as well as mining and mineral, legislation; laws on black affairs and Baster, Coloured, and Nama relations; the liquor supply and hotel accommodation; the jurisdiction of the Supreme Court of South West Africa; the regulation of public health and identity documents; and Walvis Bay's parliamentary and provincial representation.[14]

The administrator of the Cape used his Proclamation R202 powers in various ways. He dealt with mundane matters concerning the administration of a local authority, that is, the Walvis Bay municipality. More important, in April 1978 he issued Proclamation 87, which modified or repealed the ordinances of the South West African Legislative Assembly and related proclamations, made ordinances of the Cape Provincial Council specifically applicable to Walvis Bay, and determined the extent to which provincial legislation would apply in Walvis Bay.[15]

Walvis Bay was administered as part of the Cape Province until January 1980, when the state president established the office of the director for the territory of Walvis Bay through exercise of his Section 38 powers.[16] The

---

gazette, the administrator could amend or repeal any proclamation so issued by him, and, if necessary, declare any proclamation issued by him under paragraph 3 as a whole to be of retrospective effect.

When compared with the powers vested in the state president under Section 38, the powers of the administrator were extremely limited in scope and time. His powers extended only to matters entrusted to the Cape Provincial Council. The administrator could not interfere with parliamentary legislation because it fell within the exclusive legislative jurisdiction of the state president. Furthermore, those powers would terminate on June 30, 1978, with the exception of any proclamation issued prior to that date, which would remain in force. However, any laws of the South West African Legislative Assembly that were in harmony with those of the Cape Provincial Council remained in force by virtue of the provisions of paragraph 2(2).

13. He acted according to the powers vested in him by Proclamation R202. However, the comprehensive interpretive function of paragraph 4 of Proclamation R202 obviated the need for adapting or modifying many of the laws in force in Walvis Bay at the time.

14. *See* Proc. R226 (1977) as amended by Proc. 75 (1978) and Proc. R179 (1978); Proc. 344 (1977); Proc. R205 (1977) and Proc. R69 (1979); Proc. R310 (1977) as amended by Proc. R173 (1978); Proc. R204 (1977); Proc. R336 (1977); Proc. R203 (1977); Proc. 120 (1978); Proc. 78 (1980); Proc. R202 (1977), para. 5, read in conjunction with Proc. R250 (1977) and Proc. R248 (1977).

15. Proc. 87 (1978), Administrator of Cape Province, Official Gazette (Cape Province), No. 3990, Apr. 13, 1978.

16. Proc. R191 (1979); Proc. R270 (1979).

director was appointed by the state president. His functions were those that the administrator of the Cape Provincial Council would have performed in Walvis Bay or in connection with it. The director had greater independence than either the administrator or the Provincial Council. Whereas the Cape administrator or Provincial Council could only perform certain functions subject to the approval of state officials, the director could perform any of his tasks without prior approval. The state president could also from time to time instruct the director to perform any other function that might be necessary. All of this meant that when the first director took office in May 1980, Walvis Bay had a unique legal status different from that of Namibia.

Thus, with the 1977 change in the administration of Walvis Bay, the laws of the Cape Provincial Council applied in Walvis Bay, though the state president could still make laws for Walvis Bay and, from 1980 on, instruct the director to perform certain other functions that might fall beyond the scope of those carried out by the administrator and the Provincial Council. In addition, the director had more independence than the administrator or the Provincial Council. Walvis Bay was no longer subject to the laws of the South West African Legislative Assembly, and although it fell under the Cape Provincial Council, it was not subject to the executive controls that were normally exercised by the council's administrator or executive committee. Even with this legislative mechanism in place, the implementation of Proclamation R202 at times resulted in peculiar applications of the law in Walvis Bay, with the result that one observer characterized Walvis Bay as "where the law is made to seem a bewildering ass."[17] Indeed, it appeared that little thought had been given to the mechanisms that would be most useful for implementing those changes that transfer to Cape administration implied. Two days after Proclamation R202 took effect, for example, Walvis Bay Town Clerk Jan Wilken said, "We have been given no indication as to how Walvis Bay will be governed. It's all up in the air."[18] Soon, however, a new dispensation applied in everything from taxation to housing.

Judicial Administration

The system of judicial administration changed after Proclamation R202 was issued. Until then, Walvis Bay, like Namibia, fell under the jurisdiction of the South West Africa Division of the South African Supreme Court.[19] It was then transferred to the Cape Division of the Supreme Court.[20] Not until November

17. Daily Telegraph, May 19, 1981.
18. Star, Sept. 3, 1977.
19. *See supra* chapter 3 at 54–55. Cape Times, Nov. 20, 1980.
20. Cape Times, Nov. 20, 1980.

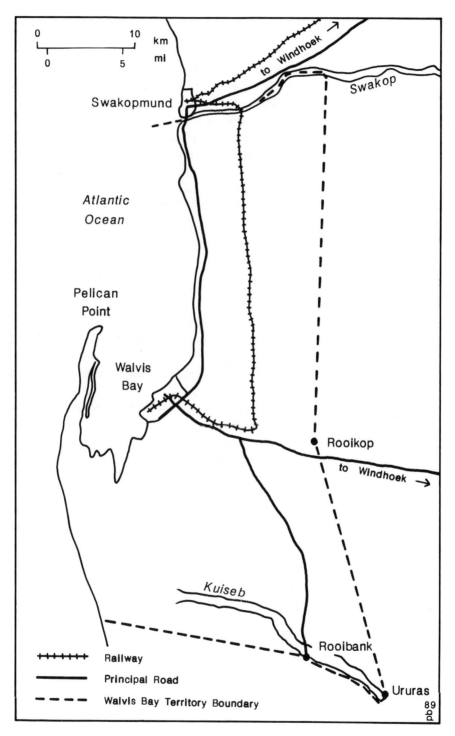

Map 4. Walvis Bay territory in the 1980s

1980, however, did Cape Division judges hear their first case from Walvis Bay. They did so as a circuit court of the division.[21]

In spite of the change in jurisdiction, the boundaries of the Walvis Bay magisterial district, of which the Walvis Bay territory composed approximately one tenth of the land area, were not adjusted.[22] This left the magistrate of Walvis Bay with jurisdiction on either side of an international boundary and over an area controlled by two different governments. Although according to an April 1978 government notice,[23] the SADF continued to include Walvis Bay in the Swakopmund magisterial district, a 1978 large-scale map of Namibia from the surveyor-general's office in Windhoek indicated that the nonannexed portion of the magistracy was transferred to the district of Swakopmund.[24] This also created a curious anomaly in the electoral system that caused confusion.

Fiscal Affairs

During the years when Walvis Bay was administered from Windhoek, the municipality incurred substantial debts to the South West African administration. Once Proclamation R202 appeared, protracted negotiations followed, and in 1981 the South African government undertook to pay the R14.5 million owed by the Bay.[25]

Of more immediate concern to residents of the Bay was the change in tax laws. After the proclamation took effect, South African tax laws became applicable. Death duties that did not exist in Namibia now obtained in Walvis Bay.[26] As for income tax, residents were required to pay Namibian rates for part of the year and South African rates for the remainder.[27] This caused much confusion among residents, who were unsure how to calculate the amount owed. As South African taxes were 35 percent higher than Namibian taxes, their imposition was particularly resented.[28] Residents complained that the South African government had breached its oft-made promise that the people

21. *Id.*

22. Republic of South Africa, House of Assembly Debates, June 6, 1978 (question to minister of Coloured relations); Windhoek Advertiser, Sept. 7, 1977; Windhoek Advertiser, Oct. 4, 1977.

23. GN 259, Gov't Gazette 5966 (Apr. 7, 1978).

24. Surveyor-General, South West Africa, Map of South West Africa (large-scale) (1978).

25. Namib Times, July 24, 1981.

26. Windhoek Advertiser, Sept. 9, 1977; Namib Times, Nov. 2, 1982.

27. Windhoek Advertiser, Sept. 9, 1977.

28. Windhoek Advertiser, Sept. 12, 1977; Windhoek Advertiser, Mar. 29, 1979; Star, May 20, 1978; Rand Daily Mail, Mar. 8, 1978; Windhoek Advertiser, Mar. 23, 1981; Star, Mar. 31, 1981; Namib Times, Apr. 3, 1981.

of Walvis Bay would not be worse off once the area began to be administered from Cape Town.[29] Eventually, the South African government sanctioned a temporary refund of income tax for the residents of Walvis Bay.[30]

The South West African administration also disapproved of the shift to the South African tax system, complaining by 1984 that Namibia had lost millions of rand in income tax from private citizens and businesses, especially the fishing industry.[31]

The Franchise

Before 1977, the white residents of Walvis Bay elected a representative to the South West African Territorial Assembly.[32] In the reshuffling that followed publication of Proclamation R202, the South African government assigned white residents first to the Namaqualand constituency, then to Green Point in Cape Town, and finally to their own separate constituency.

For parliamentary purposes, the Bay became part of the Namaqualand electoral district on September 1, 1977.[33] Even so, on November 30 of that year, when the first South African election since the transfer took place, Walvis Bay voters were unable to cast ballots, because the Namaqualand voters' roll had closed on August 31, the day before Proclamation R202 took effect.[34] For a time, the whites of Walvis Bay had no representation in the South African Parliament or the Cape Provincial legislature. (It was commonly, although incorrectly, assumed that they also had no representation in the South West African Legislative Assembly.) However, only part of the electoral division of Walvis Bay was transferred to Namaqualand. Part remained in Namibia and continued to be represented in the South West African Legislative Assembly. The part that had not been transferred was mainly a remote desert research station at Gobabeb, south of Walvis Bay, with reportedly only four voters.[35]

In 1981, in an electoral delimitation that took place before the South African elections in April, the South African government transferred Walvis Bay, with its 2,976 registered white voters, from the Namaqualand electoral district to the Cape Town constituency of Green Point.[36] Not all the Walvis

29. *Id.* (to all sources cited above).
30. Namib Times, July 24, 1981.
31. Rand Daily Mail, Feb. 25, 1978.
32. *See supra* chapter 3 at 56.
33. Rand Daily Mail, Oct. 4, 1977.
34. Windhoek Advertiser, Sept. 7, 1977.
35. *Id.;* Windhoek Advertiser, Oct. 4, 1977; Rand Daily Mail, Oct. 4, 1977.
36. Cape Times, Mar. 14, 1981; Rand Daily Mail, Mar. 26, 1981; Star, Mar. 31, 1981; Sunday Times, Apr. 19, 1981; Cape Times, Apr. 22, 1982.

Bay voters were pleased with this electoral maneuvering. Said one hotelier, "I think many people prefer to see themselves as South West Africans."[37] Other residents echoed his sentiments.[38]

In February 1982, South African Minister of Internal Affairs J. C. Heunis indicated that Walvis Bay would become a separate Cape constituency with representation in the South African Parliament and in the Cape Provincial Council. He added that Walvis Bay was an important part of the Republic with much potential for industrial development.[39] The real reason for the change, however, was to bolster support for the ruling National Party (NP) in Parliament and the Cape Provincial Council. The government assumed that the two new seats created would go to NP candidates. The opposition Progressive Federal Party (PFP) was well aware of this and criticized the plan to form a new constituency with only three thousand voters—less than a third of the minimum required for any other South African parliamentary seat.[40] The government was not deterred. The legislation was enacted in July 1982, and the office of the director of Walvis Bay was abolished on September 30.[41] In the by-elections that followed in November, the NP scored victories in the new constituency, which thereafter remained an NP stronghold.

Proclamation R202 also changed the franchise of Walvis Bay's Coloured residents. They became part of the Cape Town Tafelberg electoral division for the South African Coloured Persons Representative Council (CRC) elections. Coloured leaders complained that they wanted Walvis Bay to be part of Namibia, which they considered their country.[42] Coloureds were left without any vote at all when the CRC was abolished in 1979. They did not regain the vote until 1983, when the South African government created the (Coloured) House of Representatives of the South African Parliament. As a result of this change, Coloureds who were active in Namibian politics could no longer vote in Namibia.[43]

Once the House of Representatives was established, Narraville was incorporated into the southern Cape for electoral purposes. Seeking treatment similar to that accorded whites, Coloured residents petitioned the Delimitation Commission to have the area classified as a separate constituency.[44] The commission refused the request without giving any reasons.

37. Star, May 9, 1981.
38. *See, e.g.,* Windhoek Advertiser, Mar. 30, 1981.
39. Namib Times, June 15, 1982.
40. Cape Times, Feb. 8, 1982.
41. BBC, Oct. 2, 1982.
42. Guardian, May 3, 1978.
43. Windhoek Advertiser, Nov. 7, 1977.
44. Johannesburg, home service in Afrikaans, 1700 GMT, June 18, 1984; BBC, June 20, 1984.

The only Indian inhabitant of Walvis Bay found himself in a position similar to that of the Coloureds. After Proclamation R202 took effect, he could vote in South Africa's Indian Council elections.[45] That council too was subsequently abolished and eventually replaced by the (Indian) House of Delegates of the South African Parliament.

As for Walvis Bay Africans, who like all Africans in South Africa had no parliamentary representation, the South African government viewed them as Namibians even if they were born in Walvis Bay. According to a senior Walvis Bay official, the 8,212 African inhabitants reported in the 1980 census did not "belong to South Africa."[46] All carried Namibian identity documents and were classified as migrant laborers from various African homelands in Namibia. They were part of the Namibian political system and were expected to seek representation in Namibia through the South African–created political structures. There they were entitled to vote in local homeland elections. The people of Kuisebmond had no doubt about where they belonged, however, and insisted that they were Namibians.[47]

Labor

In September 1977, major South African industrial legislation became applicable in Walvis Bay. The Industrial Conciliation Act of 1956, which never applied in Namibia, meant that there could be no multiracial trade unions in Walvis Bay and that through job reservation the government could restrict any particular job to a specific racial group.[48] Similarly, the Native Labour (Settlement of Disputes) Act of 1953, which did not apply to Namibia, excluded all Africans from being "employees," made all strikes by Africans illegal, and restricted Africans to forming factory-based work committees or liaison committees.[49] The labor situation changed somewhat when amended South African legislation legalizing black trade unions became applicable in Walvis Bay in 1979 and 1981.[50]

Meanwhile, the imposition of South African legislation in Walvis Bay increased discrimination. The South African Natives (Abolition of Passes and

45. Financial Mail, Mar. 19, 1982.
46. Namib Times, May 11, 1982; Namib Times, June 15, 1977.
47. Rand Daily Mail, Aug. 27, 1979.
48. Industrial Conciliation Act No. 28 of 1956. Proc. R26 (1977) made the act applicable to Walvis Bay.
49. Native Labour (Settlement of Disputes) Act No. 48 of 1953. Proc. R226 (1977) made the act applicable to Walvis Bay.
50. On July 5, 1978, the South West African labor laws were amended to allow all members of the population to be members of trade unions. SOUTH WEST AFRICA PRESS RELATIONS OFFICE OF THE ADMINISTRATOR GENERAL, SWA/NAMIBIA SURVEY 6 (June 1980) [hereinafter cited as SWA/NAMIBIA SURVEY (June 1980)].

Coordination Documents) Act of 1952 became applicable.[51] It replaced the series of individual passes necessary under Namibian law with the more stringent requirement of the South African passbook. The passbook included information about the holder's identity as well as all his permits, such as those for work and residence. Police were entitled to see the passbook on demand, and if the holder was without the book or some aspect of it was out of order, he could be arrested, fined, and sent back to his homeland. Although the police had similar powers before the law on passbooks was extended, use of the books made it easier to ensure that workers remained employed by the firms to which they were contracted and that they lived in the proper area.

Eventually, because the South African pass law system was impossible for the government to enforce to its satisfaction, South Africa abolished the pass laws in 1986 and replaced passbooks with national identity documents. Supposedly aimed at "orderly urbanization," the new legislation made it more difficult for the residents of South Africa's "independent" African homelands, considered foreign nationals, to obtain work in South Africa. The South African government did not, however, treat Namibian workers in Walvis Bay as foreign nationals.[52]

In spite of the change in Walvis Bay's status, a regional office of the South African Department of Home Affairs was not opened in Walvis Bay until June 1985. Before that, Walvis Bay's residents had obtained their identity documents, passports, and other official documents from the department's office in Windhoek.[53]

Under the new legal dispensation, the position of Coloureds was especially peculiar. Coloured people from the Republic of South Africa needed permits to live in, work in, and visit Walvis Bay.[54] The South African Department of Coloured Relations took over the function of issuing these permits from the South West African administration after Walvis Bay began to be administered from Cape Town. The permits were issued in terms of the Control over the Entry and Residence of Prohibited Persons Ordinance of 1970.[55] This meant that Walvis Bay was the only part of South Africa where influx-control regulations pertained to Coloureds. Meanwhile, security legislation that was the same in Namibia as in South Africa itself continued in force. In this way, a single system of control was maintained.

51. Natives (Abolition of Passes and Coordination Documents) Act No. 67 of 1952. Proc. R205 (1977), in force from Jan. 1, 1978, made the law applicable to Walvis Bay.

52. Namib Times, Jan. 20, 1987.

53. Johannesburg, home service in English, 1115 GMT, June 20, 1985; BBC, June 22, 1985.

54. Rand Daily Mail, Sept. 8, 1981.

55. *Id.*

Housing

From 1977 on, South African housing legislation, which was more discriminatory than the Namibian legislation, obtained in Walvis Bay. The South African government applied legislation in 1979 requiring that every person be issued an identity document that classified him by race.[56] In 1986, national identity documents were introduced. Like passbooks, these documents were to be shown to the authorities on demand. They also facilitated the implementation in 1979 of the cornerstone of South African apartheid legislation, the Group Areas Act, which established designated areas in which members of particular racial groups could live.[57] In 1979, the Walvis Bay town council called upon the South African government to promulgate the act for the Bay.[58] That year, the act was abolished in Namibia, where de facto segregation continued to exist.[59]

The council was alarmed that Coloured residents, unable to find accommodation in overcrowded Narraville, were moving into empty houses and flats in white residential areas. The municipality initially denied reports that it was trying to remove Coloureds from white areas.[60] Later, Town Clerk Wilken and the mayor merely said that they were enforcing restrictive covenants in the deeds of the premises that prohibited their sale or leasing to blacks.[61] Already, in 1977, the municipality had insisted that the landlords evict their Coloured tenants. It had also refused to sell electricity to the Coloureds.

By 1979 landlords still had not complied, and the number of Coloured tenants continued to grow. White residents lodged an increasing number of complaints. In response, the town council went further. It petitioned the South African government to have the Group Areas Act applied to Walvis Bay.[62] This was in keeping with the terms of Proclamation R202, which stipulated that existing South African legislation could only be put into force in Walvis Bay by proclamation.[63]

The South African government did not honor the council's request and did not issue the requisite proclamation extending the Group Areas Act to

56. Republic of South Africa, House of Assembly Debates, Apr. 17, 1979. The legislation applied was ostensibly the Population Registration Act, No. 29 of 1970.

57. *See* L. THOMPSON & A. PRIOR, SOUTH AFRICAN POLITICS 68 (1982).

58. Windhoek Advertiser, Oct. 16, 1976; Cape Times, Oct. 16, 1979.

59. Daily Telegraph, May 19, 1981; Windhoek Observer, May 23, 1981; Rand Daily Mail, May 25, 1987.

60. Rand Daily Mail, Aug. 27, 1979.

61. *Id.;* Windhoek Advertiser, Apr. 14, 1983.

62. Namib Times, Sept. 17, 1982; Windhoek Advertiser, Oct. 17, 1982.

63. Proc. R202 (1977).

Walvis Bay. Nevertheless, in 1981, the town council gave the police "a free hand to take firm action in terms of the Group Areas Act."[64] Evictions followed, and one landlord was prosecuted, convicted, and imprisoned.[65] Walvis Bay had no prison at the time, and he was incarcerated in neighboring Swakopmund, a place across an international boundary where his actions were not a crime.

More evictions followed.[66] Even so, in 1983, there were reports of forty-nine Coloured families still in the white areas.[67] By then, the town council had taken the position that the Group Areas Act applied only to the area that constituted the municipality in 1952 when the act was first promulgated.[68] Meanwhile, the municipality cut off water and electricity supplies to houses and flats occupied by Coloureds in the white areas, thus forcing many out.

In keeping with its segregationist policies, the town council put Kuisebmond under a separate community council in 1980. The town council then denied observer status to the management committee of Narraville.[69] In spite of long-standing petitions from leaders of the black communities that they be allowed to become part of Namibia, the town council then established both Narraville and Kuisebmond as separate municipalities.

The stringent enforcement of apartheid legislation drew ire from leaders of the black communities, who insisted that Walvis Bay was part of Namibia,[70] as well as from a few whites.[71]

Other Aspects

Of the host of other changes that followed the publication of Proclamation R202, almost none occurred as soon as the proclamation was issued. Only the Department of Posts and Telecommunications began on schedule to sell South African stamps instead of the cheaper South West African ones.[72] However, Walvis Bay remained in the South West African telephone directory issued by the South West African Postmaster General's Office. That directory appeared after Proclamation R202 was published under the title *South-West Africa/Namibia and Walvis Bay.*[73]

64. Namib Times, May 1, 1981.
65. Rand Daily Mail, Sept. 11, 1978.
66. Windhoek Advertiser, Oct. 22, 1981.
67. Cape Argus, Apr. 9, 1983; Windhoek Advertiser, Apr. 12, 1983.
68. Windhoek Advertiser, Sept. 17, 1982; Windhoek Advertiser, Oct. 17, 1982.
69. Rand Daily Mail, Aug. 27, 1979.
70. Guardian, May 3, 1978; Rand Daily Mail, Sept. 11, 1978; Star, May 20, 1978.
71. Windhoek Advertiser, Dec. 3, 1980; Daily Despatch, Dec. 3, 1980; Sunday Times, Dec. 7, 1980.
72. Star, Sept. 3, 1977.
73. *See, e.g.,* SOUTH WEST AFRICA DEP'T OF POSTS AND COMMUNICATIONS, SOUTH-WEST AFRICA/NAMIBIA AND WALVIS BAY 1985.

As regarded arts and entertainment, Walvis Bay remained part of the South West Africa Performing Arts Council. It continued to receive South West African Broadcasting Corporation (SWABC) radio programs instead of South African programs. When SWABC television came into operation in 1981, it served Walvis Bay from Swakopmund.[74] SWABC treated Walvis Bay as part of Namibia for purposes of news and weather reports. Similarly, South African Broadcasting Corporation (SABC) broadcasts inside the Republic of South Africa continued to treat Walvis Bay as part of Namibia for weather reports.

Despite declarations in some South African and South West African official publications that Walvis Bay was part of South Africa,[75] physical manifestations of that status did not immediately follow the publication of Proclamation R202. Motor vehicle license plates were changed to indicate that Walvis Bay was part of the Cape in 1978.[76] Not until that year was a signpost erected at the halfway mark on the bridge over the Swakop River to remind the traveler from Swakopmund that he was entering South African territory,[77] though no physical barriers or border guards marked the boundary. Even with these changes, advertisements by Walvis Bay businesses continued to refer to the Bay as part of South West Africa/Namibia.[78]

Of more pressing concern to Walvis Bay's residents was the town council's zeal to enforce the South African Prohibition of Mixed Marriages Act[79] and the Immorality Act,[80] which prohibited interracial marriage and sex. The acts no longer applied in Namibia.[81] However, Walvis Bay's interracial couples lived in fear of prosecution until South Africa abolished the acts in 1985.[82]

The hoteliers in Walvis Bay also objected to the imposition of those acts and other such restrictive legislation as the South African Liquor Act,[83] which limited the sale of liquor to certain times, and South African anti-gambling

74. Star, Mar. 31, 1981.
75. *See supra* chapter 3 at 57–60; REPUBLIC OF SOUTH AFRICA, YEAR BOOKS (1978–87). By 1987, such publications still featured maps of Namibia without an international boundary shown around Walvis Bay and maps of South Africa and the Cape Province without insets for Walvis Bay.
76. Star, Jan. 7, 1978.
77. Namib Times, Dec. 17, 1982.
78. *See, e.g.,* 8 Namibia Brief (Third Quarter 1987) (advertisement for Namib Sun Hotels facing page 16). Maps in such publications did not show an international boundary around Walvis Bay. *See, e.g., id.*
79. *See generally,* THOMPSON & A. PRIOR, *supra* note 57, at 36–37.
80. *Id.*
81. The Prohibition of Mixed Marriages Act and the Immorality Act were abolished on Oct. 14, 1977. SWA/NAMIBIA SURVEY (June 1980), *supra* note 50, at 6.
82. Washington Post, Dec. 10, 1982.
83. Windhoek Advertiser, Oct. 3, 1980.

laws. They complained of losing their clientele, mainly fishing industry workers and military personnel, to Swakopmund, where gambling was allowed and the restrictions on the sale of alcohol and on the mixing of the races did not apply. Hoteliers also charged that they were economically disadvantaged in comparison to hoteliers in Swakopmund, who as residents of Namibia could apply for hotel subsidies and low-interest loans from the South West African government.[84] Later, although the South African Liquor Board had authority over establishments selling liquor, the Namibian legislation continued to apply.[85]

All these changes had residents up in arms about the "second-rate treatment" they had received since the Cape began to administer Walvis Bay.[86] Said one resident, "We're a great deal worse off."[87] This dismal outlook was no doubt compounded by a precipitous decline in the economic fortunes of Walvis Bay that coincided with the publication of Proclamation R202.

Economic Significance of Walvis Bay

During the years following the publication of Proclamation R202, Walvis Bay's economic fortunes deteriorated. This was the result of the collapse of the fishing industry from years of overexploitation. After 1977, the pilchard almost vanished, though in 1987 reports indicated that smaller fish were to be found in much reduced quantities. Although the number of anchovy initially increased while that of the pilchard declined, overfishing also depleted the anchovy stocks. In the late 1970s and early 1980s, emergency conservation measures went into effect, but they were too late. By 1982, the anchovy catch was at its lowest since anchovy fishing began in 1968.[88]

As the stocks disappeared, so did the fish-processing companies. Canneries closed. Of the seven operating in 1977, none was left by 1981. In that year, the canning of pilchards was banned.[89] Not until 1986 was some activity resumed.

As trawling for whitefish was a relatively small-scale enterprise at the time of the pilchard collapse, much attention was diverted there. When the administration in Windhoek—by 1987 the quotas for all the waters off the Namibian coast, including those off Walvis Bay, were still determined by

84. Rand Daily Mail, May 22, 1981.
85. Windhoek Advertiser, Oct. 3, 1980.
86. Star, Mar. 31, 1981.
87. *Id.*
88. R. MOORSON, WALVIS BAY: NAMIBIA'S PORT 32 (1984).
89. *See also* Namib Times, May 17, 1983.

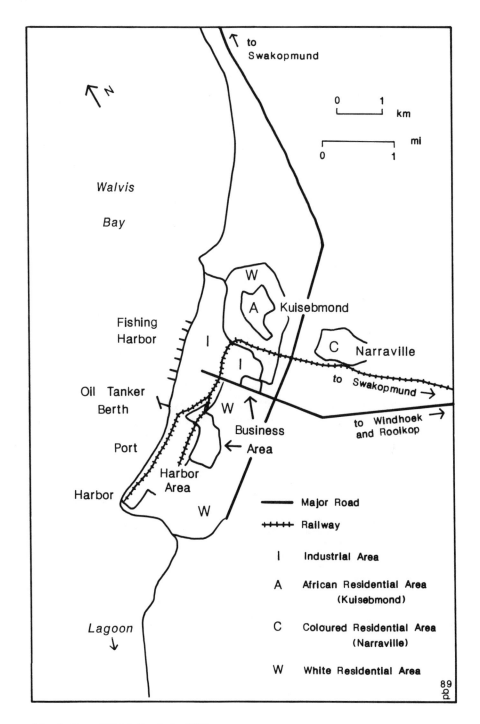

to
Swakopmund

N

0   1
km

0   1
mi

Walvis

Bay

W

A   Kuisebmond

Fishing
Harbor

I

I

C   Narraville

Oil Tanker
Berth

to Swakopmund →

W

to Windhoek
and Rooikop →

Port

Business
← Area

Harbor
Area

Harbor

W

Major Road

++++ Railway

I   Industrial Area

A   African Residential Area
       (Kuisebmond)

C   Coloured Residential Area
       (Narraville)

W   White Residential Area

Lagoon
↓

89
pb

Map 5. Port of Walvis Bay in the 1980s

South West African authorities—established its first hake quotas in 1982, South African and foreign enterprises rushed to take their share.[90]

Companies were keen to minimize losses. As catches declined, the companies, at the expense of individual owners, consolidated their hold on the industry, taking larger and larger portions of the total quota at the expense of small private owners.[91] When the industry collapsed, companies that had done nothing to diversify in spite of warnings that the fishing industry was heading for disaster endeavored to diversify, but their efforts could not rescue the Walvis Bay economy.[92]

The collapse of the fishing industry brought economic disaster for the work force. Black workers, who were least able to cope with the loss of revenue, were the most severely affected.[93] Once the pilchard disappeared, the number of fishermen dropped from eight hundred in 1976 to four hundred in 1980.[94] Walvis Bay fish factories also began to compete with the local Coloured handline fishermen.[95] The expanding economic crisis forced hundreds of residents of Narraville and Kuisebmond into penury and starvation. Children were fainting from lack of food, and there was no longer much water, electricity, or heating in the townships because the municipality had disconnected them from many homes for lack of payment.[96]

The hardest hit by the decline in the economy were cannery workers. The number of cannery workers declined from seven thousand in the mid-1970s to slightly more than one thousand in 1980.[97] Even these were unemployed when all the canneries closed the following year. That left only one hundred workers employed in the remaining fish meal and fish oil factories.[98]

The closing of the canneries had negative effects upon businesses and

90. SOUTH WEST AFRICAN SHIPPING AND FISHING INDUSTRY REVIEW 1982.

91. Windhoek Advertiser, July 10, 1981.

92. *See, e.g.,* Windhoek Advertiser, June 12, 1980; Windhoek Advertiser, Nov. 13, 1980; Namib Times, Nov. 28, 1980; Financial Mail, Nov. 5, 1980; Citizen, Mar. 14, 1981; Windhoek Observer, Nov. 7, 1981.

93. University of Stellenbosch, Transport Research Centre, Report of an Investigation into the Potential Development at Walvis Bay 23 (1977) [hereinafter cited as Stellenbosch Report]; Windhoek Advertiser, Apr. 18, 1980; Financial Mail, Dec. 5, 1980; Windhoek Advertiser, Mar. 16, 1981.

94. Stellenbosch Report, *supra* note 93, at 23; Windhoek Advertiser, Apr. 18, 1980; Financial Mail, Dec. 5, 1980; Windhoek Advertiser, Mar. 16, 1981.

95. Windhoek Advertiser, Feb. 12, 1980; African Business, Apr. 1980; Namib Times, July 24, 1981.

96. Windhoek Advertiser, Aug. 28, 1984.

97. Rand Daily Mail, Sept. 7, 1977; Windhoek Advertiser, Sept. 7, 1977; Financial Mail, Dec. 5, 1980.

98. Citizen, Mar. 14, 1981.

services, which relied upon worker spending. Numerous businesses closed.[99] To compound problems, the number of dockworkers also decreased as a result of a shift by the port to containerized cargo transport in 1977.[100]

In 1983, the port was working at only 20 percent of capacity.[101] The majority of visitors were foreign trawlers.[102] Virtually the only freighter traffic was a weekly coastal container service, a bimonthly ro-ro (roll-on, roll-off service), and a few break-bulk vessels. South African naval vessels were, however, a frequent sight. By 1987, there was no substantial improvement.

Accompanying the lack of employment was a decrease in population. In addition to migrant workers, who by law were compelled to leave once they were without jobs, black residents of the townships, as well as whites, left on a massive scale. The population shrank from twenty-seven thousand in 1976 to eighteen thousand in 1980.[103] As the Sakekamer's chairman put it, "Everything has just gone bang."[104] In 1978 and 1979, hundreds of houses and 75 percent of the flats in white residential areas were vacant.[105] By 1987, despite a small improvement in fishing stocks, no major economic turnaround had occurred.[106]

It became apparent meanwhile that Walvis Bay was part of a long-term South African government economic strategy based upon the assumption that Walvis Bay would remain South African if Namibia became independent. In 1980, state building, which had all but ceased in 1977, began again with vigor. Facilities were improved in the black townships. This was in keeping with the town council's determination to maintain strict segregation. Housing and schools were built, as well as a sports complex and police station in Narraville.[107] A R2-million prison was also constructed.

Substantial funds were also invested in improving the port and its transport infrastructure. In 1980, a new heavy-duty rail link was completed between Walvis Bay and Swakopmund. At a cost of R9 million, it replaced a low-capacity coastal line.[108] In 1982, a two-year, R15-million harbor im-

99. Windhoek Advertiser, Sept. 15, 1978; Windhoek Advertiser, Nov. 6, 1979; Star, May 9, 1981.

100. Windhoek Advertiser, Apr. 14, 1978; Feb. 15, 1980.

101. Namib Times, Mar. 22, 1983.

102. *Id.*

103. Namib Times, Nov. 28, 1980; Windhoek Advertiser, Feb. 17, 1981; Star, May 9, 1981.

104. Windhoek Advertiser, Sept. 15, 1978.

105. Windhoek Advertiser, Sept. 15, 1978, Feb. 15, 1980.

106. *See* Pieters, *Restructuring Namibia's Fisheries,* 1 IN FORMATION 39–68 (1987–88).

107. Namib Times, July 24, 1981.

108. Windhoek Advertiser, June 13, 1980; Windhoek Observer, June 14, 1980.

provement project began to rebuild and deepen three of the berths to accommodate large tankers and freighters.[109] A quay for small craft was constructed, and all crane and rail lines were relaid.

A joint project of the South West African state development corporation ENOK (Eerste Nasionale Ontwikkelings Korporasie), the Oceana fishing group, and Woker Freight Service resulted in a R2-million cold storage facility, which opened in June 1982.[110] Constructed in a converted shed at the harbor, the facility was part of a move to begin exporting meat from Namibia by refrigerated rather than live transport. This facility and a R13-million abattoir and freezing plant built by the same group at Gobabis, east of Windhoek, would give an independent Namibia the ability to process most of its meat and export the frozen or refrigerated product.[111] The anomaly of the situation—namely, that the South West African state development corporation built a plant in a foreign country—went unnoticed in the press and by the international community. As the factory at the Bay offered the only alternative to canning or to the overland trade with South Africa, South African control of the Bay would keep the meat industry firmly under South African domination. By 1987, the cold storage facility was nowhere near capacity, and much of it was being used for venison and fish instead of beef.

In 1981, the South African government also began to attempt to lure business to Walvis Bay and away from Namibia through various incentive programs.[112] This caused much distress among Namibian business interests. The South African–appointed South West African administrator-general also objected to the economic difficulties the South African plan would create.

By mid-year, ENOK's managing director reported that twelve new "industries" had located in Walvis Bay.[113] He admitted that some of them competed directly with enterprises in nearby Swakopmund. Discussing the various incentive programs, the mayor of Walvis Bay said, "I am emphatic that the economy of the Walvis Bay enclave has been saved from total collapse by the timely transfer of its administration to the Cape."[114]

Despite attempts to attract business and industry, the economy of the Bay did not improve much during the 1980s, and the municipality hoped that

109. BBC, Jan. 19, 1982; Namib Times, May 7, 1982; Windhoek Advertiser, May 13, 1982; Telegraph, July 19, 1982; Namib Times, Oct. 19, 1982.

110. Namib Times, June 4, 1982.

111. Windhoek Observer, Mar. 31, 1983.

112. Windhoek Advertiser, July 24, 1981; Windhoek Observer, Aug. 14, 1982; Windhoek Advertiser, Oct. 8, 1982.

113. Windhoek Advertiser, Oct. 8, 1982.

114. Namib Times, July 24, 1981.

tourism would draw revenue. Walvis Bay authorities assumed that, with segregated facilities, the Bay would attract whites from Swakopmund and the rest of Namibia, where such restrictions had been abolished, as well as from the Republic of South Africa. Accordingly, much to the chagrin of Walvis Bay's black communities, in 1987 a pier and tidal pool for whites were completed. Tourist brochures stressed the attractions of the Namibian coast beyond the borders of the Walvis Bay territory and noted that the Bay was the site of the annual South West Africa Yachting Championships.[115]

Strategic Significance

While its economic fortunes declined, Walvis Bay's strategic importance grew. On August 15, 1977, just two weeks before the publication of Proclamation R202, Walvis Bay was transferred to the unified South West Africa Command of the SADF, a move that was contrary to the proclamation's intent of firmly establishing Walvis Bay as South African.[116] Walvis Bay became central to the SADF strategy of creating an army of Namibians, the South West Africa Territorial Force (SWATF), under SADF command. In 1981, the SADF started conscripting black as well as white Namibians, who were sent to Rooikop, across an international border, for ten months of training[117] followed by a year of active service in the SWATF. In addition, at the end of 1982, the commanding officer at Walvis Bay indicated that military facilities at Walvis Bay would be further expanded in 1984.[118] The multimillion-rand project would include a new military base and the rebuilding of existing accommodations near Walvis Bay's lagoon. As a result, the 2 SA Infantry Battalion would move to Rooikop, where the South African government was expanding facilities.

In 1977 the South African government enlarged the naval installations at Walvis Bay harbor, and on November 1, the South African navy established a separate command at the harbor.[119] South African warships began to call frequently at the Bay and conducted exercises there; a naval firing range was just south of the Bay.[120]

115. *See, e.g., Walvis Bay* (n.d. but still being distributed by the town clerk in 1986) (brochure describing attractions and facilities of Walvis Bay).

116. INTERNATIONAL DEFENCE AND AID FUND FOR SOUTHERN AFRICA, APARTHEID'S ARMY IN NAMIBIA 18 (1982) [hereinafter cited as APARTHEID'S ARMY].

117. *Id.* at 53–54; Windhoek Advertiser, Jan. 19, 1981; Star, Apr. 4, 1981.

118. Windhoek Advertiser, Nov. 26, 1982.

119. APARTHEID'S ARMY, *supra* note 116, at 11; Namib Times, Oct. 31, 1980.

120. INTERNATIONAL DEFENCE AND AID FUND FOR SOUTHERN AFRICA, THE APARTHEID WAR MACHINE 64 (1980); Namib Times, Apr. 7, 1981.

In 1979, the South African navy geared its strategy to coastal defense. Walvis Bay became the first port to be garrisoned with the newly formed marines, a specialized outfit made up of national servicemen and supported by members of the local Citizen Force, all under the command of Permanent Force officers.[121] In addition to the marine platoon, the unit included a diving team, explosives disposal specialists, experts in ship searches, two armed harbor patrol boats, early warning surveillance devices, and mobile radar. In the 1980s, South African gunboats also began patrolling the inshore fishing grounds on a regular basis. They were present in all the waters off the Namibian coast and not just in those off Walvis Bay.[122]

The navy's activities included more than securing the port. Walvis Bay became central to South African naval involvement in the rest of Namibia and in Angola as the South African navy's advance, or forward, base on the west coast.[123] The importance the SADF placed on the harbor was illustrated by the activation of the marines in August 1978. The marines at Walvis Bay were there in a counterinsurgency role similar to that of their comrades in the army on Namibia's northern border. "They get danger pay, but they are in effect on border duty," said the naval officer then in command at Walvis Bay.[124]

Also stationed at Walvis Bay was 131 Marine Protection Unit (MPU). Established in 1980, 131 had as its chief functions the protection of a national keypoint, in-depth harbor protection, the control of shipping, coastal patrols and operations, and the general security of Walvis Bay.[125] There was a communications center with all the necessary transport infrastructure. Using several patrol boats, the unit conducted regular checks and inspections of the ships going in and out of harbor and lying at the outer anchorage. Already in 1981, marines who had received intensive counterinsurgency training served in the so-called operational area in northern Namibia. The authorities announced plans to send more units in the future.[126] The marines, too, became involved in regulating offshore shipping.

In 1987, the militarization of the Walvis Bay territory was continuing unabated. Walvis Bay had a full-fledged military airfield with ample room to expand into the desert if suddenly necessary for operations involving high

121. Star, Apr. 28, 1979.
122. Windhoek Advertiser, Apr. 26, 1979; BBC, Apr. 27, 1979; Windhoek Advertiser, Apr. 26, 1979; BBC, Apr. 27, 1979.
123. Namib Times, Aug. 24, 1982.
124. Star, July 21, 1979.
125. Paratus, Sept. 21, 1983.
126. Cape Times, Jan. 1, 1981; BBC, Jan. 1, 1981.

speed jet aircraft.[127] In 1983 a police checkpoint was established at the harbor, and passes were required for all.[128] Meanwhile, the SADF and the South African Transport Services (formerly SAR&H) remained under unified South West African regional command.

Perhaps of all the changes that have beset Walvis Bay since the late 1970s, the most significant was the transformation of the issue of sovereignty over that sleepy desert territory into a question that vexed the international community. At stake was nothing less than de facto control over all of Namibia.

127. Cape Times, Oct. 25, 1982. By 1987, although the airport located at Rooikop was still military, it had a passenger terminal. See *Walvis Bay, supra* note 115; Windhoek Observer, Apr. 11, 1987.

128. Windhoek Observer, Mar. 31, 1983.

CHAPTER FIVE

The Dispute

The proclamation of 1977, transferring the administration of Walvis Bay to the Cape Province, set off an international controversy over the legal status of Walvis Bay. This change came at a time when Namibian independence was already the subject of worldwide attention.

Namibian Independence

After the United Nations revoked South Africa's authority to administer the South West Africa mandate, South Africa continued to occupy the territory.[1] During the mid-1970s, the Portuguese colonies of Mozambique and Angola became independent. This raised hopes of majority rule among those still living under white minority regimes in southern Africa. By the time Prime Minister Vorster of South Africa announced his government's position on Walvis Bay in April 1976, South Africa's fortunes in the region were sinking. Its invasion of Angola had been a failure; military aid from the United States never materialized because the Senate passed the Clark Amendment prohibiting covert aid.[2] In January 1976 the

1. *See generally supra* chapter 1.
2. *See generally* W. MINTER, KING SOLOMON'S MINES REVISITED: WESTERN INTERESTS AND THE BURDENED HISTORY OF SOUTHERN AFRICA (1986).

United States, Britain, and France had voted in favor of U.N. Security Council Resolution 385, which provided for U.N. -supervised and -controlled elections in Namibia by August 31.

South Africa thwarted this plan by proposing its own internal constitutional settlement with the avowed goal of achieving Namibian independence. For this it sponsored the Turnhalle Conference, so named for the building in Windhoek where it was held. The conference was attended by the pro–South African political parties that South Africa allowed to operate in Namibia. SWAPO, which observers then believed would win any free election, was excluded. The parties produced a constitution, and an "interim government" that would supposedly lead Namibia to independence took power.[3]

By April 1977, the permanent members of the Security Council—the United States, Britain, and France—as well as West Germany and Canada, which were then also on the Council, had expressed their displeasure with the interim government. The five became known as the Western Contact Group.[4] They intervened in the negotiating process in the hope of settling the Namibian issue so as to satisfy both South Africa and SWAPO. The Contact Group indicated that the Namibian internal parties would receive international recognition only if they won a U.N.-supervised election in which SWAPO was also a participant. Amid rising international expectations that Namibia would soon become independent, South Africa began to change its treatment of Walvis Bay.

Walvis Bay

South Africa's Tactics
Prime Minister John Vorster of South Africa, speaking before the South African Parliament on April 23, 1976, said, "I do not want there to be any misunderstanding whatsoever about this. Walvis Bay belongs to South Africa."[5] He indicated that he was thinking of repealing Act 24 of 1922 and administering Walvis Bay as part of the Cape Province. Three weeks later a revised Shipping Board Act (No. 74 of 1976) referred to Walvis Bay as a "South African port."[6]

---

3. *See generally* NAMIBIA SUPPORT COMMITTEE, TURNHALLE (London 1977); NAMIBIA SUPPORT COMMITTEE, SOUTH AFRICA'S SHAM ELECTIONS IN NAMIBIA (1979).

4. *See generally* H. HUNKE, NAMIBIA: NEGOTIATIONS AND "ELECTIONS" (Swedish Development Agency 1979).

5. Republic of South Africa, House of Assembly Debates, April 23, 1976, col. 5278.

6. Act No. 74 of 1976. The act it replaced, Shipping Board Act No. 20 of 1929 (as amended by Act No. 19 of 1965), included Namibia as a unit and made no distinction between Lüderitz and Walvis Bay.

In June 1977, the South African government amended the South West Africa Constitution Act of 1968.[7] The new act, No. 95, gave the South African state president unlimited authority to administer and legislate for Namibia by proclamation and to control "the Administration of Walvis Bay."[8] South Africa's amendment of the act of 1968 implied its recognition of the strategic and economic importance of Walvis Bay to an independent Namibia. The 1968 act had given substantial powers to the all-white South West African Parliament and South West African Legislative Assembly. The new act made possible the appointment of an administrator-general for Namibia who was to have full delegated authority and who would oversee the preparations for U.N.-recognized independence. On August 31, the state president exercised his powers under the act by issuing Proclamation R202, which provided that as of the following day, the same day that the administrator-general assumed his duties in Windhoek, "Walvis Bay shall cease to be administered as if it were part of the Territory and shall again be administered as part of the [Cape] province."[9]

The South African position on Walvis Bay has remained unchanged since Vorster's 1976 statement.[10] After Proclamation R202 appeared, Vorster deplored a report that a U.N. Security Council debate over South Africa's action would soon occur, stating that any negative Security Council action would make further discussions with the five Contact Group members pointless. "What is more," he said, "it [the Walvis Bay territory] was always recognized by all countries as belonging to South Africa. The ownership of Walvis Bay was never disputed even in the hottest debates in the United Nations."[11] When the Security Council passed Resolution 432 in July 1978, calling for "the early reintegration of Walvis Bay into Namibia," Vorster said that "the decision has no force of law" and that "only a decision of the South African Parliament can bring about a change in the status and possession of the territory."[12] He was only willing to negotiate the use of the harbor with a pro–South African government in Windhoek.

Vorster's successor, P. W. Botha, maintained this position, often stressing the military and strategic importance of the Bay to South Africa.[13] So

7. South West Africa Constitution Act No. 39 of 1968.
8. Act No. 95 of 1977.
9. Proclamation R202 (1977).
10. *See supra* note 2 and accompanying text.
11. Rand Daily Mail, Sept. 9, 1977.
12. Daily Telegraph, July 29, 1978.
13. *See, e.g.*, Windhoek Advertiser, July 30, 1979 ("The international status of Walvis Bay has of course remained unchanged for years, namely that it is South African territory."); Namib Times, June 2, 1981 (South Africa would negotiate with a friendly government in an independent

valuable did he consider the Bay that South African Foreign Minister Roelof "Pik" Botha on several occasions indicated South Africa's intention to respond militarily throughout the region to protect it.[14] Moreover, such action would be taken without regard for international opinion, as Deputy Minister of Defence W. N. Breytenbach indicated in July 1987.[15]

SWAPO's Reaction

Even before Vorster announced his intention to transfer the administration of Walvis Bay from Windhoek to Cape Town, SWAPO maintained that Walvis Bay was Namibian. It expressed that view, for example, in its draft constitutional proposals of August 1975.[16] In May 1976, in symbolic response to Vorster's stated plan, SWAPO held its annual congress in Walvis Bay. The next congress, which took place in Windhoek in March 1977, condemned South Africa's intentions.[17] SWAPO's deputy chairman said in June that as far as Walvis Bay was concerned, Namibians could not be bound to honor nineteenth-century colonial boundaries to which they had not consented and, moreover, that "South Africa's claim for the Bay is an expansionist venture and it could be used as a base for possible aggression against Namibia under SWAPO leadership."[18] He also indicated that Walvis Bay would be liberated, if necessary, as would the rest of Namibia.

When South Africa issued Proclamation R202, a SWAPO spokesman in New York read a statement to reporters gathered at the United Nations. SWAPO appealed urgently to the United Nations to take appropriate measures to prevent the consolidation of "this criminal action by South Africa."[19] SWAPO's publicity director in London issued a statement on the same day, emphasizing that Walvis Bay was an integral part of Namibia and its only seaport: "South Africa wants to hold on to it [the Bay] in order to sabotage our

---

Namibia only over the use of the harbor facilities.); Rand Daily Mail, May 7, 1982 (The legal status of Walvis Bay had never been disputed by any country and had been recognized by the League of Nations and the ICJ.); Star, Sept. 24, 1982 (Walvis Bay would remain part of South Africa, but South Africa recognized that Walvis Bay was important not only to South Africa but also to Namibia because it was a strategic modern harbor.).

14. *See, e.g.,* Johannesburg in English for Abroad, 1600 GMT, Mar. 18, 1978, BBC, Mar. 20, 1978; Roelof Botha: The "Ominous Message" of Zimbabwe for South West Africa/Namibia, Johannesburg in English for Abroad, 2100 GMT, Feb. 28, 1982, BBC, Mar. 2, 1982; Star, Oct. 16, 1982.

15. Namibian, July 3, 1987.

16. SWAPO, Discussion Paper on the Constitution of Independent Namibia (Lusaka 1975) (unpublished paper).

17. Windhoek Advertiser, Mar. 30, 1977.

18. Rand Daily Mail, June 15, 1977; Sunday Telegraph, June 26, 1977.

19. Windhoek Advertiser, Sept. 2, 1977.

own future. . . . We reiterate our demand for the total liberation of the whole of Namibia."[20]

In the weeks that followed, SWAPO spokesmen around the world made similar arguments. Then, on April 24, 1978, SWAPO President Sam Nujoma announced at the U.N. General Assembly's Special Session on Namibia, "SWAPO has maintained and still maintains that Walvis Bay is an integral part of Namibia. Therefore, to us the question of Walvis Bay is not negotiable and cannot be compromised."[21]

Since that time, other SWAPO officials have reiterated the claim that the Walvis Bay territory is Namibian and have recognized the economic and strategic significance of Walvis Bay to a free Namibia. As Nujoma complained in 1984, "They [the South African authorities] . . . hope that Namibia will be entirely dependent for the import and export of our goods on Walvis Bay which is controlled by South Africa."[22] Thus, by 1987, he held fast to the view that SWAPO was fighting to "liberate each and every inch of Namibia, including Walvis Bay."[23]

The International Reaction

The international community also responded to Proclamation R202. On the day the proclamation was issued, State Department spokesman Hodding Carter III said, "We regard this unilateral move by South Africa as untimely and unhelpful in terms of the negotiations currently under way on the transfer of power in Namibia."[24] United Nations Secretary-General Kurt Waldheim said that same day that South Africa's decision to take over the administration of Walvis Bay was unfortunate at a time when efforts were being made to resolve the entire Namibian problem.[25]

The United Nations reacted to the South African plan for Walvis Bay in various ways. After Vorster first announced his position on Walvis Bay in 1976, the Western Contact Group, fearing perhaps to disrupt negotiations with South Africa regarding Namibian independence, took no action. During the week following publication of the proclamation, Contact Group representatives denied having approved a proposal that the Security Council challenge South Africa's claim to sovereignty over Walvis Bay.[26] Although not publicly disputing the legality of South Africa's claim, the Western powers reportedly

20. *Id.*
21. Namibia Bulletin, No. 1, at 22 (1978).
22. Rand Daily Mail, Aug. 25, 1984.
23. Namibian, July 31, 1987.
24. New York Times, Sept. 3, 1977.
25. *Id.*
26. Windhoek Advertiser, Sept. 9, 1977.

stressed the port's significance to the economic and political stability of an independent Namibia. As the only deep-water port along the Namibian coastline, Western diplomats were said to have argued, it had become accepted— by practice and convention—as an integral part of the territory.[27]

Displeased with the failure of the Western powers to act, the U.N. Council for Namibia, the legal government of Namibia, objected on September 7, 1977, "in the strongest terms to this unilateral attempt by South Africa to destroy the territorial integrity of Namibia. Walvis Bay has always been an integral part of Namibia and South Africa has no right to change its status or to appropriate it as part of its own territory."[28] The council condemned South Africa's behavior as illegal, an act of colonial expansion, and a violation of Namibia's territorial integrity. "The independence of Namibia cannot be complete without the recovery of Walvis Bay from South African control,"[29] it said. The council also called for a meeting of the Security Council to debate South Africa's "annexation" of Walvis Bay. Until this time, U.N. General Assembly and Security Council resolutions had made no explicit reference to Walvis Bay. The issue had been neither discussed during the South West Africa cases nor considered by international scholars.

As the Contact Group continued to negotiate with South Africa about Namibian independence, no such Security Council meeting occurred. However, in Resolution 32/9 of November 4, 1977, the General Assembly condemned the annexation as illegal and declared Walvis Bay to be "an integral part of Namibia, with which it is inextricably linked by geographical, historical, economic, cultural and ethnic bonds."[30] The Declaration on Namibia, adopted overwhelmingly by the Assembly's Special Session on Namibia in April/May 1978, described the annexation as "an act of aggression against the Namibian people" and South African military bases in the Walvis Bay territory as "a threat to the national security of Namibia."[31]

The Security Council finally took up the Walvis Bay issue on July 27, 1978. Nujoma argued that because of the United Nations' role as guardian of national self-determination, "swapo therefore requests this Council to ensure, by committing itself to expediting the immediate withdrawal of all enemy troops and administrative machinery from Walvis Bay, that it is speedily and unconditionally restored to Namibia."[32] The South African foreign

27. Star, September 10, 1977.
28. Namibia Bulletin, No. 3, at 5–6 (1977). For the authority of the council, see *supra* chapter 1 at 8.
29. Namibia Bulletin, No. 3 (1977).
30. U.N. GAOR Res. 32/9(D) §§6–8 (1977).
31. U.N. GAOR Res. S9/2 §11 (1978).
32. 10(2) Objective: Justice 13 (1978).

minister reminded the Security Council, however, that on the insistence of South Africa the Western Contact Group had excluded all reference to Walvis Bay in its final published settlement proposals for Namibia.[33] Indeed, it was on the basis of those proposals that the Security Council later initiated the transition process that has since failed (Resolution 431, 27 July 1978)[34] and adopted the U.N. secretary-general's report on attaining Namibian independence[35] and Resolution 435 of September 29, 1978.[36]

Nevertheless, the Security Council unanimously adopted Resolution 432, declaring that the territorial integrity of Namibia had to be assured through "the reintegration of Walvis Bay within its territory."[37] The Council indicated that it would fully support steps "to ensure the Bay's early reintegration into Namibia."[38] The Council also decided to remain seized of the matter until full reintegration was achieved. In the interim, South Africa was not to use Walvis Bay "in any manner prejudicial to the independence of Namibia or the viability of its economy."[39]

This resolution, which the Contact Group endorsed, failed to indicate when Walvis Bay would be reintegrated into Namibia, leaving open the possibility that Walvis Bay would be excluded from the transition to independence and kept under South African control. An independent Namibian government could then "negotiate" the future of the territory as best it might. Thus South Africa might be allowed to dictate terms through refusing to place the status of Walvis Bay on the negotiating agenda.

Presumably fearing to disrupt the negotiating process for Namibian independence, the Contact Group was at first vague about when the Walvis Bay issue would be settled. Secretary of State Cyrus Vance explained when speaking for the Contact Group in the Security Council debate, "We consider that the 'steps necessary' [to ensure early reintegration of Walvis Bay into Namibia] are negotiations between the two parties directly concerned."[40] Accordingly, Resolution 435 of September 1978, which approved a Western plan for independence, did not mention Walvis Bay, leaving the issue open to negotiation.[41] The United States hardened its position under the Reagan administration. In November 1981, for example, Chester Crocker said the

33. *Id.* U.N. Doc. S/12636 is reprinted in *id.*
34. U.N. SCOR Res. 431 (1978).
35. U.N. Doc. S/12827.
36. U.N. SCOR Res. 435 (1978). *See infra* note 41 and accompanying text.
37. U.N. SCOR Res. 432 §1 (1978).
38. *Id.* at §2.
39. *Id.* at §3.
40. 10(2) Objective Justice (1978).
41. U.N. SCOR Res. 435 (1978).

question of Walvis Bay would have to be negotiated between the South African government and a future independent government of Namibia.[42] Regardless of this question of timing that so concerned the United States, both sides clung tenaciously to their positions.

The Arguments of the Parties

South Africa and Its Supporters

On September 26, 1977, the South African Department of Foreign Affairs issued a memorandum presenting its position on Walvis Bay to all diplomatic missions and consular missions without diplomatic representation in the country.[43] Based upon chain of title events, the argument ran as follows. Commander Dyer took possession of Walvis Bay in March 1878. On December 14, British letters patent were issued to annex Walvis Bay to the Cape Colony.[44] Some six years later, the governor of the Cape, acting under the authority of the letters patent, annexed Walvis Bay to the Cape. The South Africa Act of 1909, which united the British colonies of the Cape Colony and Natal with the former Boer republics of the Transvaal and the Orange Free State to form the four provinces of the Union of South Africa, provided that the provinces would *"have the same limits as the respective Colonies at the establishment of the Union.* Thus, as part of the Colony of the Cape of Good Hope, Walvis Bay . . . became part of the Cape Province and consequently part of the Union of South Africa and ultimately part of the Republic of South Africa."[45]

After World War I, South Africa began to administer what had been German South West Africa as a class C mandate under the League of Nations. Article 2 of the mandate agreement provided that South Africa could administer the territory "as an integral portion of the Union of South Africa."[46] Even though Walvis Bay was not part of the mandate, in 1922, for administrative convenience, South Africa began to administer it as if it were part of the mandated territory.

The South West Africa Affairs Act of 1922 noted that "the port and

42. Windhoek Advertiser, Nov. 3, 1981.
43. Republic of South Africa, Department of Foreign Affairs, The Legal Status of the Port and Settlement of Walvis Bay, 151/121 (19), Sept. 26, 1977 [hereinafter cited as South African Memorandum].
44. *Id.* at 194. This was an incorrect statement of the law. The letters patent did not annex Walvis Bay to the Cape. They merely authorized the annexation. *See* 70 BRITISH AND FOREIGN STATE PAPERS 495–96.
45. South African Memorandum, *supra* note 43, at 194 (emphasis in memorandum).
46. *Id.* at 193.

settlement of Walvis Bay *which forms part of the province of the Cape of Good Hope* shall be administered *as if it were part* of the mandated territory and *as if* inhabitants of the said port and settlement were inhabitants of the mandated territory."[47] The act indicated that the governor-general's power to legislate for the Cape, deriving from Act No. 35 of 1884, could now *"be delegated by the Governor-General to the Administrator of the mandated territory."*[48] A proclamation of September 15, 1922, published by the governor-general also declared that Walvis Bay, *"which forms part of the province of the Cape of Good Hope,* shall be administered *as if it were* part of the mandated territory."[49] It also stipulated, "I do further . . . *delegate* to the Administrator of the mandated territory . . . the powers conferred upon the Governor-General by Section 2 of Act No. 35 of 1884 of the Cape of Good Hope."[50] By Proclamation 30 of October 2, 1922, the administrator of South West Africa indicated in the official *Gazette* that the said delegation had occurred and that "the said port and settlement of Walvis Bay *shall be deemed* to form portion of the district of Swakopmund."[51]

According to the memorandum of 1977, "the position therefore is that, since it was expedient and convenient, Walvis Bay, though part of the Republic of South Africa, has since 1922 been administered as if it were part of the Territory of South West Africa. No *divestment* of title or sovereignty has taken place as is clearly shown by the words and phrases [in the documents cited above]."[52] Proclamation R202 *"confirms* and *reiterates"* this legal position and declares that it is "expedient and desirable again to administer and legislate for the port and settlement" of Walvis Bay as part of the Province of the Cape of Good Hope.[53]

A Department of Foreign Affairs document with the same file number as the memorandum contended that Walvis Bay was internationally recognized as belonging to South Africa,[54] offering three arguments to support this. First, "there is hardly any book of reference which does not recognize the fact that Walvis Bay does not form part of the territory of S.W.A."[55] The eight annexures offered as proof included descriptions of Walvis Bay from such publica-

47. *Id.* (emphasis in memorandum).
48. *Id.* (emphasis in memorandum).
49. *Id.* (emphasis in memorandum).
50. *Id.* at 192 (emphasis in memorandum).
51. *Id.* (emphasis in memorandum).
52. *Id.* (emphasis in memorandum).
53. *Id.* (emphasis in memorandum).
54. Republic of South Africa, Department of Foreign Affairs, General Recognition of the Status of Walvis Bay, 151/121 [hereinafter cited as General Recognition].
55. *Id.* at 1.

tions as the *Statesman's Year-Book, 1976–77, Webster's New Geographical Dictionary,* and the *Encyclopaedia Britannica* (11th edition). Second, a map in *National Geographic* magazine and others published by the United Nations indicated an international boundary around Walvis Bay or a line of demarcation that was not referred to as an international boundary.[56] Third, even the U.N. General Assembly recognized that Walvis Bay was "not formally a part of Namibia."[57] When it adopted Resolution 31/143 on December 17, 1976— the Implementation of the Declaration on the Granting of Independence to Colonial Countries and Peoples—it approved the Report of the Special Committee on the Situation with Regard to the Implementation of the Declaration on the Granting of Independence to Colonial Countries and Peoples. Chapter IX of that report dealt with Namibia, and the annexure to the document, a working paper prepared by the U.N. Secretariat, read, "The area of the Territory is approximately 824,296 square kilometres, including the area of Walvis Bay (1,124 square kilometres) which, although not formally a part of Namibia, is administered together with it."[58]

Various articles on Walvis Bay that appeared in South African publications also held to the chain of title and administrative convenience arguments but either embellished them or raised new points.[59] According to these articles, three factors that supported South Africa's claim to Walvis Bay were its valid annexation of the Bay as terra nullius, land that belonged to no state;[60] its unchallenged occupation of the area;[61] and its incorporation of the Bay into South Africa by due constitutional processes.[62] The colonial boundaries of Walvis Bay had to be allowed to stand, moreover, because colonial boundaries in Africa are often arbitrary and a majority of Latin American and Afro-Asian countries, including members of the Organisation of African Unity,

---

56. *Id.* The document did not call attention to the disclaimer on both maps of Namibia (Annexures I, J), which read, "The boundaries and names shown on this map do not imply official endorsement or acceptance by the United Nations."

57. General Recognition, *supra* note 54, at 1.

58. *Id.*

59. Brooks, *The Legal Status of Walvis Bay,* 2 S. AFR. Y.B. INT'L L. 188 (1976); D. PRINSLOO, WALVIS BAY AND THE PENGUIN ISLANDS: BACKGROUND AND STATUS (Pretoria: Foreign Affairs Association 1977); Botha, *Walvis Bay: Miscellany,* 12 COMP. & INT'L L.J. S. AFR. 255 (1979); Faris, *The Administration of Walvis Bay,* 5 S. AFR. Y.B. INT'L L. 63 (1979).

60. D. PRINSLOO, *supra* note 59, at 20; Botha, *supra* note 59, at 255 (noting valid annexation but not using term *terra nullius*); Brooks, *supra* note 59, at 186–90; Faris, *supra* note 59, at 63–64 (not using term *terra nullius*).

61. D. PRINSLOO, *supra* note 59, at 13, 20; Botha, *supra* note 59, at 255–56; Brooks, *supra* note 59, at 186–90.

62. D. PRINSLOO, *supra* note 59, at 13–14; Botha, *supra* note 59, at 256–58 (discussing question of recognition); Brooks, *supra* note 59, at 186–90.

"have accepted that colonial boundaries must, under international law, continue to be the boundaries after independence."[63]

Any claim that continued South African presence in Walvis Bay would interfere with the Namibian people's exercise of self-determination had to be rejected,[64] according to the articles, as inapplicable to a town the size of Walvis Bay with a largely transient population. In addition, Walvis Bay was an integral part of an independent South Africa, so "neither the people nor the enclave can be regarded as aspiring or moving towards self-determination or independence,"[65] and "as it has never been constitutionally part of SWA, but part of South Africa, self-determination cannot be stretched to imply the cession or transfer of sovereignty from South Africa to an independent SWA/Namibia."[66]

Finally, the articles stated that because the United Nations recognized SWAPO as the official representative of the Namibian people and the reactions of both SWAPO and the international community to Proclamation R202 were negative, South Africa sought "a means whereby recognition formerly granted [by the international community] can be enforced."[67] This means was the principle of estoppel, which one supporter of South Africa described as follows: "In the international sphere this would mean that were one state to recognise the sovereignty of some state over a specific territory, and, on the strength of that recognition, the state recognised were to act in terms of such recognition, the recognising state would be estopped from later denying its recognition of sovereignty over the territory."[68] In the case of Walvis Bay, the elements of estoppel were satisfied by prior recognition of South Africa's sovereignty in international agreements and reference works as well as by South Africa's expenditure of capital to develop industries in and around Walvis Bay and the loss to be incurred if South Africa's claim were to be thwarted.[69]

SWAPO *and Its Supporters*
In opposing South Africa's claims, SWAPO refrained from issuing a memorandum comparable to the South African memorandum of 1977. It adhered instead to declarations of broad legal principles in official publications and

---

63. Brooks, *supra* note 59, at 191. A nearly identical statement is found in D. PRINSLOO, *supra* note 59, at 22.

64. D. PRINSLOO, *supra* note 59, at 23; Botha, *supra* note 59, at 264–65.

65. D. PRINSLOO, *supra* note 59, at 23.

66. *Id.*

67. Botha, *supra* note 59, at 260. For a discussion of estoppel, *see infra* chapter 9.

68. Botha, *supra* note 59, at 260.

69. *Id.* at 260–61.

statements that could be translated into detailed arguments should the issue come before some international tribunal or other body.[70] Its position had four components. First, the original British title upon which South Africa bases its chain of title argument had no consensual element. It is therefore either invalid or no longer able to support a colonialist claim. Second, South Africa abandoned its sovereignty over Walvis Bay by transferring it to the South West African administration and leaving it there for fifty-five years. Third, Walvis Bay is geographically, economically, and historically a part of Namibia. At most, South African jurisdiction was colonialist and extended to Walvis Bay only before the Bay was transferred to the South West African administration. Under modern international law, all colonial peoples are entitled to self-determination. No state may recolonize any territory or people, especially when recolonization would entail reimposing apartheid—partially abandoned in Namibia—which the ICJ declared in its 1971 advisory opinion on Namibia contravened the purposes and principles of the U.N. Charter. Fourth, the United Nations has demanded that Namibia become independent with territorial integrity. History, economics, and strategic considerations demonstrate that this cannot be achieved if Walvis Bay is not part of Namibia.

The U.N. Council for Namibia took a position that agreed with that of SWAPO. A 1976 memorandum prepared for the office of the commissioner for Namibia argued that Walvis Bay was no longer South African but had become "an integral part of Namibia."[71] Three factors contributed to this conclusion. First, the administration of Walvis Bay from Windhoek since 1922 had resulted in voluntary divestment of title. Second, "the effective integration of Walvis Bay, a non-self-governing territory, in Namibia, a contiguous territory of ethnically and culturally kindred people, constituted the attainment of substantial self-determination, as defined by the General Assembly, for Walvis Bay."[72] Therefore, South Africa "cannot now reduce or abolish the self-determination Walvis Bay has attained by terminating its integration into Namibia."[73] Third, in light of U.N. resolutions demanding national unity and territorial integrity for non-self-governing territories, and especially for Namibia, "South Africa may not separate Walvis Bay from the Territory in which it has been incorporated or deny the Territory the port which is tied

---

70. *See, e.g., supra* notes 18–23 and accompanying text; *see generally* SWAPO, Namibia Today (formerly Namibia News, vols. 1–10, 1977–87).

71. Legal Status of Namibia, United Nations Interoffice Memorandum from Elizabeth S. Landis to Séan MacBride, United Nations commissioner for Namibia, June 9, 1976 [hereinafter cited as Council for Namibia memorandum].

72. *Id.* at 2. This argument mistakenly identified Walvis Bay as a non-self-governing territory. *See infra* text accompanying notes 79–80.

73. Council for Namibia memorandum, *supra* note 71, at 2.

historically to the Territory and is necessary for the Territory's economic survival and development."[74]

Neither SWAPO nor the Council for Namibia endorsed the memorandum of 1976 as representing its official stance. Both instead restricted themselves to declaring broad principles. When South Africa issued Proclamation R202, the council declared that the proclamation was null and void because it interfered with the territorial integrity of Namibia and the Namibian people's right to self-determination.[75]

Scattered sympathizers around the world also supported SWAPO in their writings.[76] In general, they argued that South Africa had relinquished its title because (1) the original British annexation failed to satisfy criteria of international law prevailing at the time, and South Africa's chain of title was thus defective;[77] (2) estoppel barred South Africa from undoing the integration of Walvis Bay into Namibia that it had effected from 1922 to 1977;[78] (3) the boundaries of non-self-governing territories granted independence may be determined on the basis of precolonial sovereignty, which showed Walvis Bay to be part of what is today Namibia;[79] and (4) South Africa violated the duties imposed upon it by the U.N. Charter to administer Walvis Bay, a non-self-governing territory, as a "sacred trust" and thus forfeited its sovereignty over Walvis Bay.[80]

74. *Id.*

75. *See supra* notes 28–29 and accompanying text.

76. Huaraka, *Walvis Bay and International Law,* 18 INDIAN J. INT'L L. 160 (1978); Goeckner & Gunning, *Namibia, South Africa, and the Walvis Bay Dispute,* 89 YALE L.J. 903 (1980); K. Asmal, Walvis Bay: Self-Determination and International Law, United Nations Council for Namibia, Seminar on Tenth Anniversary of the Namibia Opinion, Peace Palace, The Hague (June 22–24, 1981) (unpublished paper).

77. Huaraka, *supra* note 76.

78. Goeckner & Gunning, *supra* note 76, at 904–10; K. Asmal, *supra* note 76, at 28–30. An attempt at gathering facts that satisfied the elements of estoppel while refraining from articulating the legal arguments is found in E. Landis, If It Quacks Like a Duck . . . Walvis Bay, Namibia, and Estoppel (June 19, 1981) (unpublished paper).

79. Goeckner & Gunning, *supra* note 76, at 916–18. This article listed three criteria for determining whether a territory is non-self-governing. These were: (1) the territory must be geographically separate from the administering state; (2) its people must be ethnically or culturally distinct from those of the administering state; and (3) its status must be arbitrarily subordinate to that of the administering state. Applying these criteria to Walvis Bay, the authors concluded that Walvis Bay is a non-self-governing territory (NSG) and that as an NSG it is entitled to self-determination. The U.N. Council for Namibia memorandum, *supra* notes 71–74, also identified Walvis Bay as an NSG. This argument is flawed, however. There is no need to determine if Walvis Bay is an NSG. It is undisputed that the unit of decolonization with which the United Nations must deal is Namibia. It remains to be determined only whether Walvis Bay is part of that unit. This cannot be established by suggesting that Walvis Bay is an NSG.

80. Goeckner & Gunning, *supra* note 76, at 918–20. This flawed argument also echoes that made in the U.N. Council for Namibia memorandum, *supra* note 72. It is inappropriate to suggest

Two major difficulties beset much of the writing on both sides of the Walvis Bay dispute. First, it was frequently replete with historical and legal inaccuracies.[81] Even the South African memorandum of 1977 incorrectly recited the chain of title events, reporting that the Bay was annexed to the Cape in 1878[82] though it had remained annexed to Her Majesty's dominions until 1884. Second, authors on both sides were little more than polemicists, unable to appreciate the dynamic nature of international law or to recognize the ways it has evolved over the centuries from a colonialist legal order that denied sovereignty to indigenous peoples to one that accorded them full sovereign rights. It is these changing concepts of sovereignty, however, that are applicable to the Walvis Bay dispute.

---

that Walvis Bay is an NSG and that therefore because South Africa violated its duty toward Walvis Bay, its sovereignty is terminated. There is no doubt about the illegality of South Africa's long administration of Namibia. Again, the only question to be determined is whether Walvis Bay is part of Namibia, the internationally recognized unit of decolonization.

81. For legal inaccuracies, *see, e.g., supra* text accompanying notes 79–80.
82. *See supra* text accompanying notes 45–53.

CHAPTER SIX

The Colonialist Heritage

The problem of title to Walvis Bay reflects how concepts of sovereignty have changed in international law. Sovereignty is the right of a people to exercise exclusive hegemony over a particular area of land. Denying sovereignty to indigenous peoples was the legal technique most used by Europeans to impose colonialism. After World War II, as the old order collapsed, the concept of sovereignty was applied to all the world's peoples. This shift in theory and practice has had various consequences in the case of Walvis Bay.

Jurisprudential Considerations

From medieval times, the sovereignty of indigenous peoples has been a subject of lively debate in the Western legal tradition. Two major schools of thought emerged. The naturalists believed that all peoples of the world shared certain inalienable rights, whereas the positivists denied such rights to indigenous peoples and argued that international law applied only to Christian, later civilized, peoples.

Among those who argued that non-Christians were capable of exercising sovereignty was Thomas Aquinas (1227–74), who wrote that dominion derived from the law of men, whereas the differences between the faithful and the pagans came from divine law. As divine law was the product of grace, it did not annul human law, which arose from natural reason.[1] A contemporary of Aquinas, Sinibaldo Fieschi (d. 1254), later Pope Innocent IV, also recognized the rights of non-Christians.[2]

The English theologian John Wycliffe (ca. 1324–84) took the opposite view.[3] Although the Council of Constance (1414–18) condemned the application of Wycliffe's position to the Poles and Lithuanians, his opinions were widely accepted in Europe. As the Europeans discovered new lands in the fifteenth and sixteenth centuries, however, the question of sovereignty stirred contention among scholars.

The Naturalists

In the sixteenth century, a group of Spanish publicists emerged who acknowledged the sovereignty of non-Christian peoples. Francisco de Vitoria (1480–1546) claimed that the Indians of the Americas owned all their lands and that the Spanish had no more title to those lands than the Indians would have had to Spain if they had discovered it.[4] That the Indians had rejected the gospel preached to them by the Spanish did not give Spain a right to occupy their lands. In his *De Indis relectio prior de Indis novitur inventis,* Vitoria maintained that Europeans could not force the Indians to embrace Christianity and that there should be no foreign intervention in their lives unless it was in their own interest.[5]

Vitoria's pupil Domingo de Soto (1494–1560), confessor of Charles V, suggested that "there can be no difference between Christians and pagans, for the law of nations is equal to all nations."[6] Bartolomé de Las Casas (1474–1566) argued before Charles V in 1542 that the conquest of the Indies was tyrannical, unlawful, and unjust.[7] Some forty years later, Baltasar Ayala (ca. 1548–84) maintained that God had not given sovereignty over the earth to Christians alone but to all reasonable creatures.[8] Consequently, infidelity was not an adequate justification for warring with non-Christians and depriving them of their lands.

1. Aquinas, Summa theologica sec. Q. 10, art. 10 (Venice 1593).

2. E. Nys, Les Origines du droit international ch. VII (1894).

3. *Id.*

4. C. Salamon, De l'occupation des territoires sans maitre §14 (1889); 1 T. Walker, A History of the Law of Nations §120 (1899).

5. Vitoria, De Indis relectio prior de Indis novitur inventis. *See generally* L. Hanke, The Spanish Struggle for Justice in the Conquest of America (1949); J. Scott, The Spanish Origin of International Law (1934).

6. J. Mackintosh, Dissertation on the Progress of Ethical Philosophy 60 (Edinburgh 1862); E. Nys, *supra* note 2, at ch. VII.

7. J. Mackintosh, *supra* note 6, at 60.

8. H. Hallam, Introduction to the Literature of Europe in the Fifteenth, Sixteenth, and Seventeenth Centuries II.IV.89 (London 1855).

Publicists in other countries also recognized the sovereignty of non-Christians. The Frenchman Jean Bodin (ca. 1530–94) argued in his *De la republica* (1574) that non-Christian states had sovereignty.[9] The Italian-born jurist Alberico Gentili (1522–1608), who was forced to flee to England because of his heretical views, believed that Spain's title to the Americas was the product of an unjust war.[10] He claimed that international law derived from the principles of natural law and was universally applicable. Following upon this notion, the Dutch scholar Hugo Grotius (1583–1645) wrote in his *De mare liberum* (1609) that "[non-European] rulers, though heathen, are legitimate rulers, whether the people live under a monarchical or a democratic regime. They are not to be deprived of their sovereignty over their possessions because of their unbelief, since sovereignty is a matter of positive law, and unbelief is a matter of divine law, which cannot annul positive law."[11]

German jurists expressed similar views in the seventeenth, eighteenth, and nineteenth centuries. Samuel Pufendorf (1632–94) argued that "every man is, by nature, equal to every man, and consequently not subject to the dominion of others."[12] J. Gunther (1778) and J. Kluber (1762–1837) agreed that no nation, whatever its level of culture, had the power to take property from another, even if that second nation was one of savages or nomads.[13] August Heffter (1796–1880) echoed this sentiment, declaring that no power had the right to impose its laws upon nomadic or savage peoples.[14]

Nineteenth-century France produced several writers who supported the sovereign rights of indigenous inhabitants. Paul Pradier-Fodéré (1827–1904) claimed in 1863 that Christians had no right to occupy countries inhabited by less civilized people, even if such people were savages.[15] C. Salamon (1889) expressed the view that barbarous and savage people exercised rights of sovereignty and that such sovereignty, even if rudimentary, was enough to make any occupation of their country wrongful.[16] Henry Bonfils (1835–97) and Gaston Jèze (1896) favored the absolute right of indigenous peoples to "sovereignty, sometimes rudimentary but real nevertheless," because any other rule would sanction the notion that "might is right" under the pretext of civilization.[17] Frantz Despagnet (1857–1906) argued that an uncivilized

9. J. BODIN, DE LA REPUBLICA (Paris 1576).
10. A. GENTILI, DE IURE BELLI I.xix (T. Holland ed.) (Oxford 1877).
11. H. GROTIUS, DE MARE LIBERUM cap. II (Amsterdam 1712).
12. S. PUFENDORF, OF THE LAW OF NATIONS VII.VII.III (Oxford 1710).
13. J. KLUBER, DROIT DES GENS MODERNES DE L'EUROPE §125A (Paris 1831).
14. A. HEFFTER, DAS EUROPÄISCHE VÖLKERRECHT §70 (Berlin 1867).
15. P. PRADIER-FODERE, LE DROIT DE GENS DE VATTEL §209 (Paris 1863).
16. C. SALAMON, *supra* note 4, at §80.
17. H. BONFILS, MANUEL DE DROIT INTERNATIONAL PUBLIC (P. Fauchille 7th ed. 1914); G. JEZE, ETUDE THEORIQUE ET PRATIQUE SUR L'OCCUPATION COMME MODE D'ACQUERIR LES TERRITOIRES EN DROIT INTERNATIONAL 112 (1896).

people did not forfeit its rights of sovereignty.[18] Territory controlled by any power, however barbarous and rudimentary, was not terra nullius.

All these publicists thus held that any land inhabited by people who were linked by some political organization, no matter how primitive or crude, was not terra nullius.

The Middle Ground

In contrast to the exclusive naturalists, certain publicists maintained that indigenous peoples were entitled to sovereignty in limited instances.[19] The Swiss jurist Emmerich de Vattel (1714–67) believed that states could take possession of uninhabited or ownerless lands. They might also seize those lands that would exceed the needs of pastoral or nomadic peoples if such peoples were to decide to cultivate the soil. In such cases, however, the occupying state had to have need of more land. Accordingly, he wrote, "When the nations of Europe, which are too confined at home, come upon lands which the savages have no special need of and are making no present and continuous use of they may lawfully take possession of them and establish colonies in them."[20] Nearly a century later, the English jurist Robert Phillimore (1810–1885)[21] subscribed to Vattel's view, as did the French jurist Eugène Ortolan (1851).[22]

Writing some forty years after Vattel, Georg Friedrich von Martens (1756–1821), a professor at the University of Göttingen, suggested that natural law did not allow Christians to take areas effectively occupied by indigenous peoples against their will, "although in fact too many examples of such appropriation exist."[23] This rule did not apply to land occupied by nomads.

In the nineteenth century, the Portuguese jurist Silvestre Pinheiro-Ferreira (1769–1846)[24] and the German jurist Johann Bluntschli (1808–81)[25] adopted the position that civilized states could occupy the land of indigenous peoples as long as those peoples did not forcibly resist the occupiers.

18. F. Despagnet, Cours de droit international public §396 (C. de Boeck 4th ed. 1910).

19. Members of this school are often referred to as *eclectics*. However, because the term also has a pejorative connotation in some circles, it is best avoided.

20. E. Vattel, The Law of Nations I §§81, 207, 209; II §97 (Chitty trans. London 1834).

21. R. Phillimore, Commentaries upon International Law §CCXLII (3d ed. 1879).

22. E. Ortolan, Des moyens d'acquerir le domaine international §76 (Paris 1851).

23. G. Martens, Recueil general de traites et autres actes relatifs aux rapports de droit international §§36–37 (1817).

24. S. Pinheiro-Ferreira, Notes on Vattel §§203, 209 (1839).

25. J. Bluntschli, Das moderne Völkerrecht der civilisirten Staaten §280 (1868).

The Positivists

The predominant juridical opinion denied sovereignty to non-Christian peoples. The positivists derived their arguments from Machiavelli, considering force the basis for all law. They questioned whether international law was law at all because it lacked sanctions. They reasoned, moreover, that even if it was law, it afforded non-Christians no protection because such people had no knowledge of European law and lacked military might. The positivists thus concluded that the purpose of international law was to regulate the relations of Christian states among themselves. Its principles applied only to white, Christian, civilized peoples, civilization often being equated with military strength. So-called primitive peoples were objects of the law, and civilized European states could possess their land, their property, and even their persons.

The sixteenth-century Spanish scholar Juan Ginés de Sepúlveda (ca. 1490–1574) argued against the naturalist Bartolomé de Las Casas at a 1542 conference before Charles V, maintaining on behalf of the Spanish colonists that their conquest of the New World was lawful. In his *Apologia pro libro de justis belli,* Sepúlveda claimed that the infidelity of an indigenous people furnished an adequate rationale for a just war; the passive or active resistance of non-Christians to the gospel was casus belli for a bellum justum.[26]

Later positivist writers also eschewed concepts of natural law. They believed that international law derived from Christian civilization because it was the product of relations among Christian states. To support this claim they cited continuous hostility between Christian and Muslim states and sporadic contact between Christian and Buddhist states. Arising from Christian civilization, international law did not apply to other peoples. The American jurist Henry Wheaton (1785–1848), for example, claimed that "the public law, with slight exceptions, has always been, and still is, limited to the civilized and Christian people of Europe or those of European origin."[27]

In spite of the notion that Christianity was the source of international law, by the second half of the nineteenth century positivist writers often replaced Christianity with civilization as the criterion that made a people subject to international law. Only civilized states were entitled to membership in the international community. The Englishman William Hall (1835–94) believed that because international law arose from "the special civilization of modern Europe such states only can be presumed to be subject to it as are inheritors of that civilization."[28] His compatriot John Westlake (1828–1913) equated sov-

---

26. J. SEPULVEDA, APOLOGIA PRO LIBRO DE JUSTIS BELLI (Rome 1550).
27. H. WHEATON, ELEMENTS OF INTERNATIONAL LAW (C. Phillipson 5th ed. 1916).
28. W. HALL, A TREATISE ON INTERNATIONAL LAW (A. Higgins ed. 1924).

ereignty with culturally chauvinistic notions of civilization and claimed that there was no sovereignty "where [Europeans] find no native government capable of controlling white men under which white civilization can exist."[29] He defined the international community as consisting of only those states "of European blood, that is all the European and American states except Turkey, and of Japan."[30] Thomas Lawrence (1849–1919), another Englishman, maintained that all territory whose inhabitants were not members of the family of nations and subject to international law was terra nullius. In his view, it was irrelevant that the occupants of the area had "some slight degree of civilization and political coherence."[31] The Portuguese jurist Martens-Ferrão (1890), whom Westlake quoted with approval, echoed Lawrence with his argument that "native chiefs, half or wholly savage, [do not] possess any constituted sovereignty, that being a political right derived from civilization."[32]

Thus, although naturalist ideas persisted in international legal circles, positivist thought prevailed in state practice.

State Practice

The manner of acquiring non-European lands in international law changed over time. In the fifteenth and sixteenth centuries, state practice conformed to the juridical view that lands occupied by non-Christian peoples could be acquired by Christians. The papal bulls of this period reflected this notion.[33] They did not grant title to territory but the right to conquer it. Whereas Spain and Portugal advanced grants to conquer as valid claims to territory, other European rulers whom the bulls excluded from vying for the wealth of the New World and the East accorded them little legal authority. England, France, and Holland claimed that the pope had no power to make such grants. Grotius echoed their views in *De mare liberum,* arguing that the pope lacked authority over the inhabitants of previously unknown parts of the world.[34]

By the end of the fifteenth century, the English, French, and Dutch were

29. J. WESTLAKE, I INTERNATIONAL LAW (1910).
30. *Id.*
31. T. LAWRENCE, THE PRINCIPLES OF INTERNATIONAL LAW §74 (P. Winfield 7th ed. 1923).
32. J. WESTLAKE, *supra* note 29, at I.vi.
33. *See, e.g.,* R. PHILLIMORE, *supra* note 21, at §CCXXXI; J. SCHMAUSS, I CORPUS JURIS GENTIUM ACADEMICUM 114 (Leipzig 1830); E. HAZARD, HISTORICAL COLLECTIONS 3 (Philadelphia 1792). For further discussions of the modes of acquiring territories, see M. LINDLEY, THE ACQUISITION AND GOVERNMENT OF BACKWARD TERRITORY IN INTERNATIONAL LAW (1926); R. JENNINGS, THE ACQUISITION OF TERRITORY IN INTERNATIONAL LAW (1963).
34. H. GROTIUS, *supra* note 11, at ch. VI.

disregarding the bulls. In 1495, Henry VII of England sent out the Cabots. French and Dutch explorers followed them. The three nations soon became embroiled in arguments with Spain in the West and Portugal in the East over the rights claimed by Spain and Portugal under the papal bulls.[35]

The refusal of the English, French, and Dutch to acknowledge papal authority created the need for an alternative doctrine to regulate international affairs. As the vastness of the New World made it impossible for European powers to occupy large tracts effectively, nations emphasized the fact of discovery and based their claims to great areas upon trivial acts. There arose a rule of international law that discovery by the representative of one power excluded all others from the discovered area. Discovery in this context meant an intentional act of exploration or navigation accompanied by a sighting, a landing, and some additional act or acts making or recording such a visit but excluding acts expressing possession.

Under this rule of international law the European powers made many extravagant arguments,[36] but by the end of the eighteenth century they abandoned discovery as a means of supporting their claims.[37] Occupation had become a desideratum; discovery conferred only an inchoate title that had to be perfected within a reasonable time by occupation. Consequently, when Duminy attempted to annex Walvis Bay for the Dutch in 1793, his symbolic acts were insufficient to confer title. Similarly, Alexander's efforts at annexation for the British three years later had no legal effect because he merely raised the flag, fired three volleys, and turned over some soil.

By the time of Dyer's annexation nearly a century later in 1878, five principles of international law concerning the acquisition of territories had become entrenched. These were accretion, prescription, conquest, cession, and occupation. Only the last two were applicable to Britain's actions.

Accretion, Prescription, and Conquest

Accretion, "the increase or enlargement of the territory of a state mainly through the action of its rivers or the ocean," was irrelevant in the case of

---

35. *See, e.g.,* CAMDEN, THE HISTORIE OF THE MOST RENOWNED AND VICTORIOUS PRINCESS ELIZABETH, LATE QUEENE OF ENGLAND II.116 (London 1630); E. PAYNE, I HISTORY OF THE NEW WORLD CALLED AMERICA 223 (1892); W. PRESCOTT, 3 HISTORY OF THE CONQUEST OF MEXICO 1 (1843).

36. Johnson v. M'Intosh, 21 U.S. (8 Wheaton 543, 575–76) (1823); E. PAYNE, *supra* note 35, at 214, 224–25, 238–40; W. PRESCOTT, 2 HISTORY OF THE REIGN OF FERDINAND AND ISABELLA THE CATHOLIC 9 (1838); J. STORY, COMMENTARIES ON THE CONSTITUTION OF THE UNITED STATES §1 (T. Cooley 4th ed. 1870).

37. *See, e.g.,* T. TWISS, THE OREGON QUESTION EXAMINED 110 (London 1846); WHEATON, *supra* note 27, at 271.

Dyer's actions at Walvis Bay,[38] as was prescription, "the acquisition of sovereignty over territory through continuous and undisturbed exercise of sovereignty over it during such a period as is necessary to create under the influence of historical development the general conviction that the present condition of things is in conformity with international order."[39]

Conquest, a means of acquiring territory long recognized in international law, required the absence of any formal transfer of sovereignty by the previous European or indigenous ruler[40] as well as the taking of the area by force with the intention and the ability to retain the area as its sovereign. As the English fought no battles with the indigenous inhabitants of what became the Walvis Bay territory, conquest did not occur.

Cession

Another mode of territorial acquisition was the completion of treaties of cession with indigenous rulers. Cession was the transfer of sovereignty over a territory by mutual agreement.[41] Although such treaties were concluded by European nations competing for African trading stations during the seventeenth century, they were most widely used in the colonial scramble of the last quarter of the nineteenth century. These treaties were of three types: (1) treaties of complete cession, (2) treaties implying a protectorate, and (3) treaties establishing a protectorate. The British employed the last of these in the case of Walvis Bay.

Treaties of Complete Cession. In treaties of complete cession, native rulers relinquished all authority over their lands. Examples of treaties of complete cession were the two identical treaties concluded by Great Britain in May 1884 with Mankoroane, chief of the Bathlaping, and Montsia, chief of the Barolong.[42] The British never concluded a similar agreement with indigenous rulers in Walvis Bay.

Treaties Implying a Protectorate. Treaties implying a protectorate contained no direct reference to the sovereignty of the European power or the

38. N. HILL, CLAIMS TO TERRITORY IN INTERNATIONAL LAW AND RELATIONS 163 (1945). On Dyer's actions, see *supra* chapter 2 at 36–37.

39. N. HILL, *supra* note 38, at 156.

40. In re Southern Rhodesia, (1919) A.C. 211, 221; GROTIUS, *supra* note 11, at III; W. HALL, *supra* note 22, at IX.§204.

41. R. PHILLIMORE, *supra* note 21, at ch. XIV.

42. *Compare* E. HERTSLET, 17 HERTSLET'S COMMERCIAL TREATIES: A COMPLETE COLLECTION OF TREATIES AND CONVENTIONS 21–22 (London 1890) [hereinafter cited as HERTSLET'S COMMERCIAL TREATIES] *with* E. HERTSLET, MAP OF AFRICA BY TREATY 290 (1909).

protectorate established, but merely implied the hegemony of the colonizer over an area. The provision implying the supremacy of the European power was often a stipulation that the chiefs would not make treaties or other agreements with foreign nations or cede the land they inhabited to them without permission from the contracting nation. The 1888 agreement between Britain and Lobengula of the Ndebele was, for example, such a treaty.[43] The British never concluded a treaty implying a protectorate with the indigenous peoples of Walvis Bay.

Treaties Establishing a Protectorate. In a treaty establishing a protectorate, indigenous rulers ceded control of their lands in exchange for the promise that the colonizer would protect them. Such treaties created regimes of capitulation, that is, they articulated the rights and duties of the parties. In 1885, for example, the Germans in South West Africa entered into treaties of protection with the Red Nation, the Rehoboth Basters, and the Herero.[44]

The British concluded such treaties in 1886 with indigenous rulers on the Somali Coast.[45] One of these also included a number of articles specifically restricting the powers of the indigenous rulers in local affairs, such as the administration of justice, resource development, and commerce.[46]

In the case of Walvis Bay, the Palgrave-Herero agreement of 1876 fits the paradigm of a treaty establishing a protectorate. As such, it supports South Africa's claim that its chain of title to Walvis Bay derives from a valid cession. In 1872, Kamaherero, probably at the instigation of German missionaries, sent a request for protection to Governor Henry Barkly, asking him to "extend a helping hand to our people" and arbitrate in the friction between the Orlam and the Herero.[47] Two years later, he sent another letter, this time seeking protection from the Dorsland Trekkers. Whether Kamaherero fully understood the implications of these letters or whether they were entirely the product of missionary meddling, on their face both appeared to constitute requests for protection. Neither, however, was a treaty establishing a protectorate, as there was no agreement between the parties, and indeed, the Colonial government initially ignored these petitions.

43. 79 BRITISH AND FOREIGN STATE PAPERS 868. See also 66 BRITISH AND FOREIGN STATE PAPERS 650; 67 BRITISH AND FOREIGN STATE PAPERS 89 (treaty between Britain and West African rulers); 70 BRITISH AND FOREIGN STATE PAPERS 333; 78 BRITISH AND FOREIGN STATE PAPERS 758 (treaty between Britain and rulers of Zululand).

44. 76 BRITISH AND FOREIGN STATE PAPERS 506; G. MARTENS, II TRAITES ET AUTRES ACTES RELATIFS AUX RAPPORTS DE DROIT INTERNATIONAL 479–82 (2d series).

45. 77 BRITISH AND FOREIGN STATE PAPERS 1265.

46. *Id.* at 1263.

47. XXXIII BRITISH PARLIAMENTARY PAPERS 238 (1840).

When the Colonial government, then bent upon annexation, purportedly acted upon the letters and sent Palgrave to Damaraland and Namaland, the result was his September 1876 agreement with the Herero, in which the Herero allegedly requested that a resident be sent to their country, agreed to grant a reserve, and ceded those parts of the coast that the Colonial government desired.[48] Embodied as it was in a letter to the governor, even though Palgrave wrote it and it repeated the formulas popular then for such treaties, this agreement may be said to have constituted a treaty establishing a protectorate. At the time, this type of petition or letter was legally sufficient to transfer sovereignty from indigenous rulers to the Crown.

Although the Palgrave-Herero agreement appears to have been a valid treaty establishing a protectorate, that does not necessarily mean that the agreement was completed in accordance with the rules for the proper conclusion of treaties of cession that prevailed at the time.

Validity of Treaties of Cession. There is some authority for the proposition that agreements such as that between Palgrave and the Herero were completed in a manner that conflicted with the rules prevailing then for the proper conclusion of treaties of cession. Certain jurists argue that the validity of such agreements depended upon the colonizer's compliance with four conditions.

First, the supreme local authority in the area had to be party to the agreement.[49] There had occurred disputes between colonizing states in cases where one power had accepted from a subordinate ruler a cession of rights he had no authority to give. Great Britain almost lost its rights to some territory on the Niger by concluding a treaty with a subordinate ruler at Boussa. The French contended that the ruler at Boussa was the client of a ruler at Nikki. The powers reached an understanding that Britain would lose its rights if another colonizing state extracted a treaty from the ruler at Nikki. This set off a race to Nikki that the British won.[50] Second, the treaty had to be made or agreed to by the individual or individuals who, in accordance with the laws of their people, had or might reasonably be expected to have the authority to make the cession. In the Delagoa Bay Arbitration, for example, Portugal challenged a treaty of cession upon which Britain based its claim to the territory on the ground that the local Tembe ruler with whom it was made did

---

48. *See supra* chapter 2.

49. *See, e.g.,* 98 BRITISH AND FOREIGN STATE PAPERS 382; F. SHAW, A TROPICAL DEPENDENCY 355 (1905); 73 BRITISH AND FOREIGN STATE PAPERS 1242, 1298.

50. F. SHAW, *supra* note 49, at 355.

not have the power to conclude the treaty under the law and custom of his people.[51] Third, the agreement had to be executed in the form usually employed by the indigenous inhabitants for acts of a public nature.[52] This usually meant that the treaties were written, even though many indigenous peoples were not literate. Fourth, the contracting parties should understand the nature of the agreement. In the Delagoa Bay Arbitration, for example, the Portuguese argued that what the British claimed were treaties of cession were thought by the indigenous inhabitants to be lists of goods promised them.[53] Since there might have been doubt that the contracting local ruler knew what he was agreeing to, the European power often included a clause noting the effort made to inform the local ruler of the effects of his act.[54]

Some jurists argue, the views of the positivists notwithstanding, that these rules adhered to by the European powers in their dealings with local rulers were rules of law because of the universality of the practice of establishing a protectorate based on an agreement with such rulers. They argue further that the importance attached by the European powers to treaties of cession with local rulers indicated that they did not consider the lands inhabited by such people to be terra nullius.[55]

According to such thinking, the Palgrave-Herero agreement did not constitute a valid treaty of cession because it failed to satisfy the four criteria for such a cession.[56] First, the supreme local authority was not a party to the agreement. The land Kamaherero purported to transfer was not his to give because it was not under his control. The Peace Treaty of Okahandja, which pronounced the Herero the dominant power in Damaraland, did not disturb Orlam ascendancy in Namaland, which included Walvis Bay. At the time of the Palgrave-Herero agreement, the people of what became the Walvis Bay territory owed allegiance not to Kamaherero but to Jan Jonker Afrikaner or other Nama/Orlam leaders. Palgrave's mission to the Orlam was unsuccessful, and Palgrave, who in keeping with the state practice of the day endeavored to extract the legally requisite agreements from indigenous rulers before Britain would annex the territory, never obtained an agreement binding under the prevailing standards of international law from those entitled to give

51. C. 1361 at 95 (1875).

52. *See, e.g.,* XXXIII British Parliamentary Papers 238 (1840); Hertslet's Commercial Treaties, *supra* note 42, at III.894; Lambermont, *Arbitrage concernant l'ile de Lamu,* 22 Revue de droit international et de legislation compare 351, 354 (1890).

53. *See also* C. 3108 (1882); 81 British and Foreign State Papers 995–97; 85 British and Foreign State Papers 680.

54. *See, e.g.,* Hertslet's Commercial Treaties, *supra* note 42, at I.146; 77 British and Foreign State Papers 19.

55. *See, e.g.,* M. Lindley, *supra* note 33, at 43–44.

56. *See supra* notes 49–53 and accompanying text.

it. During his mission, he never even attempted to enter into any type of agreement with the people of what later became the Walvis Bay territory.

If Kamaherero was not the supreme local authority in the area, then the second criterion for creating a valid treaty of cession was not met either: the treaty was not agreed to by the individual who, according to the laws of his people, might have been able to make the cession. Since the first two criteria were not met because Kamaherero was the wrong person with whom to make the treaty, it is irrelevant whether the agreement was in a form usually employed by the Herero for acts of a public nature or whether the contracting parties understood the nature of the agreement. When viewed in this way, the South African claim that it acquired Walvis Bay through a treaty of cession valid under then prevailing standards of international law must fail.

A better view, however, is that in accordance with the positivist thinking of the day European powers did not consider such treaties to be agreements with independent states having international validity but regarded them instead as administrative acts over terra nullius by the colonizing nation that served notice on European rivals that a particular territory was being occupied. Support for the proposition that this was the real purpose of concluding treaties of cession with African rulers comes from Article 34 of the Berlin Act of 1885, which provided that a signatory was to notify all other signatories of new territorial acquisitions so that the latter might, if necessary, make good any claims of their own.[57]

In relations among European countries, such notice was useful. It enhanced the legal position of any power that had properly taken possession of or established protection over territory during the period of reasonable delay within which it was perfecting its administration of the area. Notice also made it possible for other European powers to advance any claims they had regarding the territory before the acquiring nation had taken definitive action in the area.

Many examples of notice are found in the practice of European powers about the time of the Berlin Conference.[58] From 1843 to 1880, the Dutch concluded some four hundred treaties and conventions with local rulers in Asia and informed the British accordingly.[59] In August and September 1884, Germany informed Britain that the emperor had placed South West Africa under his protection.[60]

57. C. 4361 at 312 (1885); C. 4730 (1886).
58. For further example, see 75 BRITISH AND FOREIGN STATE PAPERS 780–81; 77 BRITISH AND FOREIGN STATE PAPERS 1103; HERTSLET'S COMMERCIAL TREATIES, *supra* note 42, at II.682; F. DESPAGNET, *supra* note 18, at §394.
59. C. 3109 at 44 (1882).
60. 75 BRITISH AND FOREIGN STATE PAPERS 538, 546.

If it is assumed that notice was the reason colonizing powers concluded treaties of cession with local rulers, this explains the zeal of Britain and the Cape Colony to have Palgrave, cloaked with legal authority as special commissioner, extract such agreements from indigenous leaders. It also accounts for Germany's purchase of what became German South West Africa from indigenous rulers such as Josef Frederiks of Bethanie.

This interpretation of state practice also supports a finding that the Palgrave-Herero agreement constituted a valid treaty of cession; the case comports with the position that the four conditions for the validity of such treaties were not rules of international law but notice-giving devices for the benefit of European powers.

Regarding the requirement that the supreme local authority in the area should be party to the agreement, state practice reveals that only when an area was sought by two colonizing powers, as in the race to Nikki, did it matter whether the local ruler was actually the supreme local authority; when a European power had an uncontested claim to a territory, a treaty with any local ruler seemed to have fulfilled the notice function. In some situations a treaty with a ruler in a neighboring region would have been more valuable to the colonizers than a treaty with the supreme local ruler if the strength of the neighboring ruler was such that his opposition to colonial rule could destabilize the entire region.

In the case of Walvis Bay, Germany made no objection to Palgrave's agreement with the Herero, so that agreement sufficed to give notice to other European powers. Palgrave's mission to the Orlam, of whom the people of Walvis Bay were clients, failed, and he never attempted to extract any agreement from the people of Walvis Bay. Perhaps he ignored them because they were numerically insignificant; all the other groups he visited had sufficient size and strength to disrupt South West African life, including European trade, by becoming involved in war. As the Herero were a powerful people, their acquiescence helped Britain and the Cape to consolidate control over the area.

If it is accepted that in uncontested cases a treaty by a colonizer with any local authority was sufficient for supplying notice to other European powers, the Palgrave-Herero agreement was an adequate instrument for fulfilling the second criterion for notice, that is, that the cession had to be agreed to by individuals who had the authority to do so in accordance with the laws of their people. If a power was going to conclude an agreement with the Herero, it was necessary to obtain, as Palgrave did, the assent of Kamaherero and most of the other Herero leaders.

When the third and fourth criteria for creating a valid treaty of cession are considered, it becomes clear that the real purpose of these requirements was to give notice to other European powers. As mentioned, these criteria were that the agreement be in the form the indigenous inhabitants usually employed for acts of a public nature and that the contracting parties understand the nature of the agreement. The Herero, like the other indigenous peoples of sub-Saharan Africa, were not literate, so it is implausible to argue that writing was a form usually employed for acts of a public nature. It was, of course, the form that Europeans used for this purpose, and they preferred it to oral evidence of title, which led to evidentiary problems in disputed cases. Moreover, treaties like the Palgrave-Herero agreement were always written in a European language but only infrequently in the relevant African language as well. Even if such agreements were in the local language, the local people probably could not read it anyway; in the case of the Herero, missionary education had done little to spread literacy. African signatures were often only a thumbprint or, as in the Germany–Josef Frederiks and Palgrave-Herero agreements, an X. The illiteracy of local rulers and the uncertainty about whether there were any indigenous people capable of explaining the agreement to them support the argument that Europeans did not care if local rulers like Kamaherero understood the agreement they signed as long as the colonizers had a document sufficient for giving notice to other European nations. The British authorities knew that Kamaherero and his people did not understand the nature of the agreement; indeed, Britain informed Portugal that the Herero had ceded territory claimed by Portugal because they had "no idea" of Portugal's claims.[61] This lack of understanding also explains Kamaherero's later statements that the land did not belong to the whites, who believed they had "bought it" with "a piece of paper."[62]

In 1893, Lord Lugard furnished an account of the agreement-making process that might have applied to Palgrave's dealings with the Herero. After recalling words of friendship exchanged between himself and "a savage chief," he wrote, "then I put down on paper what was the pith of the contract between us; that is a treaty as I consider it."[63] Similarly, in his letter to the governor, Palgrave memorialized his agreement with the Herero as he saw fit.

The clause at the end of such treaties noting that the indigenous leaders understood the agreement was a legal fiction which served the notice function vis-à-vis other European powers. This explains Palgrave's insistence that after they were read aloud by Lewis, Kamaherero agreed to the definitions of the boundaries, saying, "These are the boundaries. Mr. Lewis has described

---

61. *See supra* chapter 2, note 101 and accompanying text.
62. *See supra* chapter 2, note 104 and accompanying text.
63. Lugard, *Treaty-Making in Africa,* 1 GEOGRAPHICAL J. 53 (1893).

them correctly, as well as those of the part we wish to keep for our own occupation and uses."[64]

If the real purpose of the requirements for treaties of cession was to give notice, thereby aiding the colonizing powers in regulating their relations inter se, the Palgrave-Herero agreement satisfied the prevailing requirements of international law for a valid cession. Accordingly, Britain annexed Walvis Bay pursuant to a valid treaty of cession. Viewed in this way, South Africa's derivative claim was sustainable.

Occupation

The last method by which European powers acquired foreign territories was through occupation. This required the settlement of terra nullius with the object of incorporating that territory into the national domain and exercising sovereignty over it. The two conditions of occupation were that the occupied territory had to be terra nullius and that the occupation had to be real or effective. In defining terra nullius, the views of the positivists prevailed. Accordingly, Europeans did not recognize the sovereignty of "noncivilized" peoples to the lands they occupied at the time the Europeans encountered them.

In *Johnson v. M'Intosh* (1823),[65] for example, the U.S. Supreme Court addressed the question of the validity of claims made to land granted to private individuals by the original Native American inhabitants; these grants conflicted with claims Virginia made under its 1609 charter. The Court held that the Native Americans' rights at the time of the grant were only rights of occupancy remaining to them after the discovery and annexation of the territory by the British. The Court noted that "while the different nations of Europe respected the rights of the natives, as occupants, they asserted the ultimate right of dominion to be in themselves; and claimed and exercised, as a consequence of this ultimate dominion, a power to grant the soil, while yet in possession of the natives."[66] The Court then acknowledged the validity of a similar title in Holland, Portugal, and Spain.

For effective occupation, it was not essential that the occupying power have sufficient force to repel foreign intrusion or that it be efficiently exploiting the land. It was necessary only that the Europeans exercise sufficient governmental control over the land to protect life and property there. For example, in 1872, the United States informed Haiti that because that country could not demonstrate "an actual possession and use" of the island of Ne-

64. G. 50–'77 at 40–41. According to one source, Lewis was illiterate. J. WILKEN & G. FOX, THE HISTORY OF THE PORT AND SETTLEMENT OF WALVIS BAY, 1878–1978 (1978).
65. Johnson v. M'Intosh, *supra* note 36, at 543.
66. *Id.*

vassa or "an extension and exercise of jurisdiction and authority over it," Haiti's claim to proprietorship of and sovereignty over the island was not admissible.[67]

In the Delagoa Bay Arbitration, Britain argued against Portugal that "as far as the Governor of the fortress, in the name of his sovereign, can and does exercise authority and jurisdiction, so far the country and its inhabitants are under the control and government of the country to which that fortress belongs. That control and government cease at the moment and at the places where the jurisdiction no longer exists, and the authority no longer is or can be exercised."[68] In his decision, the arbitrator recognized the British argument in his finding for the Portuguese, citing Portuguese occupation of various points on the Bay and Portugal's use of force against the Dutch and Austrians in upholding its claim of sovereignty over and exclusive right of trading at the Bay. In another case, in 1877, the British notified the Portuguese government that, with regard to the interior of the African continent for which no treaties existed, Britain refused to acknowledge that the notion of sovereignty could be separated from that of bona fide occupation and de facto jurisdiction of a continuous and nonintermittent kind.

The African Conference of Berlin in 1884–85 supported the validity of this type of acquisition of territory. At the conference, statesmen and jurists acknowledged that an essential condition for the validity of a title was the control and administration of the territory. In his opening remarks Bismarck said, "So that an occupation may be considered effective, it is, furthermore, desirable that the acquirer manifest, after a reasonable delay, by positive institutions, the will and the power to exercise its rights there and discharge the obligations which result from it."[69]

The conference accepted the pith of Bismarck's words as a rule applicable to the territories with which the conference dealt. It expressed the rule in Chapter VI of the Final Act, the Declaration Relative to the Essential Conditions to Be Observed in Order that the New Occupations on the Coast of the African Continent May Be Held to Be Effective. Article 35 of the chapter noted: "The Signatory Powers of the present Act recognize the obligation to insure the existence of authority in the regions occupied by them on the coasts of the African Continent sufficient to protecting existing rights and, as the case may be, freedom of trade and of transit under the conditions agreed upon."[70]

67. J. Moore, A Digest of International Law 575 (1906).
68. C. 1361 at 5 (1875).
69. C. 4361 at 3 (1885).
70. C. 4739 (1886).

In accepting this rule, however, the conference merely formalized what was by then the internationally recognized norm. As the British foreign minister wrote in his post-conference report, "No attempt is made by the Conference to interfere with existing maxims of International Law; dangerous definitions have been avoided, and international duties on the African coasts remain such as they have been hitherto understood."[71]

Under the law of occupation as it then existed, the power seeking to perfect its title had to install an administration sufficient to protect life and property within a reasonable time after first formally taking possession or announcing a claim to exclusive control. What constituted a reasonable time varied from case to case. In his *International Code,* the American scholar David Dudley Field (1805–94) argued for a twenty-five-year period after discovery during which the discovering nation could meet the requirement of actual possession.[72] The Italian jurist P. Fiore (1868) echoed these views, but such proposals giving a fixed limit received little support from the international community.[73]

Instead, the generally accepted rule was that what constituted a reasonable time depended upon such factors as the difficulty of establishing political control and effecting colonization in the discovered area, the relation of other nations to the land in question, and the urgency of the need for governmental institutions there. According to Hall, an inchoate title was valid against other claimant states for such a period as, "allowing for accidental circumstances or moderate negligence, might elapse before a force or a colony were sent out to some part of the land intended to be occupied."[74]

Whether a power's administration over the land to which it claimed title was sufficient depended upon the circumstances. If the territory had a large population or was frequented by many traders, elaborate administrative machinery might be necessary. If the area was remote, small, or unable to support more than a small or transitory population, only a rudimentary administrative organization was required.

In the case of Walvis Bay, although Dyer's symbolic acts of annexation were insufficient to confer title by occupation of terra nullius, physical acts meeting the requirement of effective occupation may be said to have occurred in a reasonable time thereafter through the appointment in 1878 of the first of a series of resident magistrates for the Walvis Bay territory. Arguably, this

---

71. C. 4631 at 12 (1885).

72. D. FIELD, OUTLINE OF AN INTERNATIONAL CODE §176 (1876).

73. P. FIORE, NOUVEAU DROIT INTERNATIONAL PUBLIC (P. Pradier-Fodéré trans. Paris 1868); H. BONFILS, *supra* note 17, at §554 (P. Fauchille 7th ed. 1914).

74. W. HALL, *supra* note 28, at II.II.

administration was sufficient because of the small, isolated nature of the territory and its capacity to support only a small European and transitory indigenous population. The requirements for occupation were met in this instance. These factors support a finding that British and, derivatively, South African title to Walvis Bay arose from an occupation of terra nullius that was valid according to the rules of international law of the time.

It appears then that at the end of the nineteenth century there existed what may be termed a common law of the abrogation of the natural law rights of indigenous peoples. When measured against this standard, British practice with regard to Walvis Bay complied with accepted state practice concerning the acquisition of territory by cession or occupation. Accordingly, the title of Britain and, derivatively, that of South Africa was valid.

The cultural chauvinism and juridical positivism that supported this state of affairs continued well into the twentieth century; as international law then evolved, it did nothing to disturb the validity of South Africa's title to Walvis Bay.

CHAPTER SEVEN

Brave New Legal Order?

At the turn of the twentieth century, a Western-educated African and Caribbean elite began a campaign of political resistance to colonial rule, and Pan-Africanism was born. Later, the rhetoric surrounding the Paris Peace Conference of 1919 and the League of Nations encouraged blacks by emphasizing the concept of self-determination. In practice, however, the old legal order remained intact, and the international community did not question South African sovereignty over Walvis Bay.

Pan-Africanism

British rule in India gave rise to a Western-educated elite with a political conscience and the finances to send its children to Europe for higher education. By the end of the nineteenth century, a similar elite had emerged in West Africa and South Africa, as well as in the Caribbean.[1] Members of these black groups came together in the metropolitan countries, which became centers of black intellectual and political dialogue. This ferment gave rise to the first organized

---

1. In South Africa, members of this new elite group came together in 1912 to form the first independence movement in Africa, the South African Native National Congress, now the African National Congress. *See generally* T. LODGE, BLACK POLITICS IN SOUTH AFRICA SINCE 1945 (1983).

international black movement against colonialism. A 1900 conference in London, which protested unsuccessfully against the treatment of Africans in the Rhodesias and South Africa, used the term Pan-Africanism for the first time.[2]

The outbreak of the First World War temporarily disrupted Pan-Africanist activities. In the longer term, however, the war strengthened nationalist and Pan-Africanist sentiment. Thousands of Africans served in the armed forces as soldiers or construction workers, acquiring new skills and learning new organizational techniques. Allied propaganda that railed against German colonialism, Woodrow Wilson's championing of self-determination, and the success of the October 1917 Russian Revolution also encouraged Africans.

The First World War similarly politicized Afro-Americans. By the end of the war, a movement had arisen among black Americans, many of whom had seen combat, to ensure the rights of Africans throughout the world.[3] They held meetings across the country and, on behalf of their African brethren, petitioned Woodrow Wilson, whose domestic record on civil rights was poor.[4]

W. E. B. DuBois went to France to arrange for a Pan-African Congress to be held concurrently with the Paris Peace Conference, as well as to lobby for African rights.[5] After opposition from the American delegates to the peace conference, in the end, fifty-seven delegates from fifteen countries—nine African countries and colonies sent a total of twelve delegates—attended the congress, which met from February 19 to 21, 1919. The congress made several recommendations, including that the members of the Paris Peace Conference hold Africa's land in trust for Africans and prevent the exploitation of African labor and the depletion of Africa's natural resources. The congress' goals were politically evolutionary rather than revolutionary, with no immediate independence envisioned.[6]

In 1921, DuBois organized the second Pan-African Congress, which was held in London, Brussels, and Paris. The congress' aims were gradualistic, as those of the first congress had been. The congress petitioned the League of Nations for "local self-government for backward groups, deliberately rising as experience and knowledge grew to complete self-government

2. C. LEGUM, PAN-AFRICANISM 25 (1963).
3. *See* U. UMOZURIKE, INTERNATIONAL LAW AND COLONIALISM IN AFRICA 55 (1979).
4. On Wilson's domestic policy, see M. STEINFELD, OUR RACIST PRESIDENTS: FROM WASHINGTON TO NIXON (1972); R. GARRETT, THE PRESIDENTS AND THE NEGRO (1982).
5. Dubois, *The Pan-African Movement,* in HISTORY OF THE PAN-AFRICAN CONGRESS 13–15 (G. Padmore ed. 1963).
6. T. WALLBANK (ed.), DOCUMENTS ON MODERN AFRICA 27 (1964).

under the limitation of a self-governed world."[7] Thus, it sought to have an African appointed to the Permanent Mandates Commission and asked the League of Nations to take "a firm stand on the absolute equality of races."[8]

DuBois organized the third Pan-African Congress in 1923. Held in London and Lisbon, the congress called for a role for Africans in their government, the abolition of the slave trade and the liquor traffic, and the development of Africa for the benefit of Africans.

The colonial powers prevented the occurrence of a fourth congress planned for a French-owned ship that would call at various Caribbean ports. The fourth congress eventually took place in New York in 1927 and reiterated the calls made at the third congress. France objected to plans to hold a fifth congress in Tunis—it would have been the first on the African continent— suggesting instead a site in France. The Great Depression then interfered with the organization of further congresses, although Pan-Africanist activities continued in Europe, North America, and the Caribbean.

The Pan-African congresses were not meetings of states and were not attended by the colonial powers, but they did serve to publicize the rigors of colonialism. Although the congresses did not move states to take up the cause of Africans in international fora, the resolutions of the congresses and the attention they received furnished various humanitarian organizations with information for advancing the Africans' interests. Eventually, the views expressed at these congresses established the basis for the anticolonial order in international law. At that time, however, the congresses exerted only a moral influence because international law remained captive to the interests of the colonial powers. The international community was not yet prepared to address the problems raised by the congresses, such as racial discrimination and loss of land and sovereignty.

The League of Nations

The Paris Peace Conference of 1919 did not inquire into the validity of the title to the possessions of colonial powers. With the exception of German sovereignty over the Kionga Triangle, which Portugal successfully challenged, the peace conference and the League of Nations accepted as given the boundaries of Germany's colonies as they had been at the beginning of the war. Also implicitly recognized was British and therefore, derivatively, South African sovereignty over Walvis Bay, which was not a part of what became the South

7. U. Umozurike, *supra* note 3, at 55.
8. *Id.*

West Africa mandate.[9] The Union of South Africa thus controlled both the Bay and the mandated territory. This recognition of the status of Walvis Bay by the League of Nations did not create the status or give legal effect to it, however. Rather, it presumed that the Bay's status had been created according to the rules of international law as they existed at the time when the status originated. The lack of objection at the peace conference to the Bay's status did not create a new principle of international law; rather, the nineteenth-century international legal principles regarding the acquisition of territory remained in effect. The conference and the League contributed, however, to the growth of the nascent principle of self-determination.

At the beginning of World War I, the Allied and Associated Powers hesitated to appeal to the idea of self-determination. That outlook changed when the United States entered the war in the summer of 1917. By then Woodrow Wilson's position on the issue was well known; as early as May 1916, he had said that "every people has a right to choose the sovereignty under which they shall live."[10]

Wilson announced his Fourteen Points to a joint session of Congress on January 8, 1918. Although not expressly mentioned, self-determination was implicit in seven of the points. In later speeches Wilson reiterated his position, advocating the creation of a League of Nations and the abrogation of arbitrary power. Instead of being merely a political phrase, self-determination was to be "an imperative principle of action which statesmen will henceforth ignore at their peril."[11]

The British also extolled self-determination. On June 29, 1917, Lloyd George said, "When we come to settle who must be the future trustees of those uncivilized lands, we must take into account the sentiment of the people themselves."[12] After consulting the dominions, the cabinet, the parliamentary opposition, and labor leaders, on January 5, 1918, he stated about the German colonies that "the general principle of national self-determination is . . . as applicable in their cases as in those of European occupied territories."[13]

9. The mandate for South West Africa of December 17, 1920, contained no boundary description, and the presumption was that there was to be no divergence from the boundaries of German South West Africa, the title to which Germany had renounced in the Treaty of Versailles. I. BROWNLIE (ed.), AMERICAN BOUNDARIES 1277 (1979).

10. R. BAKER, 6 WOODROW WILSON 220 (1938); A. LINK, WILSON: CAMPAIGN FOR PROGRESSIVISM AND PEACE, 1916–1917, 25 (1965); *see also* J. SCOTT, OFFICIAL STATEMENTS OF WAR AIMS AND PEACE PROPOSALS 52 (1921).

11. M. SHUKRI, THE CONCEPT OF SELF-DETERMINATION IN THE UNITED NATIONS 66 (1965).

12. H. TEMPERLEY, 2 A HISTORY OF THE PEACE CONFERENCE OF PARIS 227 (1921).

13. *Id.*

The czar of Russia was meanwhile overthrown, and the provisional government led by Lvov proclaimed on April 10, 1917, that Russia wished to establish a lasting peace based on the right of nations to self-determination.[14] Then, a repudiation of self-determination by Miliukov, the Russian foreign minister, and his government's willingness to comply with the secret treaties with the Allies allowed Lenin to attack the government openly. This was one of many events leading to the October revolution. Once the Bolsheviks gained control of the government, they revealed the secret treaties. On November 15, 1917, the new government issued the Declaration of the Rights of the Peoples of Russia, which supported the right of Russia's nationalities to self-determination, including secession and the organization of independent states.[15] Thus the success of the Russian Revolution popularized the concept of self-determination.

Self-determination and nonannexation were major issues at the Paris Peace Conference. Independence as a manifestation of self-determination was emphasized. Although Article 119 of the Treaty of Versailles required Germany to renounce "all her rights and titles over her overseas possessions" in favor of the principal Allied and Associated Powers, the delegates to the conference agreed, over the objections of the South Africans and others, that these powers should not annex the colonial possessions of the losers.[16]

Instead, in the paternalistic mode of the day, the conference created the mandates system, according to which the "advanced nations" were to guide the former colonial possessions to independence at an unspecified date once the advanced nations deemed them capable of entering the community of nations.[17] This system in effect recognized the inchoate right of self-determination in the "backward peoples" of the world, departing from the positivist view that international law regulated only the relations of Western states and non-Western states of Western culture. It was an ideological halfway house between independence and nonrecognition.

Discussions about mandates at the peace conference revolved around Wilson's Fourteen Points and the South African Jan Smuts's 1918 work *The League of Nations: A Practical Suggestion*. Smuts, a South African cabinet minister and erstwhile member of the Imperial War Cabinet in London,

14. *See* J. SCOTT, *supra* note 10, at 96; see also F. GOLDER, DOCUMENTS OF RUSSIAN HISTORY, 1914–1917, 341 (1927).

15. Lasserson, *The Development of Soviet Foreign Policy in Europe, 1917–1942*, INT'L CONCILIATION 10 (1943).

16. Treaty of Versailles, art. 119.

17. J. SMUTS, THE LEAGUE OF NATIONS: A PRACTICAL SUGGESTION (1918). On Smuts, see generally W. HANCOCK, SMUTS (2 vols.) (1962, 1968).

argued that the world should reconstruct itself on the basis of the principles of nationality and self-determination. He believed that such new states as Finland, Poland, Czechoslovakia, and Yugoslavia were advanced enough to become independent with the aid of the victorious powers. The League would ensure that large and small states received equitable treatment and that their minorities received protection. Smuts felt that other civilized areas, like Lebanon, Syria, Transcaucasia, and Mesopotamia, needed guidance and that areas with national and religious divisions like Armenia and Palestine should be supervised by an international commission. For such states he suggested mandate status in place of "any policy of national annexation."[18] With regard to the former German colonies in Africa and the Pacific, however, he maintained that they were "inhabited by barbarians, who not only cannot possibly govern themselves, but to whom it would be impracticable to apply any ideas of political self-determination in the European sense."[19]

Smuts's ideas impressed Wilson, who embodied some of them in his second draft of the League Covenant. Unlike Smuts, however, Wilson extended the principle of self-determination to all colonies through the mandate system. At the conference, Wilson declared that the purpose of the system was to assist the mandates in achieving "self-government and self-dependence."[20]

Although Wilson's draft of the League Covenant referred to the "principle of self-determination," the covenant as adopted did not include the phrase.[21] Still, the mandates system theoretically represented an international recognition of the notion that ultimately the principle of self-determination applied to all the world's peoples, regardless of what the Western powers saw as their stage of development. In the case of supposedly undeveloped peoples, the mandatory power held the full exercise of that right in trust for them until they were capable of acting for themselves. This was implicit in the words of Article 22 of the Treaty of Versailles, the League Covenant, which incorporated the mandates system and made it applicable to peoples "not yet able to stand by themselves."[22] The fundamental principle of the article was that the "well-being and development of such peoples [in the mandated territories] form a sacred trust to civilization."[23] Article 22

18. J. SMUTS, *supra* note 17. *See generally* A. ZIMMERN, THE LEAGUE OF NATIONS AND THE RULE OF LAW 209–14 (1936).

19. *Id.*

20. D. MILLER, 2 THE DRAFTING OF THE COVENANT 104 (1928).

21. *Id.*

22. Covenant of the League of Nations, art. 22, *reprinted in* F. NORTHREDGE, THE LEAGUE OF NATIONS, Appendix A, 324–25 (1986).

23. *Id.*

also divided the former German and Turkish colonies into A, B, and C mandates according to the level of civilization—from highest to lowest—that the nations at the conference believed the indigenous inhabitants had attained. Article 23 of the covenant required signatories to establish fair labor practices and "ensure just treatment of the native inhabitants of territories under their control."[24]

There were several major differences between the mandate system and annexation. Theoretically, the mandate system prohibited the mandatory, which exercised authority on the League's behalf, from committing various acts that an owner of territory could do lawfully. Mandatories did not have the power to annex, cede, or otherwise dispose of mandated territories without the consent of the League Council.

Mandatories were restricted in recruiting and training indigenous inhabitants. In addition, the indigenous inhabitants did not acquire the nationality of the mandatory ipso facto. The central principle of the arrangement was that of trusteeship for the mandate's indigenous inhabitants, "peoples not yet able to stand by themselves under the strenuous conditions of the modern world."[25] In the case of C mandates, the mandatory had the right to administer the territory "as an integral portion" of itself, although this right was to be exercised for the protection of the indigenous inhabitants.[26]

The phrase "as an integral portion" in relation to C mandates did not imply annexation. Rather, it indicated a permissible mode of administration that was not to disturb the obligations of the "sacred trust of civilization."[27] The Permanent Mandates Commission repeatedly rejected any act or suggestion implying that a mandatory had sovereignty over a mandated territory. It objected, for example, when the preamble to the Portuguese–South African treaty of 1926, delimiting the boundary between South West Africa and Angola, provided that "the Government of the Union of South Africa, subject to the terms of the said mandate, possesses sovereignty over the territory of South-West Africa lately under the sovereignty of Germany."[28] In 1927 and 1930, the League Council passed resolutions stipulating that mandatory powers did not have sovereignty over their mandates.

The mandate system was responsible for a new international accountability in the form of obligatory annual reports by the mandatory to the League

24. Covenant of the League of Nations, art. 23, reprinted in *id.* at 326.
25. Covenant of the League of Nations, art. 22, *supra* note 22.
26. *Id.*
27. *Id.*
28. Treaty Series, No. 29 (1926); 123 British and Foreign State Papers 590 (1926) [hereinafter cited as South African–Portuguese Treaty].

Council.[29] With the advice and assistance of the Permanent Mandates Commission, the League Council supervised the mandate system. The commission was composed of ten ordinary members. The majority of the members were from states that were not mandatories. The commission examined the annual reports from each mandatory in the presence of the mandatory's representative, who responded to questions and supplemented the information contained in the report.

The system granted the indigenous inhabitants of mandatories a right to petition the League. They had to forward their petition through the mandatory's government, however, so that the government could attach its own comments before the commission examined the petition. This hindered the system's effectiveness. Other individuals and groups also communicated petitions to the League Council, which was mainly responsible for the system, though the League Assembly had the power to consider questions concerning it as well.

In spite of these provisions, the system was seriously limited in its ability to control the administration of the mandated territories. The Permanent Mandates Commission had no powers of sanction. If the commission believed that a mandatory was ignoring its obligations, it could only report to the League Council and leave the matter there, knowing that if its report to the council disturbed a mandatory, future dealings with that nation and the flow of information about its mandate might be adversely affected.

In addition, the Permanent Mandates Commission was unable to visit the mandated territories and interview the inhabitants. Its narrow powers to deal with petitions and—as with all League organs—limited financial resources compounded problems. As the mandatory powers were on the spot, whereas the commission was far away in Geneva, the influence exerted by the commission over the mandatory remained, throughout the life of the League, theoretical rather than practical. Nevertheless, at the time, some observers applauded the mandates system as an enlightened development in the creation of a new legal order in which internationalism triumphed over narrow nationalism.[30]

In operation, however, the mandate system was not the altruistic device it appeared to be in the League Covenant. Exploitation of the territories did not cease with the switch from colonial to mandate status. Among the worst of all mandate administrations was that of South Africa over its C mandate, South West Africa. It repeatedly disregarded the obligations imposed upon it

29. For a discussion of the League's structure, see C. Fenwick, International Law 128–38 (1924).
30. *See, e.g.*, C. Lee, Mandates: How They Are Working 31, 34 (1927).

by the mandate agreement, as in the Bondelswart Massacre and the Rehoboth Affair.[31]

South Africa in South West Africa

After the First World War, the indigenous peoples of South West Africa who had not been annihilated by the German policy of extermination began return-ing from hiding places to lands they had previously occupied. South Africa disapproved of this in its 1922 Report to the Permanent Mandates Commis-sion, noting that it had sold or allotted these lands to whites.[32]

Instead of securing the territorial rights of Africans, the South Africans continued the system of labor reserves instituted by the Germans. In May 1922, the government perpetrated what became known as the Bondelswart Massacre. The South African authorities had forced the Bondelswart people into a reserve in southern South West Africa. At the same time, the South West African administrator had promulgated a law to force them to work for whites. When the South West African authorities attempted to arrest a Bondelswart, the community refused to give him up. Fearing retribution, several thousand Bondelswart set up camp on a hill. White residents of the territory complained to the authorities that the Bondelswart constituted a threat. In response, white magistrates and police demanded that they surrender. When they refused, the South West African administrator massed troops and ordered the air force to bomb the hill from 3:00 P.M. until dawn. Thousands of Bondelswart perished, including women and children.

Although such conduct violated the terms of the mandate agreement, the League with its limited powers suggested only that South Africa establish a commission to review the incident. The report of the commission noted that the massacre occurred because of misunderstanding on both sides; it blamed the whites for being susceptible to fear.[33] Nothing more came of the matter, and the Bondelswart never received any compensation.

The Rehoboth Affair occurred shortly thereafter. It involved the Re-

31. For further accounts of the events, see I. GOLDBLATT, THE MANDATED TERRITORY OF SOUTH WEST AFRICA IN RELATION TO THE UNITED NATIONS 215–18, 222–25 (1961); J. WELL-INGTON, SOUTH WEST AFRICA AND ITS HUMAN ISSUES 284–89 (1967); A. FREISLICH, THE LAST TRIBAL WAR: A HISTORY OF THE BONDELSWART UPRISING WHICH TOOK PLACE IN SOUTH WEST AFRICA IN 1922 (1964); A. DAVEY, THE BONDELZWARTS AFFAIR (1961); A. TOYNBEE, SURVEY OF INTERNATIONAL AFFAIRS, 1920–23, 397 (1927).

32. Union of South Africa, Report of the Administration of South West Africa for the Year 1922, U.G. 21–1923 [hereinafter cited as 1923 Union Report].

33. Minutes of the Permanent Mandates Commission, 27th meeting, 3d Sess., Aug. 7, 1923; Report of the Permanent Mandates Commission 1923, min. III, 292; XI, 95, 97–100.

hoboth Basters,[34] to whom, during the First World War, South African Prime Minister General Louis Botha promised some type of self-government in exchange for their cooperation against the Germans. The Rehoboth Basters disagreed with the South West African authorities over the issue of independence, the extent of their reserve, and a government monopoly on the branding of their cattle. When they rebelled, the South West African administrator again mobilized the army and the air force, and they surrendered without bloodshed. Although the 1923 Report of the Permanent Mandates Commission criticized the state of relations between whites and blacks in South West Africa, the commission took no action.[35]

South Africa continued to disregard the welfare of the mandated territory's indigenous inhabitants in spite of its obligation to improve their situation. Labor conditions in South West African diamond mines, for example, were particularly severe, and South Africa devoted only 1 percent of the mandate's revenues to black education.[36] Indeed, from the beginning of its administration, South Africa had no intention of honoring its obligations as a mandatory.

Throughout the life of the League, South Africa maintained that South West Africa was as much under its sovereignty as the Transvaal or Natal. In 1920, South African Prime Minister Smuts reportedly said that "in effect, the relations between the South West Protectorate and the Union amount to annexation in all but name."[37] The preamble of the 1926 treaty between South Africa and Portugal that fixed the boundary between South West Africa and Angola noted that South Africa possessed sovereignty over the mandated territory.[38] On various occasions in 1926 and 1927, South African Prime Minister J. B. M. Hertzog claimed full sovereignty over South West Africa subject to the terms of the mandate.[39]

Although the Permanent Mandates Commission repudiated South Africa's claim, it acquiesced, pursuant to the passage of the 1922 South West Africa Affairs Act, in South Africa's administration of Walvis Bay from Windhoek, the capital of the mandate, as if the Bay formed part of the

34. In South West African racial/ethnic terminology the Rehobothers are Coloured.

35. Report of the Permanent Mandates Commission 1923, *supra* note 33, at III, 325; Rep. Sess. IV, OFFICIAL JOURNAL V 1412.

36. F. WHITE, MANDATES 141 (1926); Report of the Permanent Mandates Commission, *supra* note 33.

37. A detailed discussion of the position of the South African government and courts is found in J. DUGARD (ed.), THE SOUTH WEST AFRICA/NAMIBIA DISPUTE 75–82 (1975).

38. South African–Portuguese Treaty, *supra* note 28.

39. *See, e.g.,* London Times, June 9, 1927, Aug. 13, 1927; Permanent Mandates Commission, Minutes and Report of the Tenth Session 82–86, 182 (1926); Minutes and Report of the Eleventh Session (1927), ROUND TABLE 217–22 (Dec. 1927).

mandated territory. In its report to the commission in 1922, South Africa treated Walvis Bay as part of the mandate.[40] Questioned about this, the South African representative to the commission replied that South Africa had attached the Bay to the mandate for "administrative reasons."[41] By 1928, however, the South African representative said that "Walvis Bay . . . was essential to the economic development of the mandated territory" and that "the trade of South West Africa would be severely injured were it not to control Walvis Bay."[42] Moreover, he stated that "the fact of the incorporation of Walvis Bay in South West Africa" enabled the administrator of South West Africa to make representations to the prime minister of the Union on behalf of Walvis Bay.[43] In 1929, the commission accepted the South African proposition that Walvis Bay formed an integral part of the South West Africa mandate.[44]

In spite of these developments, throughout its life the League could do nothing to ensure that the legal order it purported to create was instituted in the mandated territory. Although this might have been expected in the case of supposedly uncivilized indigenous inhabitants of a C mandate, the refusal of Western states to recognize the rights of Ethiopia, an independent African state and League member, when it tried to enforce the provisions of the League Charter against its fellow member Italy, indicated that the international legal order was not yet prepared to recognize African sovereignty.

The Italian Conquest of Ethiopia

Italy, which had attempted to conquer Ethiopia (then commonly known as Abyssinia) at the end of the nineteenth century and had made colonies of Eritrea, Somaliland, and Libya, was not pleased with the League's distribution of the former German colonies. In 1925, Ethiopian Emperor Haile Selassie complained to Britain, France, and the League about an Anglo-Italian agreement by which Britain acknowledged "an exclusive Italian economic influence" in large parts of Ethiopia.[45]

40. 1922 Union Report, *supra* note 32.

41. Permanent Mandates Commission, Minutes, 6A League of Nations Publications (3d Sess.) 103 (1923).

42. Permanent Mandates Commission, Minutes, 6A League of Nations Publications (14th Sess.) 69 (1928) (remarks of South African representative).

43. *Id.*

44. Permanent Mandates Commission, Minutes, 6A League of Nations Publications (15th Sess.) 294 (1929) (requesting more information on lack of South African voting privileges in Walvis Bay).

45. U. UMOZURIKE, *supra* note 3, at 67.

In 1928, Italy and Ethiopia entered into a Treaty of Friendship that provided for the peaceful resolution of disputes arising between them.[46] That same year, Italy signed the Kellogg-Briand Pact on the Renunciation of the Use of Force in the Resolution of International Disputes. Nevertheless, in 1930, Italy occupied an oasis at Wal Wal some sixty miles inside Ethiopia; the Ethiopian military could not resist this aggression. Four years later, the forces of the two nations clashed.

In spite of Britain's urging not to raise the matter, Haile Selassie called on the League to invoke Article 11 of the League Covenant, which required League action to safeguard peace.[47] In response to international pressure, Ethiopia withdrew its appeal hoping to obtain a negotiated settlement, but Italy refused to enter into discussions and started mobilizing troops. After several Ethiopian requests for intervention, the League established a conciliation committee composed of Italy, France, and Britain. It inquired only into the Wal Wal incident and eventually found that neither state was at fault.

Meanwhile, on June 20, 1935, Ethiopia informed the League that Italy would soon invade and asked for foreign observers. The European powers, including Britain, opposed the request. Mussolini indulged in racist rhetoric against Ethiopia, asking, "Has the League of Nations become the tribunal before which all the negroes and uncivilized peoples, all the world's savages, can bring the great nations which have revolutionized and transformed humanity?"[48]

In August, Italy, France, and Britain concluded the Zeila Agreement, which, with the Ethiopian emperor's approval, gave Italy extensive economic concessions. The Italian representative to the League then argued that Italy and Ethiopia were not equal sovereign states and that a peaceful settlement was out of the question. He said that in treaties made before the League was established, Italy had acquired most of Ethiopia and that by committing offenses against Italian nationals, Ethiopia had violated its duties to the League and lost its right to League protection. He claimed that Article 22 of the covenant, which applied to mandates like South West Africa, should pertain to Ethiopia.[49]

46. Italo-Ethiopian Treaty of Amity, Conciliation and Arbitration of August 2, 1928 (94 League of Nations Treaty Series 434). *See generally* G. BAER, THE COMING OF THE ITALIAN-ETHIOPIAN WAR (1967).

47. League Covenant, art. 11, *supra* note 24, at 320–21. On the war, see generally G. BAER, TEST CASE: ITALY, ETHIOPIA AND THE LEAGUE OF NATIONS (1976); T. COFFEY, LION BY THE TAIL: THE STORY OF THE ITALO-ETHIOPIAN WAR (1974).

48. Hansard (1935) col. 29300–31.

49. Speech of 10 Oct. 1935 before the 15th Plenary Meeting of the 16th Sess. of the League Assembly.

In what was ostensibly an act of neutrality, Britain then announced an arms embargo on both sides. Other nations, including France, followed suit. This denied Ethiopia a means of self-defense, however, because Italy manufactured most of its weapons and also continued to use the British- and French-controlled Suez Canal for transporting munitions and men. At the same time, British Foreign Secretary Sir Samuel Hoare announced to the League that his country stood with the League "for the collective maintenance of the Covenant in its entirety, and particularly steady and collective resistance to all acts of unprovoked aggression."[50] France concurred with Britain.

On October 3, 1935, Italy invaded Ethiopia. The League did not meet until October 6. The next day it passed a resolution condemning the Italian action. Fifty states, including Italy's supporters, voted in favor of the resolution, whereas Italy voted against it and Austria, Hungary, and Albania abstained. The resolution prohibited exporting arms and munitions to Italy but allowed the shipment of iron, steel, petrol, and copper to continue. Italy produced its own arms, however, so the sanctions had no effect and European politicians recognized them as a sham.[51]

In December 1935, Britain and France formulated the Hoare-Laval Plan, which envisaged a transfer of the eastern portion of the Ogaden, Tigre, and Danakil to Italy and a mandate-like status for the remainder of Ethiopia under the supervision of League advisers selected by Italy, France, and Britain. Since the Ethiopians were losing badly, Canada pressed to include oil in the sanctions. Anthony Eden, who had replaced Hoare as British foreign secretary, argued successfully that the existing sanctions were effective and sufficient. Ecuador then abandoned economic sanctions on April 1, 1936, and several states followed suit. These moves were of no consequence. On May 5, the Italians reached Addis Ababa. Four days later, Italy announced that it had annexed Ethiopia and proclaimed Vittorio Emmanuele Ethiopian emperor.

Haile Selassie fled to Britain, where he was taken in because of strongly sympathetic public opinion. Appearing in June 1936 before the League of Nations, he decried both the Italians' use of chemical warfare and the League's acquiescence in Italy's aggression. Two years later, with Haile Selassie still in Britain, the British government attempted to exclude Ethiopia from the League.

Although the actions of Italy and other League members violated the principles of the League, the Latvian president of the League Council found

50. Speech of 11 Sept. 1935, *quoted in* U. UMOZURIKE, *supra* note 3, at 69–70.
51. *See, e.g.*, Manchester Guardian, Oct. 13, 1936 (statement by Lloyd George).

that it was up to individual members to determine their actions.[52] Not until World War II did the Allies attacking Italy's colonies enlist the aid of Haile Selassie, who returned to his country to join the liberation forces. By the time Ethiopia regained its independence after the war,[53] a new international legal order was taking shape.

The League's treatment of the African inhabitants of both mandated territories like South West Africa and supposedly independent states like Ethiopia was a patina of internationalism covering acts of aggression. The treaty law of the period, however, like that of the previous century, regarded indigenous peoples as having no place in the international legal order.

Developments in Treaty Law

Developments in treaty law in the early twentieth century, if applicable to indigenous peoples, would have voided titles such as that of the Union of South Africa to Walvis Bay. In such cases, the attack was not upon agreements themselves but upon the subsequent conduct of the parties to these agreements.

By that time, the basic principles of contract law had become part of international law, as in the 1914 *Island of Timor*[54] case and the 1934 *Lighthouses*[55] case between France and Greece. In *Island of Timor,* Portugal and the Netherlands disputed a portion of the boundary dividing their domains on Timor, the easternmost of the Sunda Islands in the Timor Sea near what is today Indonesia. According to a treaty of 1859, ratified in 1860, the western part of the island was Portuguese and the eastern part was Dutch. Pursuant to an 1893 treaty, a mixed commission determined the border between the two territories but failed to agree about one section. Consequently, in 1913, the two states submitted the dispute to a member of the Permanent Court of Arbitration.[56]

The arbitrator relied upon state practice as described in national codes on

---

52. LEAGUE OF NATIONS, OFFICIAL JOURNAL 338 (1938).

53. *See generally* L. MOSLEY, HAILE SELASSIE (1964).

54. Affaire de l'île de Timor, 11 R. INT'L ARB. AWARDS 481 (1961) [hereinafter cited as Island of Timor].

55. Lighthouses Case Between France and Greece, Judgment, Permanent Court of Int'l Justice, Judgment, PCIJ, Ser. A/B, No. 62, at 4 (1934) [hereinafter cited as Lighthouses]. *See generally* J. VERZIJL, 1 THE JURISPRUDENCE OF THE WORLD COURT 370–82, 483–95 (1965). The Permanent Court of International Justice came into existence on September 1, 1921. In addition to the Assembly, the Council, and the Secretariat, it was the fourth principal League organ. *See generally* M. HUDSON, THE PERMANENT COURT OF INTERNATIONAL JUSTICE (1934).

56. *See also Arbitral Award Rendered in Execution of the Compromise Signed at The Hague, April 3, 1913, between the Netherlands and Portugal Concerning the Subject of the Boundary of a Part of the Islands of Timor,* 9 AM. J. INT'L L. 240 (1915).

the law of contract. He referred to the principle that parties must perform their contractual obligations in good faith and noted the internationally recognized "coincidence of private and international law in this point."[57] Furthermore, he relied upon the views of the publicists to support the notion that parties had to discharge treaty obligations according not only to the letter of the agreement but also to the common and real intentions of the parties and the spirit of the agreement.

In *Lighthouses*, the parties had by special agreement referred the dispute to the Permanent Court of International Justice. The question for decision was whether a concession for the maintenance of lighthouses along the coasts of the Ottoman Empire, agreed between the Ottoman government and a French firm, was still operative after the Balkan Wars with regard to the Greek government. During the wars, the Balkan Allies occupied most of European Turkey, and Greece occupied the Aegean coast and islands. The court held affirmatively (10–2) on the ground that because negotiations for the concession had begun before the war, there was clearly no intention to exclude from the concession's scope the territories that Turkey's adversaries occupied by 1913.[58]

Judge Seferiades' separate opinion indicated that "contracting parties are always assumed to be acting honestly and in good faith. That is a legal principle which is recognized in private law and cannot be ignored in international law."[59] Accordingly, *pacta sunt servanda* was a general principle of international law which raised a legal presumption that treaty obligations bound the parties, who had to perform in good faith. As jurist Bin Cheng later wrote, "from the fact that it is the common intention of the parties or the spirit of the treaty that has to be respected, it follows that it is not impermissible, whilst observing the letter of the agreement, to evade treaty obligations by— what the Permanent court . . . called—'indirect means.' "[60]

In the case of Walvis Bay, since the British never performed their part of the Palgrave-Herero agreement, neither it nor the documents issued pursuant to it—namely, Dyer's proclamation, the letters patent, and the Annexation Act—would have had international legal effect.[61] Accordingly, the South African chain of title claim would have failed.

In practice, however, these rules of international law did not apply to agreements concluded by Western powers with African rulers. Since the international legal order continued to deny African rulers the sovereignty

57. Island of Timor, *supra* note 54, at 490.
58. Lighthouses, *supra* note 56.
59. *Id.* at 47. Separate opinion of Judge ad hoc Seferiades.
60. B. CHENG, GENERAL PRINCIPLES OF INTERNATIONAL LAW (1953).
61. *See supra* chapter 2 at 32–46.

accorded Western states, agreements between Western and African powers did not have the status of international treaties governed by the rule of pacta sunt servanda. In both theory and practice, Westerners still saw such treaties as binding only upon the conscience and enforceable at the whim of the Western power. As the judge in a 1914 British colonial case from East Africa noted, "I agree with the view expressed by respondents that it [the treaty] imposed moral obligations on both the contracting parties; these, however, are not cognisable in a Court of Law."[62]

Similarly, in the 1928 *Island of Palmas* case, which involved a dispute between the United States and the Netherlands regarding sovereignty over the island, Judge Huber of the PCIJ wrote of treaties with indigenous rulers that such "treaties or conventions are not capable of creating rights and obligations such as may, in international law, arise out of treaties. But, on the other hand, contracts of this nature are not wholly void of indirect effects on situations governed by international law; if they do not constitute titles in international law, they are none-the-less facts which the law must in certain circumstances take into account."[63] In practice, the international legal community persisted in viewing such agreements as treaties to the extent that they secured rights and privileges for Westerners without guaranteeing correlative obligations and duties toward indigenous peoples.

Thus, in spite of the pretense of creating a new international legal order, in the early twentieth century principles of international law still applied only to the relations of Western states among themselves. Regardless of whether Africans occupied what international law termed colonies, mandates, or states, the Western powers perpetuated the idea of the previous century that international law did not apply to indigenous peoples. In a world that permitted the commission of brutalities against South West Africans by the mandatory power and the subjugation of Ethiopia, the international legal order recognized as legally sufficient the events upon which South Africa based its chain of title claim to Walvis Bay.

War soon brought the collapse of the League and change for Africa. Growing Pan-Africanism and nationalist sentiment in the colonies; the influence of Marxism, increasingly attractive since the rise of the Soviet Union to Great Power status after World War II; tirades against colonialism from progressive groups in Europe and the United States; and the founding of the United Nations all contributed to the creation of a new international legal order that no longer recognized as valid the South African claim to Walvis Bay.

62. Ol Le Njogo et al. v. A.G. for Eastern Africa (Masai Case) E.A.P.L. 1 (1913–14).
63. Island of Palmas Case, 2 R. INT'L ARB. AWARDS 829 (1929).

CHAPTER EIGHT

The Triumph of Self-Determination

T he Second World War was a catalyst for the reassertion and strengthening of Pan-Africanist ideas, advancing notions of self-determination and equal rights that came to have primacy of place in postwar international law. The new international legal order that arose would no longer support colonialist claims like that of South Africa to Walvis Bay.

The War and Africa

Like World War I, World War II affected Pan-Africanism and African nationalism first by paralyzing organizational activity and then by accelerating and intensifying earlier nationalist trends. Initially, it disrupted international contact among Pan-Africanist groups.[1] At the same time, the colonies assumed greater economic and military importance for the Allies than ever before by furnishing them with much-needed manpower and raw materials.[2]

Once the United States entered the war, its huge commitment of material resources to the war effort worked to help modernize Africa through the construction of harbors, airports, roads, supply depots, and repair shops. Increased urbanization resulted from the

---

1. On these developments, see generally I. GEISS, THE PAN-AFRICAN MOVEMENT 363–65 (1974).

2. *See, e.g.*, U. UMOZURIKE, INTERNATIONAL LAW AND COLONIALISM IN AFRICA 79 (1979); 2 WAR AIMS OF THE UNITED NATIONS, 1943–45, 577 (1948).

rise in the demand for labor. Other changes in the wake of the colonies' economic contributions to the war were a marked increase in the size of the work force and the establishment of the first trade unions of considerable size.[3]

Through military service, Africans acquired new organizational skills. Hundreds of thousands served in the British and French armed forces.[4] Even as the number of Europeans in administrative apparatuses declined, the war demanded an expansion of administrative activities, and the civil service began to be Africanized. Military service and urbanization widened the horizons of the African people. Many ex-combatants transformed their expanded political awareness into action for African nationalist movements.[5]

Participation in the wartime economy and the armed forces also increased political consciousness among Afro-Americans in the United States and the Caribbean.[6] Encouraged by the growing independence movement in India, blacks in the Caribbean, North America, and Europe resumed the struggle for African rights. The Pan-African Congress held in Manchester in 1945 sent a memorandum to the nascent United Nations Organization, requesting that provision be made for representatives of the African colonial peoples to participate to the maximum extent possible under the U.N. Charter.[7] The memorandum also decried the administration of South West Africa by South Africa and requested that the United Nations put the territory under trusteeship.[8]

These changes in economic and political orientation occurred in the context of major changes in world politics.

The Rise of Self-Determination

During World War II, various anticolonial declarations and principles were formulated. Both the Allies and the Axis used shortwave radio broadcasting as a method of psychological warfare to criticize oppression and colonialism. In a speech on January 6, 1941, President Franklin Roosevelt recognized four freedoms for the world's peoples: freedom of speech and expression, freedom of worship, freedom from want, and freedom from fear. The Four Freedoms Speech was important for its effects on the British-American Atlantic Charter

3. *See, e.g.,* W. HAILEY, AN AFRICAN SURVEY (1956).
4. *Id.*
5. *See generally* T. HODGKIN, NATIONALISM IN AFRICA (1957).
6. *See generally* I. GEISS, *supra* note 1, at 363–84.
7. U. UMOZURIKE, *supra* note 2, at 80.
8. *Id.* at 81. A detailed examination of the 1945 Pan-African Congress is found in I. GEISS, *supra* note 1, at 363–408.

of August 14, 1941.[9] Among the Charter's eight principles was support for the right of peoples to choose their own form of government. Although the United States held that the charter was universally applicable, Churchill insisted in spite of West African petitioning that it was not relevant for British colonies.[10] Nevertheless, Clement Attlee, deputy prime minister under Churchill, interpreted the charter in a way that raised the expectations of African nationalists. He looked for "an ever-increasing measure of self-government in Africa."[11] Similarly, in February 1942, Roosevelt noted that the charter was for "all humanity."[12]

The world soon went beyond the declaration of broad principles to establish institutions for furthering them. On March 9, 1943, U.S. State Department officials compiled the Draft Declaration by the United Nations on National Independence. Its preamble made the Atlantic Charter universally applicable and indicated that the "opportunity to achieve independence for those peoples who aspire to independence shall be preserved, respected and made more effective."[13]

The declaration listed general principles to which the colonial powers were to adhere in dealing with dependent peoples. It also proposed the establishment of an international trusteeship administration for all mandated territories and for those detached from the enemy as a result of the war. The distinction between general principles applicable to all dependent territories and an administration for certain types of territories avoided disturbing the Allies' control over their colonies; later it was embodied in the U.N. Charter, which separated provisions relating to non-self-governing territories from those relating to trusteeship.

The Big Three Conference at Yalta in 1945 confirmed the division of dependent territories into two categories—trust and non-trust—classifying trust territories as either strategic or nonstrategic. These classifications reflected the demise of the League of Nations mandate system and the relation of the mandated territories to issues of war and security. The conference did not agree upon a specific trusteeship plan, leaving that instead to the forthcoming U.N. Conference.[14] Thus, the wartime conference record reveals that although the Allies recognized that colonialism demanded a postwar solution,

9. British-American Atlantic Charter, Aug. 14, 1944.

10. Hansard, Parliamentary Debates, House of Commons Official Report, Parliamentary Debates H.C. 374, cols. 67–69.

11. U. UMOZURIKE, *supra* note 2, at 81.

12. D. VAUGHAN, NEGRO VICTORY 122 (1950).

13. Draft Declaration by the United Nations on National Independence.

14. Y. EL-AYOUTY, THE UNITED NATIONS AND DECOLONIZATION: THE ROLE OF AFRO-ASIA 15 (1971).

they were not yet prepared to accord the right of self-determination to all peoples.

Self-Determination and the Postwar Legal Order

At the U.N. Conference on International Organization, held in San Francisco in May 1945, three of the four sponsoring powers—the United States, the Soviet Union, and China—claimed to be anticolonialist to different degrees. At the time, the granting of independence to Japanese-occupied colonies of European powers before the Japanese had surrendered, the reactivation of the Pan-Africanist movement, and rising nationalism in Africa and elsewhere were all contributing to the anticolonialist spirit in a world determined not to allow the difficulties that beset the League to occur again. This spirit was reflected in the U.N. Charter, which stressed the principles of self-determination and equal rights.

The preamble to the charter placed "faith in fundamental human rights, in the dignity and worth of the human person, in the equal rights of men and women and of nations, large and small."[15] Article 1 stipulated that the purposes of the document included developing amicable relations among nations, based upon "equal rights and self-determination of peoples," and achieving international cooperation in advancing and fostering respect for "human rights . . . and fundamental freedoms for all without distinction as to race, sex, language, or religion."[16] Article 55 called for international economic and social cooperation based upon "the principle of equal rights and self-determination of peoples" in a world characterized by "peaceful and friendly relations among nations."[17] Article 56 required member nations to take "joint and separate action in cooperation with the Organisation for the achievement of the purposes set forth in Article 55."[18] These provisions applied to all peoples—dependent or independent.

The charter also divided dependent territories into non-self-governing territories, those ruled by the victors of the war, and trust territories, those formerly ruled by the defeated. Chapter XI dealt with non-self-governing territories, "whose peoples have not yet attained a full measure of self-government," insisting that colonial powers accept "the principle that the interests of the inhabitants are paramount."[19] The colonial powers were to

15. 6 U.N. CIO docs. (1945), Charter of the United Nations Preamble [hereinafter cited as U.N. Charter].
16. *Id.* at art. 1.
17. *Id.* at art. 55.
18. *Id.* at art. 56.
19. *Id.* at ch. XI.

accept as a sacred trust the obligation to advance "the well-being" of the inhabitants and to submit regular reports to the U.N. secretary-general, describing in detail "economic, social, and educational conditions in the territories."[20] Such reports were then reviewed by the Special Committee on Colonialism, known also as the Committee of Twenty-four.

Chapters XII and XIII of the charter concerned trust territories. Trusteeship theoretically applied to territories that had been mandated under the League, territories removed from the jurisdiction of nations defeated in World War II, and colonies that a ruling nation voluntarily placed under the system. In practice, however, trusteeship applied only to territories in the first two categories. With the exception of South West Africa, which South Africa refused to submit to trusteeship, the administering powers of all mandated territories that had not received independence placed their mandates under trusteeship. According to Article 76 of the charter, the goals of trusteeship were "the progressive development towards self-government or independence" and promotion of respect for fundamental human rights without discrimination as to race, sex, language, or religion.[21]

Under the trusteeship system, administering states performed their obligations and advanced the goal of self-determination. Accordingly, Libya became independent in 1952. British Togoland followed suit when it became part of Ghana in 1957. The French Cameroons became independent Cameroon in 1960. The following year, Cameroon incorporated all of the British Cameroons except for a small part that joined an independent Nigeria. Also in 1961 Tanganyika gained independence, as did Rwanda and Burundi a year later. A growing nationalist spirit meanwhile led to violent opposition to colonial rule throughout Africa.

As anticolonial sentiment spread across the world and more states of what later became known as the Third World gained independence and joined the United Nations, the ranks of the organization swelled and its composition changed. At its inception, the United Nations had fifty-one members. Of those, twenty were from Latin America, eight from Asia, and three from Africa.[22] By 1970, Third World states, including those that had freed themselves from colonial rule before the founding of the United Nations, were already a majority in the body. In 1987, over 77 percent of the 159 members

20. *Id.*

21. *Id.* at art. 76.

22. Wang, *The Third World and International Law,* in SELECTED ARTICLES FROM CHINESE YEARBOOK OF INTERNATIONAL LAW 6, 12–13 (Chinese Society of International Law ed. 1983) [hereinafter cited as SELECTED ARTICLES].

were newly independent states.[23] These new states argued in favor of speedily granting independence to those areas still under colonial rule.

The lobby for swift decolonization eventually prevailed. General Assembly Resolution 637A (VII) of December 1953 included among its recommendations that "the States Members of the United Nations shall uphold the principle of self-determination of all peoples and nations."[24] In 1960, the anticolonialist lobby saw the fruition of its efforts in Resolution 1514, the Declaration on the Granting of Independence to Colonial Countries and Peoples, which applied to all dependent territories regardless of origin. It called for an end to colonialism and provided that "all peoples have the right to self-determination." In addition, "any attempt at the total or partial disruption of the national unity and the territorial integrity of a country is incompatible with the purposes and principles of the Charter of the United Nations."[25]

Promulgated at the beginning of the era in which colonial empires were dismantled, the resolution, which has been called the Magna Carta of decolonization, reflects a shift in the way the international community viewed self-determination. In the international law of the League era, self-determination was a principle that, as in the case of nationalities, was applicable preferentially—or, rather, virtually exclusively in Europe. It did not signal the rejection of colonialism in Africa, Asia, and elsewhere. In the U.N. Charter self-determination was mentioned only in Articles 1 (paragraph 2) and 73. By the time of Resolution 1514, self-determination appeared to have been transformed into a universally applicable norm, a right of all peoples.

The resolution provided that the right of self-determination applied to all dependent territories desiring emancipation, including former mandates. It did not, however, legitimate fissiparous or secessionist movements within a state. The resolution treated the right of self-determination as one of the obligations deriving from the U.N. Charter. It was not a recommendation but, rather, an authoritative interpretation of the charter. Under the resolution, the right to self-determination supplemented the notions of nondiscrimination and equality and applied to all dependent territories.

Later, many instruments of the United Nations, including a number of General Assembly resolutions concerning specific territories, referred to the resolution, as did various international instruments. As more African states gained independence and joined the United Nations in the early 1960s, the

---

23. Encyclopaedic Dictionary of International Law 413 (C. Parry, J. Grant, A. Parry & A. Watts eds. 1986).

24. U.N. GAOR Res. 637A (VII) (1953).

25. U.N. GAOR Res. 1514 (1960).

General Assembly passed Resolution 2106 (XX) of 1965, which linked the right of self-determination with the International Convention on the Elimination of Racial Discrimination of that year.[26]

By then, however—indeed, by the time Resolution 1514 was passed—an international debate had arisen over the legal consequences of General Assembly resolutions.[27] By 1966, it was settled that U.N. resolutions were not binding per se. They had the force of law only when they restated a binding rule of international law, when they had been incorporated into state practice, or when they had been so often repeated over time and had been accepted by the majority of the states of the world as binding that they had become a rule of customary international law.[28] Thus, although General Assembly resolutions were typically persuasive rather than binding, the principle of self-determination, because it was frequently cited and was accepted by most states, had become a right of peoples everywhere, a rule of customary international law.

With this issue settled, in 1966 the General Assembly issued the Covenant on Civil and Political Rights and the Covenant on Economic and Social Rights.[29] Both acknowledged that "all people have a right to self-determination" and called upon those states that were party to the covenants to "promote the realisation of that right."[30] By then, in spite of the protestations of a small number of legal scholars—most of them British—who refused to accept the right of self-determination, the international community acknowledged that right as furnishing the juridical basis for the recognition of a people as a legal entity with rights.[31] The colonial idea that peoples and territories

26. The Convention on the Elimination of All Forms of Racial Discrimination of Dec. 21, 1965 (660 U.N.T.S. 195) based on the General Assembly Declaration of the same name (Res. 1904 of Nov. 20, 1963) obliges state parties "to pursue by all appropriate means and without delay a policy of eliminating racial discrimination in all its forms" (art. 21). That convention, with over 120 ratifications, is the most ratified of all U.N. conventions.

27. *See generally* O. ASAMOAH, THE LEGAL SIGNIFICANCE OF THE DECLARATIONS OF THE UNITED NATIONS (1966); Sloan, *The Binding Force of a "Recommendation" of the General Assembly of the United Nations*, 25 BRIT. Y.B. INT'L L. 1 (1948); Vallat, *The Competence of the United Nations General Assembly*, 97 RECUEIL DES COURS 211 (1959); J. CASTANEDA, LEGAL EFFECTS OF UNITED NATIONS RESOLUTIONS (1969); Cheng, *United Nations Resolutions on Outer Space: "Instant" International Customary Law?*, 5 INDIAN J. INT'L L. 23 (1965); *see also* South West Africa Cases (Second Phase), (1966) I.C.J. Reports 171–72 (separate opinion by Van Wyk), 291–93 (Tanaka dissenting), 432–41 (Jessup dissenting), 455–57, 464–70 (Padilla Nervo dissenting); I. BROWNLIE, PRINCIPLES OF PUBLIC INTERNATIONAL LAW 14–15 (1973); Lachs, *The Law in and of the United Nations: Some Reflections on the Principle of Self-Determination*, 1 INDIAN J. INT'L L. 429, 432 (1961).

28. *See generally* J. CASTANEDA, *supra* note 27, at 175–77.

29. 6 INT'L L.M. 368.

30. *Id.* at art. 1.

31. *See, e.g.*, D. HARRIS, CASES AND MATERIALS ON INTERNATIONAL LAW 95 (1983); M. POMERANCE, SELF-DETERMINATION IN LAW AND PRACTICE (1982).

were "mere chattels to be acquired and disposed of by and for the benefit of the proprietary State"[32] was replaced by the notion that such territories were "the heritage of those who dwell within them."[33] In a statement on southern Africa in 1969, for example, the International Commission of Jurists acknowledged the right to self-determination and decried colonialism as illegal.[34]

The General Assembly issued two declarations in 1970 that encapsulated its position on the advancement of self-determination and decolonization. The Programme of Action for the full implementation of the Declaration on the Granting of Independence to Colonial Countries and Peoples [Resolution 2621 (XXV)] provided that "the further continuation of colonialism in all its forms and manifestations [is] a crime which constitutes a violation of the Charter of the United Nations, the Declaration on the Granting of Independence to Colonial Countries and Peoples and the principles of international law."[35] It also stressed the right of colonized peoples to oppose colonialism by "all necessary means."[36] The Programme of Action proposed implementing measures for the achievement of independence, rendering of material and moral assistance to freedom fighters, intensifying the crusade against financial interests that aided and abetted colonialism, and publicizing through all media the evils of colonialism and U.N. activities in support of decolonization. The Programme of Action also acknowledged and strengthened the role of the Special Committee on Colonialism in achieving independence for colonized peoples.

The General Assembly followed the Programme of Action with the Declaration on Principles of International Law Concerning Friendly Relations and Cooperation Among States in accordance with the Charter of the United Nations [Resolution 2628 (XXV)]. Stressing self-determination, the declaration obligated states to promote the goals it expressed and to assist the United Nations in attaining them.[37] The declaration recognized the right of colonized peoples to obtain assistance to allow them to become free. It confirmed that dependent territories had a separate status in international law from their colonizers and were not part of the colonized state. Although the colonizers restricted the exercise of sovereignty by the colonized, they could not destroy that right. Rather, the colonizers only illegally and forcibly suspended the

32. Lauterpacht, *Some Concepts of Human Rights,* 11 HOWARD L.J. 264, 271 (1965).
33. *Id.*
34. 2 REV. INT'L COMM. JURISTS 55 (1969).
35. U.N. GAOR Res. 2621 (XXV) (1970).
36. *Id.*
37. U.N. GAOR Res. 2628 (XXV) (1970).

rights of the colonized until the colonized regained them when they achieved self-determination. Moreover, the colonized exercised the right of self-determination in ways other than by achieving independence, that is, by free association, integration, or the free choice of a political status.

According to international law, because the covenants of 1966 were General Assembly resolutions, they bound only those states that were parties to them, whereas the declaration, prepared over seven years by a broad-based U.N. Special Committee and adopted unanimously, elevated the principles it contained to the status of rules of customary international law binding all states. The declaration referred, however, to the principle of self-determination enshrined in the charter rather than to the right of self-determination. Four years later, the Consensus Resolution on the Definition of Aggression [Resolution 3314 (XXIX)], clarified the United Nations' position on self-determination, stressing the "right to self-determination, freedom and independence" of those under "colonial and racist regimes or other forms of alien domination."[38] The right to self-determination thus became entrenched as a rule of customary international law.

Self-Determination as *Jus Cogens*

Later legal developments took the right of self-determination even further, incorporating it into the *jus cogens*—basic, fundamental, imperative, or overriding rules of international law, peremptory norms "which cannot be set aside by treaty or acquiescence but only by the formation of a subsequent norm of contrary effect."[39] According to the jurist E. Suy, jus cogens is "the body of those general rules of law whose non-observance may affect the very essence of the legal system to which they belong to such an extent that the subject of law may not, under pain of absolute nullity, depart from them in virtue of particular agreements."[40]

In 1963, the International Law Commission's commentary on Article 37 of the draft articles on the law of treaties suggested that self-determination was an example of jus cogens.[41] The commission did not include any examples of jus cogens in the article itself, however, so the only reference to self-determination appeared in the report.[42] Later, the Sixth Committee of the General

38. U.N. GAOR Res. 2314 (XXIX) (1974).

39. I. BROWNLIE, *supra* note 27, at 499–500.

40. E. Suy, *quoted* in Li, *Jus Cogens and International Law,* in SELECTED ARTICLES, *supra* note 22, at 44.

41. *Report of the International Law Commission on the Work of Its Fifteenth Session,* 2 Y.B. INT'L L. COMM. 198–99 (1963) [hereinafter cited as 1963 Report].

42. *Id.*

Assembly discussed the commission's draft articles. Speakers from many states agreed that self-determination was in the nature of jus cogens.[43] The only country to oppose this idea was Portugal, which at the time still had colonies in Africa, including Angola and Mozambique.[44]

At the first session of the U.N. Conference on the Law of Treaties, representatives of numerous governments made statements supporting the right of self-determination as part of the jus cogens.[45] Although specific examples did not appear in the text that later became Article 53 of the Vienna Convention on the Law of Treaties, this did not imply that the cases referred to when the articles were drafted were not in the nature of jus cogens. Rather, the omission of examples derived from a wish that the content of jus cogens remain open-ended so that it could "be worked out in State practice and in the jurisprudence of international tribunals."[46] As jurist Héctor Gros Espiell has pointed out, "This is the right approach, since, without prejudice to the possible existence of other means of determining the content of *jus cogens*, it implies that this content is not static or fixed but takes shape and evolves according to the criteria and principles accepted by the international community as a whole at any particular time in its historical development."[47]

The Vienna Convention on the Law of Treaties of 1969 recognizes the notion that the content of jus cogens may alter over time because of changes in the concepts composing the jus cogens that the international community acknowledges.[48] Article 53 of the convention provides that a norm of jus cogens "can be modified only by a subsequent norm of general international law having the same character."[49] Article 64 acknowledges that "if a new peremptory norm of general international law emerges, any existing

43. Official Records of the General Assembly, Twenty-first Session, Sixth Committee, 905th meeting.

44. Note verbale, Aug. 27, 1964. *See* Gonzales, *Los Gobiernos y el jus cogens: Las Normas imperativas de derecho internacional en La Sexta Comisión,* in Estudios de derecho internacional publico y privado, homenaje al Profesor Luis Sela Sempil 133 (1970).

45. F. de la Guardia & M. Delpech, El Derecho de los tratados y la Convencion de Viena 426 (1970); Nisot, *Le Jus Cogens et la Convention de Vienne sur les Traités,* 3 Revue generale de droit international public (1972).

46. 1963 Report, *supra* note 41, at 198; *see generally* J. Pastor Ridruego, La Determinacion del contenido del jus cogens 10 (1972).

47. The Right to Self-Determination: Implementation of United Nations Resolutions. H. Gros Espiell, Special Rapporteur. U.N. Doc. E/CN.4/Sub.2/405/Rev.1 at 11 (1980) [hereinafter cited as Right to Self-Determination]; H. Gros Espiell, Derecho internacional del desarrollo 26 (1975).

48. Vienna Convention on the Law of Treaties, T.S. No. 58 (1980); Cd. 7964, U.N. Doc. A/Conf. 39/27 (1969). On the convention, see I. Sinclair, The Vienna Convention on the Law of Treaties (1973).

49. Vienna Convention on the Law of Treaties, *supra* note 48, at art. 53.

. . . [law] which is in conflict with that norm becomes void and terminates."[50]

The virtual end of traditional colonialism and the change in the nature of the international community that accompanied it are in themselves the best evidence for the recognition of the right of self-determination as part of the jus cogens. The twenty-fifth session of the General Assembly touched on this issue when drafting the Declaration on Principles of International Law Concerning Friendly Relations and Cooperation Among States in Accordance with the Charter of the United Nations [Resolution 2625 (XXV)].[51] The Iraqi representative argued that the fundamental principles of international law expressed in the declaration, including that of self-determination, could be viewed as true rules of jus cogens.[52] The representative from the Netherlands opposed this suggestion, maintaining that the declaration was heterogeneous and therefore did not constitute jus cogens.[53] The U.S. representative took a similar view.[54]

As Gros Espiell has pointed out, even if one acknowledges that the declaration, which expresses desiderata for the future content of international law, was heterogeneous and therefore not jus cogens in each of its tenets, the fundamental principles of the U.N. Charter found in it, including that of self-determination, are in the nature of jus cogens.[55] These fundamental principles of the charter are termed basic in the declaration,[56] as well as in the Declaration on the Occasion of the Twenty-fifth Anniversary of the United Nations (paragraph 3)[57] and the Declaration on the Strengthening of International Security (paragraphs 2 to 6).[58] The General Assembly adopted all three

---

50. *Id.* at art. 64.

51. U.N. GAOR Res. 2625 (XXV). On this question, see generally Rosenstock, *The Declaration of Principles of International Law Concerning Friendly Relations: A Survey*, 65 AM. J. INT'L L. 713 (1971); Sahovic, *Codification des principes de droit international des relations amicales et de la coopération entre les Etats*, 137 RECUEIL DES COURS 302 (1972); Arangio Ruiz, *The Normative Role of the General Assembly of the United Nations and the Declaration of Principles of Friendly Relations*, 137 RECUEIL DES COURS 441 (1972); Johnson, *Towards Self-Determination: A Reappraisal as Reflected in the Declaration on Friendly Relations*, 3 GA. J. INT'L & COMP. L. 146 (1973).

52. Official Records of the General Assembly, Twenty-fifth Session, Sixth Committee, Summary Records of the Meetings, 1180th meeting.

53. *Id.* at 1183d meeting.

54. Special Committee (1970) on Principles of International Law Concerning Friendly Relations and Cooperation Among States, Summary Records of 110th to 114th Meetings, 114th meeting (U.N. Doc. A/AC.125/SR.110–14).

55. Right to Self-Determination, *supra* note 47, at 12.

56. U.N. GAOR Res. 2625 (XV).

57. U.N. GAOR Res. 2627 (XXV).

58. U.N. GAOR Res. 2734 (XXV).

documents without opposition on the twenty-fifth anniversary of the United Nations. This suggests not that the additional formulations, the sequences, and the corollaries that appear in a heterogeneous fashion under each of these in the Declaration on Friendly Relations are jus cogens but that the "basic principles," including self-determination, are in contemporary international law jus cogens.[59]

It is significant, too, that these resolutions were passed in 1970, before the collapse of Portuguese rule in Africa and of white minority rule in Zimbabwe. With only a few exceptions, such as South Africa, colonialism has now ended.[60] Since 1970, the continued existence of such colonialism has been universally condemned in varying degrees by the international community and international bodies, including the ICJ.

In 1976, while the Sub-Commission on Prevention of Discrimination and Protection of Minorities was awaiting the completion of two studies on self-determination that it had commissioned,[61] several scholars argued that the right to self-determination was jus cogens.[62] In 1977 and 1978, the representatives of various states that were considering the reports endorsed this view.[63] Numerous speakers at the thirty-fourth session of the U.N. Commission on Human Rights in 1978 took the same position.[64] That same year, the World Conference to Combat Racism and Racial Discrimination suggested in its Programme of Action that "the United Nations Institute for

59. H. Gros Espiell, Right to Self-Determination, *supra* note 47, at 12.

60. As the historian Leonard Thompson has written, "Commentators have described the South African situation as constituting 'domestic' or 'internal' or 'settler' colonialism. The term 'secondary colonialism' is more appropriate because it places the situation in historical perspective. In all European colonies, society was racially stratified. Some of the preconditions for secondary colonialism existed in those colonies which contained sizeable communities of European origin established as settlers in the midst of more numerous indigenous populations. The transition from primary to secondary colonialism occurred when, voluntarily or involuntarily, the metropolitan government passed into the hands of the local white community." Thompson, *The Parting of the Ways in South Africa,* in THE TRANSFER OF POWER IN AFRICA: DECOLONIZATION, 1940–1960, 417, 419 (P. Gifford & W. Louis eds. 1982).

61. The Right to Self-Determination, *supra* note 47; The Right to Self-Determination: Historical and Current Development on the Basis of United Nations Instruments. A. Critescu, Special Rapporteur. U.N. Doc. E/CN.4/Sub.2/404/Rev.1 (1980).

62. Report of the United Nations Sub-Commission on Prevention of Discrimination and Protection of Minorities, Twenty-ninth Session (1976), Doc. E/CN.4.

63. Report of the United Nations Sub-Commission on Prevention of Discrimination and Protection of Minorities, Thirtieth Session (1977), U.N. Doc. E/CN.4/1261; Report of the United Nations Sub-Commission on Prevention of Discrimination and Protection of Minorities, Thirty-first Session (1978), U.N. Doc. E/CN.4/1296.

64. Report of the Commission on Human Rights on Its Thirty-third Session, Official Records of the Economic and Social Council, Sixty-third Session, 1978, Supp. No. 4, U.N. Doc. E/1978/34.

Training and Research should organize an international colloquium on the prohibition of apartheid, racism and racial discrimination and the achievement of self-determination in international law, paying special attention to the principles of non-discrimination and self-determination as imperative norms of international law."[65]

Since 1970, the vast majority of jurists has come to accept self-determination as jus cogens.[66] They have done so based upon one of two ideas. First, the fundamental, imperative nature of jus cogens is a characteristic of the right of self-determination.[67] Second, the right of self-determination, because it is a prerequisite for the exercise and effective realization of human rights, is jus cogens.[68] Taken together, these post-1970 developments further strengthen the argument that self-determination is jus cogens.

Violations of the Jus Cogens

Since jus cogens is universally applicable, states that violate it have committed an international crime. In 1976, the International Law Commission's draft articles on state responsibility described an international crime as "a serious breach of an international obligation of essential importance for safeguarding

65. Report of the World Conference to Combat Racism and Racial Discrimination, U.N. Doc. E 79.XIV.2.

66. Among the few dissenters are G. FITZMAURICE, THE FUTURE OF PUBLIC INTERNATIONAL LAW AND OF THE INTERNATIONAL LEGAL SYSTEM IN THE CIRCUMSTANCES OF TODAY, SPECIAL REPORT (Institute of International Law 1973); Whiteman, *Jus Cogens in International Law, with a projected list,* 7 GA. J. INT'L & COMP. L. 609 (1977); M. POMERANCE, SELF-DETERMINATION IN LAW AND PRACTICE (1982).

67. *See, e.g.,* G. ABI-SAAB, THE CONCEPT OF JUS COGENS IN INTERNATIONAL LAW 13 (Geneva: Carnegie Endowment for International Peace 1967); Alexidze, *The Problem of Jus Cogens in Contemporary International Law,* SOVIET Y.B. INT'L L. 146 (1969); Kiss, *Le Droit international peut-il être considéré comme volontariste?,* 33–36 TEMIS-SYMBOLAE GARCIA ARIAS 75, 83 (1973–74); Caicedo Perdoma, *La Teoria del jus cogens en derecho internacional a la luz de la Convención de Viena sobre el derecho de los tratados,* 206–07 REVISTA DE LA ACADEMIA COLOMBIANA DE JURISPRUDENCIA 272 (1975); A. GOMEZ ROBLEDO, EL DERECHO DE AUTODETERMINACIÓN DE LOS PUEBLOS Y SU CAMPO DE APLICACIÓN (1976); Ago, *The Internationally Wrongful Act of the State Source of International Responsibility,* II:1 Y.B. INT'L L. COMM. 31–32, 49–54 (1976), U.N. Doc. A/CN.4/921; A. MORENO LOPEZ, IGUALDAD DE DERECHOS Y LIBRE DETERMINACIÓN DE LOS PUEBLOS: PRINCIPIO EJE DEL DERECHO INTERNACIONAL CONTEMPORÁNEO (1977); R. GALINDO POHL, JUS COGENS (Washington, D.C.: Organization of American States 1977); INSTITUTO HISPANO-LUSO-AMERICANO DE DERECHO INTERNACIONAL, PROCEEDINGS OF THE ELEVENTH CONGRESS, MADRID (1977).

68. *See, e.g.,* Ago, *Droit de traités à la lumière de la Convention de Vienne: Introduction,* 134 RECUEIL DES COURS at 321, note 35; 324, note 37 and sources cited therein (1971); Nahlik, *Jus Cogens and the Codified Law of Treaties,* in 33–36 TEMIS-SYMBOLAE GARCIA ARIAS 85, 101 (1973–74); T. ELIAS, THE MODERN LAW OF TREATIES 185 (1974); U. UMOZURIKE, *supra* note 2, at 85.

the right of self-determination of peoples, such as that prohibiting the establishment or maintenance by force of colonial domination."[69] Later, the commission adopted the following definition of an international crime: "an international wrongful act which results from the breach by a State of an international obligation so essential for the protection of fundamental interests of the international community that its breach is recognised as a crime by that community as a whole."[70] In the commission's view, violation of the right to self-determination fit this definition.[71]

Once a state has committed such an international crime, the other members of the international community have certain duties. The International Law Commission has indicated that "the breach by a State of an obligation deriving from the recognition by International Law of the rights of peoples to self-determination, especially a violation of the duty to refrain from establishing or maintaining colonial domination by force, is an international crime, precisely characterized as such, which gives rise to an international responsibility."[72] In the *Barcelona Traction* case of 1970, the ICJ affirmed that states are obligated to the international community and that because of the seriousness of the rights involved "all States can be held to have a legal interest in their protection; they are obligations *erga omnes.*"[73]

International responsibility takes various forms. According to the 1970 Declaration on Principles of International Law Concerning Friendly Relations and Co-operation Among States, all states "shall promote the realization of the right of self-determination, and shall respect that right, in conformity with the provisions of the Charter of the United Nations."[74] Also, "every State has the duty to refrain from any forcible action which deprives peoples . . . of their right to self-determination and freedom and independence."[75] These

69. Report of the International Law Commission on the Work of its Twenty-eighth Session, 2:2 Y.B. INT'L L. COMMISSION 1976, 75 (1977), U.N. Doc. A/31/10. *Cf.* draft version in *id.* 2:1 at 54.

70. *Id.* 2:2 at 75.

71. *Id.* 2:1 at 54.

72. *Id.*

73. Barcelona Traction case (Second Phase), (1970) I.C.J. Reports 32; *see also* separate opinion of Judge Ammoun at 304 (discussing self-determination); *In re Koch,* 30 INT'L L. REV. 496, 503. *Cf.* the position of Western jurist Gerald Fitzmaurice, articulated in 1957, that "there are cases in which over-riding rules of *jus cogens* produce a situation of irreducible obligation and demand that illegal actions be ignored or not allowed to affect the obligations of other States." Fitzmaurice, *The General Principles of International Law Considered from the Standpoint of the Rule of Law,* 2 RECUEIL DES COURS 5, 122 (1957).

74. U.N. GAOR Res. 2625 (XXV). Many other international instruments, including the two International Covenants on Human Rights, deal in a similar fashion with the question of the duties of states resulting from exercises of the right to self-determination.

75. U.N. GAOR Res. 2625 (XXV).

ideas also appear in the U.N. Definition of Aggression.[76] This means that all states have a positive legal duty to further the exercise of the right of self-determination of peoples and a negative duty to refrain from interfering with that right.[77] General Assembly resolutions 2131 (XX) and 2160 (XXI) condemn attempts to interfere with the exercise of the right as impermissible interventions.[78]

In addition, states have a duty not to recognize an illegal international situation. This rule of international law was first articulated in the *South West Africa (Voting Procedure)* case of 1955. In that case, the ICJ recognized that some acts or behavior would render a state—in that instance, South Africa—open "to consequences legitimately following as a legal sanction."[79] Similarly, in its *Namibia (Advisory) Opinion* of 1971, the ICJ stressed international nonrecognition of situations based upon illegalities.[80] The court maintained that when organs of the United Nations acting pursuant to their legally constituted authority determine that a situation is illegal, the nations to which the

76. U.N. GAOR Res. 3315 (XXIX) at annexure, art. 7.

77. A number of jurists believe that this positive duty includes the duty to display solidarity (including military aid) with colonial peoples whose use of armed struggle to achieve self-determination is legitimate under international law. The argument is that the conflict engendered by the struggle of peoples against colonial domination is not in the nature of civil war but of international armed conflict. Therefore, third states are not bound to refrain from intervening. Instead, they must become involved because of the positive obligation to aid peoples fighting colonial domination. The right of peoples to fight for their self-determination is recognized in many United Nations instruments, including General Assembly Resolutions 2625 (XXV) of Oct. 24, 1970; 2787 (XXVI) of Dec. 6, 1971; 3103 (XXVIII) of Dec. 12, 1973; 3314 (XXIX) of Dec. 14, 1974; 3382 (XXX) of Dec. 8, 1975; and 31/34 of Nov. 30, 1976. *See also* Security Council Resolutions 269 (1969), 277 (1970), 282 (1970). *See generally* Ginsburgs, *"Wars of Liberation" and the Modern Law of Nations—The Soviet Thesis,* in THE SOVIET IMPACT ON INTERNATIONAL LAW (H. Baade ed. 1965); P. PIERSON MATHY, LA LEGALITE DES GUERRES DE LIBERATION NATIONALE (1970); Iglesias Buigues, *La Prohibición general del recurso a la fuerza y las resoluciones descolonizadoras de la Asamblea General de las Naciones Unidas,* 25 REVISTA ESPANOLA DE DERECHO INTERNACIONAL 173 (1971); Zourek, *Enfin une définition de l'aggression,* 20 ANNUAIRE FRANÇAIS DE DROIT INTERNATIONAL 24 (1974); Tomasi, *La Conception soviétique des guerres de libération nationale,* in CURRENT PROBLEMS OF INTERNATIONAL LAW (A. Cassesse ed. 1975); Di Blase, *La légitimité du recours à la force dans les résolutions des Nations Unies et dans la Déclaration d'Alger,* in POUR UN DROIT DES PEUPLES (Collection Tiers monde en bref, Paris 1978).

78. U.N. GAOR Res. 2131 (XX); U.N. GAOR Res. 2160 (XXI). According to these resolutions, the principle of nonintervention protects not only sovereign states but also peoples under colonial or alien domination. *See* Bastid, *Remarques sur l'interdiction de l'intervention,* in MELANGES OFFERTS A JURAJ ANDRASSY 3 (The Hague 1968).

79. South West Africa (Voting Rights) Case, (1955) I.C.J. Reports (opinion of Lauterpacht).

80. Namibia (Advisory) Opinion, (1971) I.C.J. Reports 16, 54. In political terms, the practical effects of nonrecognition are similar to nonmilitary sanctions. *See* (1971) I.C.J. Reports at 134–37 (separate opinion of Pétren); *see also* I. BROWNLIE, *supra* note 27, at 503.

United Nations addresses a resolution have a duty to act to end that situation. Furthermore, the court noted that all cases in which a state violates peremptory norms of international law, such as self-determination and nondiscrimination, are internationally illegitimate and therefore void.[81]

Assertions of title to territory are among the acts that violation of the jus cogens renders illegitimate. Even a Security Council resolution that attempted to divide a territory in breach of the right of self-determination would be theoretically void, as would any international agreements based upon it. According to the court, "the foreign occupation of a territory—an act . . . affecting the right to self-determination of the people whose territory has been occupied—constitutes an absolute violation of the right to self-determination."[82]

In the case of Walvis Bay, the application of the jus cogens has important implications.

The Jus Cogens, South Africa, and Walvis Bay

The international community has long recognized that the South African presence in Namibia violated international law and interfered with the right of self-determination of the Namibian people. It remains to be determined whether Walvis Bay is part of Namibia. If so, the South African government is interfering with the right of self-determination of the Namibian people in the Walvis Bay territory. As in the case of the termination of the South West Africa mandate, the competent organs of the United Nations—the General Assembly, which is charged with safeguarding self-determination, and the Security Council—have declared that Walvis Bay is an integral part of Namibia. Even though Security Council Resolution 432 called for the "early reintegration of Walvis Bay into Namibia," the choice of the word *reintegration* recognized that Walvis Bay is an integral part of Namibia, as did the resolution's call for the "reintegration of Walvis Bay within its territory [Namibia]."[83] Indeed, the operation of various concepts of modern international law indicates that Walvis Bay is legally part of Namibia.

Here, however, let it be assumed that Walvis Bay is part of Namibia and that therefore the South African government is interfering with the right of self-determination of the Namibian people in Walvis Bay. Thus, South Africa's denial of their right of self-determination amounts to a breach of the jus cogens, with the result that South Africa has committed an international crime

81. *Id.* at 54–56.
82. *Id.*
83. U.N. SCOR Res. 432 (1976).

and its claims of title to Walvis Bay are void. Other states have a duty not to recognize such claims.

In sum, under modern international law, the right of self-determination of peoples is part of the jus cogens. The international order that once denied sovereignty to indigenous peoples has so changed that those who were once colonized now constitute the majority of the world's states. The colonizers' actions, like South Africa's claim to Walvis Bay, now violate international law.

CHAPTER NINE

Walvis Bay as Part of Namibia

The international community has long acknowledged that South Africa's presence in Namibia contravened international law. Not least, it violated the jus cogens by interfering with the Namibian people's right of self-determination. Accordingly, because it did so, states were under a duty not to recognize South African actions regarding Namibia. The operation of such concepts of modern international law as legal ties, intertemporal law, and estoppel makes it clear that Walvis Bay is part of Namibia. Therefore, states have a similar duty not to recognize South African claims of sovereignty over Walvis Bay.

Legal Ties

The integration of Walvis Bay into Namibia before the British annexation makes it part of Namibia for purposes of self-determination and decolonization. The operation of the modern doctrine of legal ties, moreover, gives credence to the international legal acknowledgment that the two entities are one.

Legal ties is a term used to describe patterns of political and social organization existing in a territory prior to its colonization. Once the U.N. General Assembly was granted power over dependent territories (non-self-governing and trust) and the responsibility of fostering their independence, that is, their exercise of self-determination, after World War II, it had to decide which areas or combinations of peoples were entitled to receive recognition as national units.[1] The General Assembly had various choices in creating boundaries. It frequently used boundaries created by the colonial powers. In most cases, these were arbitrary and did not reflect the geographical distribution of indigenous peoples, with the unhappy result that there was much tension among groups placed in the same polity. In the case of Nigeria, for example, the United Nations' use of colonial borders caused violent confrontation after independence.[2]

Such unsatisfactory results led the General Assembly, in creating boundaries, to examine the political and social organization that had existed before colonialism was imposed in dependent territories. In 1960, General Assembly Resolution 1514, the Declaration on the Granting of Independence to Colonial Countries and Peoples, authorized an examination into the precolonial political and social organization of dependent territories,[3] which became known as legal ties.

In its *Western Sahara (Advisory Opinion)* of 1975, the ICJ clarified the nature of the legal ties necessary to establish the sovereign rights of an indigenous people.[4] That case involved the phosphate-rich Western Sahara on the northwest coast of Africa, over which Spain had proclaimed a protectorate in 1884. From that time, Spain had administered Western Sahara as a Spanish "province," but since 1958 Morocco and thereafter newly independent Mauritania had asserted claims to the area. From 1966 on, Spain had indicated that it was prepared to decolonize the territory by putting its future status to a referendum. Spain argued against Morocco and Mauritania, both of which claimed historic rights to the area, for the independence of the territory,

1. U.N. Charter, arts. 73, 76, 85. The Assembly may perform this duty in a number of ways, including by holding free elections in such territories. *See* Western Sahara (Advisory Opinion), (1975) I.C.J. Reports 12, 29–37 (discussing ways of implementing self-determination) [hereinafter cited as Western Sahara].

2. *See, e.g.,* H. GRIMAL, DECOLONIZATION OF THE BRITISH, FRENCH, DUTCH AND BELGIAN EMPIRES, 1919–1963, 295–305 (1978) (Ghana and Nigeria became independent with colonial boundaries intact).

3. G.A. Res. 1514, 15 U.N. GAOR Supp. (No. 16) 66, U.N. Doc. A/4684 (1960); *see* Western Sahara, *supra* note 1, at 41–68 (legal ties used as term to describe historical organization). On the pre-colonial organization of the people of Walvis Bay, see *supra* chapter 2 at 1–2.

4. Western Sahara, *supra* note 1. For further discussions of this case, see Flory, *L'Avis de la Cour Internationale de Justice sur le Sahara Occidental,* 21 ANNUAIRE FRANÇAIS DE DROIT INTERNATIONAL 253 (1975); Franck, *The Stealing of the Sahara,* 70 AM. J. INT'L L. 694 (1976); Prévost, *Observations sur l'avis consultatif de la Cour Internationale de Justice relatif au Sahara Occidental ("terra nullius" et autodétermination),* 103 JOURNAL DU DROIT INTERNATIONAL 813 (1976); Riedel, *Confrontation in Western Sahara in the Light of the Advisory Opinion of the International Court of Justice of 16 October 1975,* GERMAN Y.B. INT'L L. 405 (1976).

contending that when Spain proclaimed its protectorate, Western Sahara had an identity separate from that of Morocco and Mauritania. Consequently, it had a right to modern independence. Morocco insistently repeated its claim, however, eventually bringing about the adoption of General Assembly Resolution 3293 (XXIX), which requested an advisory opinion from the ICJ.

The meaning of legal ties was a key issue in the case. As a notion that had not previously been determined with precision in international law, legal ties bore on the question of whether such ties were capable of constituting evidence of an effective display of sovereignty over the claimed territory. By fifteen votes to one, the ICJ rejected the Moroccan and Mauritanian claims, implicitly accepting Spain's argument. In analyzing this decolonization situation, the court recognized the sovereign rights of a people to the territory in which they live if at a "critical date" they had a sufficiently developed social and political organization.[5] Such organization did not have to replicate the structure of a Western state, the concept of the nation-state being a Western creation. Thus, the court rejected the view of the positivists that the concept of sovereignty applied only to "civilized" peoples in favor of the naturalist idea that "wherever a country is inhabited by people who are connected by some political organization . . . such a country is not to be regarded as *territorium nullius* and open to acquisition by Occupation."[6] The court found that in 1884, when Spain proclaimed its protectorate, Western Sahara was inhabited by people who, although nomadic, were socially and politically organized under chiefs competent to represent them. Such land was not terra nullius.

Legal ties analysis requires determination of the critical date at which political and social organization must be examined.[7] A critical date is determined in two situations. First, there is the colonial situation, in which two nations claim sovereignty over an area with no indigenous inhabitants.[8] In such cases, the court considers the claims at the date on which the second claimant attempted to establish sovereignty. It resolves the issue by deciding if the first claimant has already exerted sovereignty over the area by effectively occupying it. If the court finds that it has, the second claimant is defeated. If there was no prior effective occupation, the land was terra nullius at the critical date and the court acknowledges the second state's claim of sovereignty.

5. Western Sahara, *supra* note 1, at 39.
6. M. LINDLEY, THE ACQUISITION AND GOVERNMENT OF BACKWARD TERRITORY IN INTERNATIONAL LAW 17 (1926); *see supra* chapter 6 at 104–09.
7. Western Sahara, *supra* note 1, at 38.
8. *See, e.g.*, Minquiers and Ecrehos, Judgment, (1953) I.C.J. 47; Legal Status of Eastern Greenland, (1933) P.C.I.J. Series A/B, No. 53, at 22; Island of Palmas (United States v. Netherlands), 2 R. INT'L ARB. AWARDS 829 (1928).

Second, there is the decolonization situation, like that of Namibia, in which the General Assembly wishes to restore sovereignty to the indigenous inhabitants of an area. In such cases, a court decides upon a critical date for another reason. As the *Western Sahara* opinion noted, the court "is not . . . concerned to establish a 'critical date' in the sense given to this term in territorial disputes; for the questions do not ask the Court to adjudicate between conflicting [claims]."[9] Thus, the court establishes a critical date in order to place the controversy in its proper historical context. The court's analysis in such decolonization situations, unlike that in colonial cases, considers the history of the indigenous inhabitants of a dependent territory. Determining the critical date aids the General Assembly in creating cohesive new states by elucidating prior legal ties.[10] Hence, the date that best typifies the precolonial sociopolitical organization of the territory best serves as the critical date for legal ties purposes. In *Western Sahara*, the court suggested that the critical date could be fixed at the beginning of a series of acts that culminated in colonization instead of at the official date of colonization.[11]

As the current controversy over Walvis Bay involves decolonization, the date for legal ties analysis must be ascertained. In this context, the year 1800 can be chosen because it is prior to Jan Jonker Afrikaner's alliance with the head of the senior indigenous Nama-speaking group and before the Orlam movements had destroyed the indigenous Nama sociopolitical organization.[12] This date best exemplifies the precolonial sociopolitical organization of the territory. It may also be said to be at the beginning of a series of continuous acts that culminated in colonization, with the attendant collapse of the preexisting order that opened the way for the eventual British annexation of Walvis Bay.

With the critical date decided, the next step is to examine legal ties as they existed at that time. The legal ties analysis is a two-pronged inquiry. First, were the existing organizations sufficiently developed to possess sovereignty? Second, did the patterns of allegiance within these organizations unify the areas being examined?[13] In *Western Sahara*, the ICJ did not articulate the threshold of adequate legal ties. As the court rejected the narrow positivist view of sovereignty, however, it would accept organization that fell short of that of a classical Western state. Nevertheless, the court would not accept the presence of scattered inhabitants at the critical date as amounting to legal

9. *See* Western Sahara, *supra* note 1, at 38.
10. *See id.* at 37.
11. *See id.* at 38.
12. *See supra* chapter 2 at 23–28.
13. *See* Western Sahara, *supra* note 1, at 47–62.

ties.[14] Within the bounds of these two extremes, a court would have to undertake a case-by-case analysis using the type of evidence specified in *Western Sahara* to evaluate the social organization the indigenous inhabitants had at the critical date.

According to the ICJ in *Western Sahara,* four kinds of evidence apply to an examination of legal ties. These are (1) recognition by a foreign power; (2) a sophisticated, uniform political system; (3) a uniform cultural identity; and (4) geographical contiguity.[15] Analysis of Nama society in 1800 using these criteria reveals the existence of legal ties that confirm the General Assembly's conclusions that Walvis Bay is an integral part of Namibia.

Early explorers in Namibia recognized the existence of Great Namaqualand, including Walvis Bay.[16] This satisfies the first criterion of the legal ties test. Throughout Great Namaqualand, Nama groups had common sociopolitical structures and economic organization.[17] They had a uniform, sophisticated political system based on kinship ties and the acquisition of clients and cattle. Each group had a chief and council of elders. The chief presided over the council of elders. In times of war, he also led the men in battle and conducted peace negotiations. The council, in which the will of the majority prevailed, served as the ultimate authority within the group. Each council member headed a family group related by patrilineal descent. This family group was the main unit of Nama social organization. Thus, the second criterion of the legal ties test is met. The Nama also had a uniform cultural system. Groups shared the same language, myths, and religion.[18] They believed they were all related and expressed this genealogically. The Topnaar of Walvis Bay, for example, saw themselves as offshoots of the senior Nama lineage in the Nama myth of origin. The third criterion is also satisfied. Finally, the area inhabited by the Topnaar, including Walvis Bay, was part of the northwestern corner of Great Namaqualand. The Nama area that later became the Walvis Bay territory was contiguous with the rest of the Nama lands. In addition, the Swakop and Kuiseb rivers, which converged there, served much of Great Namaqualand and for early explorers functioned as routes connecting the Bay with the interior. Walvis Bay thus meets the fourth criterion of legal ties, geographical contiguity. Evidence for this contiguity comes from maps of that time, which placed Walvis Bay in Great Nama-

14. The court's invocation of the terra nullius test is an example of a minimum threshold test. *See supra* note 5 and accompanying text.

15. *See* Western Sahara, *supra* note 1, at 148–64.

16. *See supra* chapter 2 at 22.

17. *Id.*

18. *Id.*

qualand.[19] The court gave much weight in *Western Sahara* to the evidentiary use of such maps.[20] As all four criteria of the legal ties test are thus fulfilled, the Nama people had sovereignty over Namaland, including Walvis Bay.

In *Western Sahara,* the ICJ found that although there were indications that a legal tie of allegiance and authority had existed between the sultan and some of the nomadic peoples of the territory, these were not sufficient to confer Moroccan sovereignty. The Court also determined that Mauritania did not have a separate character from the several emirates that composed it. At the time of colonization by Spain, there had not existed between Western Sahara and Mauritania any tie of sovereignty or allegiance or of simple inclusion in the same entity. Hence, no ties existed that could modify "the application of [General Assembly] resolution 1514 (XV) [Declaration on the Granting of Independence to Colonial Countries and Peoples] in the decolonization of Western Sahara and, in particular, of the principle of self-determination through the free and genuine expression of the will of the peoples of the Territory."[21]

The relation of Walvis Bay to Namibia, however, is not the same as that of Western Sahara to Mauritania. Mauritania was composed of a number of nonhomogeneous and previously independent entities, whereas Western Sahara was never part of Mauritania and was an independent entity at the critical date. Hence, Mauritania had no legal ties that the General Assembly could rely upon to unite Western Sahara and Mauritania.[22] Although Namibia also originated from the joinder of several nonhomogeneous and previously independent entities, such as Great Namaqualand and Damaraland, Walvis Bay, unlike Western Sahara, was not an independent entity at the critical date. Rather, it was part of Great Namaqualand, one of the previously independent entities forming Namibia. Unlike Mauritania, then, SWAPO wishes to incorporate into Namibia a historical part of one of Namibia's constituent entities rather than a previously unrelated entity. Under the doctrine of legal ties, the South African claim to the Bay is defeated and the United Nations should ensure that Walvis Bay becomes part of an independent Namibia.

---

19. *See, e.g.,* J. ALEXANDER, AN EXPEDITION OF DISCOVERY INTO THE INTERIOR OF AFRICA 1 (London 1838) (map reflecting early travelers' beliefs about group names); B. TINDALL, THE JOURNAL OF JOSEPH TINDALL 194 (1959) (map for 1839–55); H. VEDDER, SOUTH WEST AFRICA IN EARLY TIMES 166 (1966) (map of Great Namaqualand ca. 1820); *id.* at 242 (map for 1820–80); J. WHITE, THE LAND GOD MADE IN ANGER 64 (1969) (depicting Topnaar area around Walvis Bay as part of Great Namaqualand in 1880).

20. Western Sahara, *supra* note 1, at 152. On the evidentiary use of maps in international law, see Weissberg, *Maps as Evidence in International Boundary Disputes,* 57 AM. J. INT'L L. 781 (1963).

21. Western Sahara, *supra* note 1, at 68.

22. *Id.* at 59.

Intertemporal Law

The concept of intertemporal law also defeats South Africa's chain of title claim. According to this concept, the original title to territory may lapse or become invalid through the operation of new applicable law, such as the law of decolonization, which arose from the right of self-determination.

Customary international law holds that the law in force at the time when a right arose or a situation occurred, not the law that obtained at the time when the dispute arose, is the law that governs a situation. According to the British jurist Sir Gerald Fitzmaurice, "It can now be regarded as an established principle of international law that in such cases the situation in question must be appraised, and the treaty interpreted, in the light of the rules of international law as they existed at the time, and not as they exist today."[23] Thus, in the case of Walvis Bay the 1884 law on the validity of the annexation applies rather than the modern law of decolonization prevailing in 1977, the year the dispute arose, and South Africa therefore has a valid claim. Judge Huber of the PCIJ articulated this principle in the seminal *Island of Palmas* case of 1928 as follows: "A juridical fact must be appreciated in the light of the law contemporary with it, and not of the law in force at the time when a dispute in regard to it arises or fails to be settled."[24]

The island of Palmas (or Miangas) is a small inhabited island lying between the Philippines and the Indonesian Nanusa Island, which at the time of the dispute was part of the Dutch East Indies. By the Treaty of Paris of December 10, 1898, which ended the Spanish-American War, Spain—having discovered Palmas early in the sixteenth century—ceded it and the Philippines to the United States. When in 1899 the United States communicated the treaty to the Netherlands, the latter did not protest the cession. In 1906, during a visit to Palmas, the U.S. commander in Mindanao found the Netherlands flag flying on the island. After diplomatic correspondence, the United States and the Netherlands submitted the issue of sovereignty to the Permanent Court of International Justice. Huber, then president of the Court, was the sole arbitrator. He found that "the Island of Palmas . . . forms in its entirety a part of Netherlands territory."[25]

---

23. Fitzmaurice, *The Law and Procedure of the International Court of Justice, 1951–54: General Principles, and Sources of Law,* 30 BRIT. Y.B. INT'L L. 1, 5–8 (1953).
24. Island of Palmas Case (United States v. Netherlands) (1928) 2 R. INT'L ARB. AWARDS 829 [hereinafter cited as Island of Palmas]. For further discussions of this decision, see Jessup, *The Palmas Island Arbitration,* 22 AM. J. INT'L L. 735 (1928); F. NIELSEN, THE ISLAND OF PALMAS ARBITRATION (1928); De Visscher, *L'Arbitrage de l'île de Palmas (Miangas),* 56 REVUE DE DROIT INTERNATIONAL ET DE LEGISLATION COMPAREE 735 (1929).
25. Island of Palmas, *supra* note 24, at 829.

Huber first restated the traditional rule by indicating that the effect of Spain's discovery of the island had to be "determined by the rules of international law in force in the first half of the Sixteenth Century."[26] He then went far beyond that to declare that if Spain had a valid claim according to the international law of that period, a court had to apply the intertemporal law: "As regards the question which of different legal systems prevailing at successive periods is to be applied in a particular case [the intertemporal law], *a distinction must be made between the creation of rights and the existence of rights.* The same principle which subjects the act creative of a right to the law in force at the time the right arises, demands that the existence of the right, in other words its continued manifestation, shall follow the conditions required by the evolution of the law."[27] Hence, Huber ruled that because of the application of intertemporal law, even if Spanish discovery of the island was sufficient to create a valid title, under the changed conditions of the nineteenth century, when Spain purported to transfer title to the United States, international law required that a reasonable period of effective occupation follow discovery for title to an area to be valid.

According to Huber, the discovery of Palmas by Spanish explorers early in the sixteenth century—in the first place, the United States based its claim as successor to Spain on Spain's discovery—may have brought the island under Spanish sovereignty. Through the application of the intertemporal law, however, the original Spanish rights were subject to the rules of territorial acquisition in existence at the time of the Treaty of Paris. By then, discovery alone created only an inchoate title that had to be perfected within a reasonable time by effective occupation of the territory. Such occupation would have to offer minimum protection of the rights of other states and their nationals in the area. Thus, discovery did not suffice to establish sovereignty, if it ever had.

If discovery had merely created an inchoate title, Spain had never perfected it by any act of occupation. Even if an inchoate Spanish title still existed in 1898, it could not prevail over "the continuous and peaceful display of authority by another state."[28] Huber found that from 1677, certain territories had been associated with the Dutch East India Company and the Netherlands by agreements acknowledging their sovereignty. At least since 1700 Palmas had been part of these territories. The Netherlands had performed various acts of state authority on Palmas between 1700 and 1898 and thereafter until 1906. The Netherlands Indian Government had considered the islands part of its

26. *Id.*
27. *Id.* at 883 (emphasis added).
28. *Id.*

possessions and had increased demonstrations of sovereignty over them before 1898. Although the acts were sporadic, Huber felt that they were sufficient manifestations of sovereignty relating to the claimed territory. This display of sovereignty had existed long enough to allow another country a reasonable opportunity to determine the state of affairs affecting its real or alleged rights.

The ICJ has upheld Huber's approach on several occasions, including the *Minquiers and Ecrehos* case of 1955.[29] In that instance, both France and Britain claimed sovereignty over the Minquiers and Ecrehos, groups of rocks and islets that lie between the British Channel island of Jersey and the coast of France. The parties based their claims upon original title going back to the eleventh century and subsequent effective displays of sovereignty. By special agreement, in 1950 the parties submitted the question of sovereignty to the ICJ. The court held unanimously that evidence of sovereignty for the period before the nineteenth century was largely inconclusive and ambiguous. Although specific probative value attached to acts that related to the exercise of jurisdiction and local administration and to legislation, "what is of decisive importance . . . is not indirect presumptions deduced from events in the Middle Ages, but the evidence which relates directly to the possession of the Ecrehos and Minquiers groups."[30]

At the beginning of the thirteenth century, the Ecrehos group was considered to be and was treated as an integral part of the fief of the Channel Islands, which were held by the king of England. They continued to be under his dominion, and at the beginning of the fourteenth century he exercised jurisdiction over them. During the nineteenth and twentieth centuries, the British authorities exercised state functions over the group. France did not show any evidence of valid title to it. The Minquiers group was part of the fief of Normont in Jersey at the beginning of the seventeenth century. Again, in the nineteenth and twentieth centuries, Britain exercised state functions over the group, whereas France did not establish any valid title. Thus, the court considered it "sufficient to state in its view that even if the Kings of France did have an original feudal title also in respect of the Channel Islands, such a title must

29. Minquiers and Ecrehos Case, (1953) I.C.J. Reports 47 [hereinafter cited as Minquiers and Ecrehos]. On this decision, see Johnson, *The Minquiers and Ecrehos Case,* 3 INT'L & COMP. L.Q. 189 (1954); Orcasitas Llorente, *Sentencia del Tribunal Internacional de Justicia de la Haya sobre soberanía de las islas "Minquiers" y "Ecréhous" en el Canal de la Mancha,* 7 REVISTA ESPAÑOLA DE DERECHO INTERNACIONAL 531 (1954); A. ROCHE, THE MINQUIERS AND ECREHOS CASE (1959); Wade, *The Minquiers and Ecrehos Case,* 50 TRANSACTIONS OF THE GROTIUS SOCIETY 97 (1955).

30. (1953) I.C.J. Reports 47.

have lapsed as a consequence of the events of the year 1204 and following years."[31]

In *Western Sahara* the court also adhered to the concept of intertemporal law and "thus judged that the original title ceases to be valid if there are new facts to be considered on the basis of new Law."[32] Thus, the doctrine of intertemporal law invalidates an original title by applying new rules that affect the root of title.

The new law of decolonization arising out of the right to self-determination displaces South Africa's claim to Walvis Bay, which is based upon nineteenth-century colonialist rules governing the acquisition of territories. This right to self-determination was, when the dispute arose in 1977, a basic right of customary international law and forms part of the jus cogens. Any right, transaction, or benefit that violates the jus cogens is null and void.[33] Thus, the new law of decolonization and SWAPO's claim based upon it supersede South Africa's claim of sovereignty to Walvis Bay. As jurist Gros Espiell noted:

> On the basis of Resolution 1514 (XV) all titles which established or were held to establish sovereignty or dominion over a colonized territory have lapsed, inasmuch as they conflict with the principle of the right of peoples under colonial and alien domination to self-determination. Under the new international order now applicable, all former colonial titles, deriving from the old obsolete international law, have ceased to exist. Today by virtue of the so-called "intertemporal law" all these situations can be resolved solely through the application of the consequences of the recognition of the right of peoples to self-determination.[34]

Even though the modern law of decolonization and the concept of intertemporal law defeat the South African claim to Walvis Bay, South Africa and its supporters[35] seek to avoid the application of this modern international law to the Walvis Bay dispute by relying upon the fact that the Organisation of African Unity (OAU) has adhered to the doctrine of *uti possidetis,* which allows colonial boundaries to stand after the end of colonialism.

Uti possidetis, the practice that pre-independence "boundaries established by law remain in being" because this is "in accordance with good

31. *Id.* at 56.
32. (1975) I.C.J. Reports 168.
33. *See generally supra* chapter 8.
34. The Right to Self-Determination: Implementation of United Nations Resolutions. H. Gros Espiell, Special Rapporteur. U.N. Doc. E/CN.4/Sub.2/405/Rev.1 at 11 (1980) [hereinafter cited as Right to Self-Determination].
35. *See supra* chapter 5 at 99–100.

policy," was first applied in Latin America.[36] In that situation it was a functional policy, described by the British jurist Hyde as follows: "When the common sovereign power was withdrawn, it became indispensably necessary to agree on a general principle of demarcation, since there was a universal desire to avoid resort to force, and the principle adopted was a colonial *uti possidetis;* that is, the principle involving the preservation of the demarcations under the colonial regimes corresponding to each of the colonial entities that was constituted as a State."[37]

The successor states of Spain agreed to apply first among themselves and later in disputes with Brazil a principle for settling frontier disputes in areas where terra nullius did not exist. The independent states viewed their titles as coextensive with Spain's former title. In the Latin American case, the principle of uti possidetis involved an implied agreement to territorial settlement based on a rule of presumed possession of the area by Spain according to administrative boundaries of 1810 for South America and boundaries of 1821 for Central America.

Unfortunately, the application of uti possidetis in Latin America did not always produce the desired results because of disputes about the concept of possession to be used and because the Spanish administrative boundaries were often unclear or hard to prove.[38] In spite of these difficulties, newly independent states in Asia[39] and Africa recognized the soundness of the basic principle as a means of avoiding disputes.

Since its founding at Addis Ababa on May 25, 1963, the OAU has been committed to recognizing the colonial borders African nations inherited at independence. Colonial frontiers were arbitrary, and colonies were thus ethnically nonhomogeneous. This lack of homogeneity led to a number of disputes among the new nations in the early 1960s—between, among others, Ghana and Togo, Ghana and the Ivory Coast, Ghana and Upper Volta, Morocco and Mauritania, Algeria and Morocco, Kenya and Somalia, Ethiopia and Somalia, Nigeria and Cameroon, Malawi and Zambia, and Malawi and Tanzania.

In an effort to create stability on the continent, Article III of the OAU's

36. I. Brownlie, Principles of Public International Law 138 (1973).

37. C. Hyde, 1 International Law Chiefly as Interpreted and Applied by the United States 499, n. 3 (1945).

38. *See* the Guatemala-Honduras Boundary Arbitration, 2 R. Int'l Arb. Awards 1322 (1933); 46 Ann. Dig. Pub. Int'l L. Cases 7 (1933–34); *see generally* Fisher, *The Arbitration of the Guatemalan-Honduran Boundary Dispute*, 27 Am. J. Int'l L. 403 (1933); Waldcock, *Disputed Sovereignty in the Falkland Islands Dependencies*, 25 Brit. Y.B. Int'l L. 325 (1948).

39. *See* L. Green, International Law Through the Cases 455 (1970); Rann of Kutch Case (India v. Pakistan) (1968) 17 R. Int'l Arb. Awards 1.

charter implicitly accepted and guaranteed the inviolability of the colonial frontiers when it noted that the purpose of the OAU was "to defend [the members'] sovereignty and independence."[40] The OAU made this acceptance explicit at the Cairo Conference of Heads of State in July 1964. The Resolution on Border Disputes Among African States issued at the conference noted that the OAU: "1. Solemnly reaffirms the strict respect for the sovereignty and territorial integrity of each state and for its inalienable right to independent existence. 2. Solemnly declares that all Member States pledge themselves to respect the frontiers existing on their achievement of national independence."[41] Thus, the heads of state, having accepted that the colonial boundaries of African states, "on the day of their independence, constitute a tangible reality," declared that "all Member States pledge themselves to respect the borders on their achievement of national independence."[42]

Subsequently, Article II of the Lusaka Manifesto of 1969 subscribed to this approach and noted that "the present boundaries of the States of southern Africa are the boundaries of what will be free and independent states."[43] The manifesto, a formal statement of policy for the decolonization of southern Africa, was the product of a conference of fourteen heads of state of East and Central Africa. Later, both the OAU and the United Nations adopted the manifesto.

South Africa cannot, however, invoke the OAU's practices regarding uti possidetis in order to support its claim to Walvis Bay for two reasons. First, South Africa cannot elevate the practice of the OAU to a rule of international law binding on all states. Second, South Africa, which is not a member of the OAU, cannot invoke a practice applying to members because, according to international law, *pacta tertiis nec nocent nec prosunt*, a state cannot claim any rights to a treaty to which it is not a party unless it is the clear intention of the parties thereto to confer such rights.[44]

Moreover, even if the principle of uti possidetis binds the OAU's members in international law, the principle "is by no means mandatory and the States concerned are free to adopt other principles as a basis of settlement."[45]

40. Organisation of African Unity, Charter, art. III (1963).

41. Organisation of African Unity, Resolution on Border Disputes Among African States, Cairo, July 21, 1965, O.A.U. Doc. AHG/Res. 16(1).

42. *Id.*

43. 1 Basic Documents of African Regional Organisations 143–44 (L. Sohn ed. 1971).

44. *See, e.g.*, Vienna Convention on the Law of Treaties, Treaty Series No. 58 (1980); Cmd. 7964; U.N. Doc. A/Conf. 39/27 (1969), *reprinted in* 63 Am. J. Int'l L. 878 (1969); 8 Int'l L. M. 679 (1969).

45. I. Brownlie, *supra* note 36, at 138.

Thus, in view of international doctrine and practice, it is improper for a state to assert, as South Africa's claim to Walvis Bay does, that "colonial boundaries must, under international law, continue to be the boundaries after independence."[46]

A secondary colonial state[47] like South Africa cannot rely upon uti possidetis to mask its breach of the jus cogens through its disregard for the right of self-determination. Indeed, the General Assembly's Declaration on the Granting of Independence to Colonial Countries and Peoples, Resolution 1514 (XV) of 1960, anticipated the arguments that a colonial state like South Africa would raise in cases of this type. It stipulated that "any attempt aimed at the total or partial disruption of the national unity and the territorial integrity of a country is incompatible with the purpose and principles of the Charter of the United Nations."[48]

Hence, the operation of the concept of intertemporal law demonstrates that Walvis Bay is part of Namibia for decolonization purposes. Uti possidetis is not applicable in this situation, and South African claims based upon it must fail.

Estoppel

The South African administration of Walvis Bay as part of South West Africa from 1922 to 1977 made Walvis Bay part of the mandated territory through the operation of international estoppel.

Estoppel, also called preclusion in civil law systems and well known in municipal law, is the rule that a party which has acquiesced in a certain situation or has taken a particular position with respect to it cannot later act inconsistently. This rule has become universally recognized in the international legal order of the last half of the twentieth century. As the British jurist Lord McNair has written: "It is reasonable to expect that any legal system should possess a rule designed to prevent a person who makes or concurs in a statement upon which another person in privity with him relies to the extent of changing his position, from later asserting a different state of affairs."[49] The Permanent Court of International Justice first applied the principle in relation to the acquisition of territorial sovereignty in the *Eastern Greenland* case (1933).[50] More recently, the court has invoked it in the *Temple of Preah Vihear*

46. Brooks, *The Legal Status of Walvis Bay,* 2 S. Afr. Y.B. Int'l L. 187, 191 (1976).
47. *See supra* chapter 8, text accompanying note 60.
48. U.N. GAOR Res. 1514 (XV) (1960).
49. A. McNair, The Law of Treaties 485 (1961).
50. Legal Status of Eastern Greenland Case (Denmark v. Norway) (1933) P.C.I.J., Ser. A/B, No. 53.

case (1962),[51] the *North Sea Continental Shelf* case (1969),[52] and the *ICAO Council* case (1972).[53]

In *Eastern Greenland* the government of Norway proclaimed part of Eastern Greenland to be under Norwegian sovereignty. The government of Denmark sought a decision that the proclamation had no legal effect because all of Greenland was already under Danish sovereignty, as Norway itself had recognized by treaty and otherwise. This recognition was most notable in an oral statement by the Norwegian minister of foreign affairs to his Danish counterpart "that the Norwegian Government would not make any difficulties in the settlement of the question" of extending Danish economic and political interests over Greenland.[54]

The court held (12–2) that it was "beyond all dispute that a reply of this nature given by the Minister of Foreign Affairs on behalf of his Government in response to a request by the diplomatic representative of a foreign Power, in regard to a question falling within its province, is binding upon the country to which the Minister belongs."[55] Through the operation of estoppel, Norway was thus "under an obligation to refrain from contesting Danish sovereignty over Greenland as a whole and, *a fortiori* to refrain from occupying a part of Greenland."[56]

The *Temple* case involved title to the area in which the Temple of Preah Vihear is located—a promontory of the Dangrek Mountains, which form the boundary between Thailand and Cambodia. According to a February 13, 1904, treaty between Siam (as Thailand was then known) and France (of which Cambodia was then a protectorate), the frontier was to follow the watershed line. A mixed commission was established to carry out the delimitation. At its last meeting in January 1907, it did not complete its task. Meanwhile, a French survey team had been commissioned by the Siamese government to map the area. The maps, published in Paris in 1908, were widely distributed, and copies were sent to the Siamese government. On the map, the Preah Vihear promontory appeared on the Cambodian side. By 1935 it was discovered that careful adherence to the watershed line would have put the promontory in Siamese territory. The French protested unsuccessfully that

51. Temple of Preah Vihear Case, (1962) I.C.J. Reports 6.
52. North Sea Continental Shelf Case, (1969) I.C.J. Reports 3, 26.
53. I.C.A.O. Council Case, (1972) I.C.J. Reports 46.
54. Legal Status of Eastern Greenland Case (Denmark v. Norway) (1933) P.C.I.J. Ser. A/B, No. 53, at 71. For discussions of this case, see Hyde, *The Case Concerning the Legal Status of Eastern Greenland*, 27 AM. J. INT'L L. 732 (1933); O. SVARLIEN, THE EASTERN GREENLAND CASE IN HISTORICAL PERSPECTIVE (1964).
55. (1933) P.C.I.J. Ser. A/B, No. 53, at 73.
56. *Id.*

Thai custodians were stationed at the temple, and after Cambodia achieved independence the new state tried unsuccessfully to establish authority in the area. Thus, the case came before the ICJ, which delivered its judgment on June 15, 1962.[57]

The court determined (9–3) that the temple was in Cambodian territory and that Thailand had to remove all military and civil personnel stationed on the promontory. The main issue was the significance to be attached to the French map of 1908—that is, whether the parties had accepted the map and the frontier line it established. Thailand denied that it had done so. The court, noted, however, that although the Siamese authorities had had much time in which to object, "They did not do so, either then or for many years, and thereby must be held to have acquiesced."[58]

The court also rejected Thailand's contention that it had made an error, because such a plea "cannot be allowed as an element vitiating consent if the party advancing it contributed by its own conduct to the error, or could have avoided it, or if the circumstances were such as to put that party on notice of possible error."[59] Thailand also sought to justify its failure to object by arguing that at all material times it had been in possession of Preah Vihear through certain "acts on the ground."[60] The court indicated that most of these acts were those of local provincial authorities. It therefore concluded that Thailand by its conduct had accepted the map and was estopped from asserting nonacceptance of it. In addition to the lengthy discussions about estoppel and the significance to be accorded maps in treaty interpretations, the decision is important for the emphasis it placed upon stability as a main goal in settling boundary disputes.

Since estoppel affects issues of title, a further question arose among jurists as to whether estoppel is a procedural, or evidentiary, rule or a substantive one.[61] If it is a procedural, or evidentiary, rule and relevant solely to the question of proof, then it can influence issues of title only in a particular dispute before a competent tribunal. If, however, it is a substantive rule, it

57. Temple of Preah Vihear Case, (1962) I.C.J. Reports 6. For discussions of this case, see Johnson, *Judgment of May 26, 1961, and June 15, 1962, The Case Concerning the Temple of Preah Vihear*, 11 INT'L & COMP. L.Q. 1183 (1962); Kelly, *The Temple Case in Historical Perspective*, 39 BRIT. Y.B. INT'L L. 462 (1963); Pecourt Garcia, *El Principio del "estoppel" y la sentencia del Tribunal Internacional de Justicia en el caso del templo de Preah Vihear*, 16 REVISTA ESPAÑOLA DE DERECHO INTERNACIONAL 153 (1963); Weissberg, *supra* note 20, at 793–803.

58. (1962) I.C.J. Reports 6.

59. *Id.*

60. *Id.*

61. On this debate, see sources cited in Bowett, *Estoppel Before International Tribunals and Its Relation to Acquiescence*, 33 BRIT. Y.B. INT'L L. 176, no. 1, 2 (1957).

presumably affects title in an absolute sense, regardless of whether there is an issue before a court.

Although prior to *Temple* there were many competing views, beginning with the separate opinions in that case substantial authority arose for the proposition that estoppel is a rule of substantive law. As vice president of the ICJ Alfaro wrote:

> In my judgment, the principle is substantive in character. It constitutes a presumption *juris et de jure* in virtue of which a State is held to have abandoned its right if it ever had it, or else that such a state never felt that it had a clear title on which it could base opposition to the right asserted or claimed by another State. In short, the legal effects of the principle are so fundamental that they decide by themselves alone the matter in dispute and its infraction cannot be looked upon as a mere incident of the proceedings. . . . The primary foundation of this principle is the good faith that must prevail in international relations.[62]

According to this view, estoppel can shift title. Estoppel seems especially apposite in such cases as that of Walvis Bay, where the question of title to territory is bound up with the issue of self-determination of peoples and where failure to allow estoppel to shift title would interfere with the right of self-determination and therefore with the jus cogens. Such an interpretation would comport with the court's concern in *Temple* for stability as a major object of boundary dispute settlements.

Although legal scholars have not always agreed about the incidence and effects of estoppel, they are in accord about what three elements must exist before a party can invoke estoppel against an adversary. These are that (1) a state party, aware of a right that could be enforced, must choose not to assert it or must assert it ineffectively; (2) the party must know that its nonassertion or ineffective assertion may be interpreted as an abandonment of the right; and (3) the party must induce other parties to rely on the nonassertion or ineffective assertion of the right sufficiently that belated enforcement would prejudice or harm them.[63] By its administrative, executive, political, and economic conduct with regard to the Bay over time, South Africa has integrated Walvis Bay into Namibia. Indeed, its actions satisfy all three elements of estoppel.

Under the colonialist legal order, Britain, through valid annexation, had what constituted an enforceable right to incorporate Walvis Bay into itself.[64]

---

62. (1962) I.C.J. Reports at 41 (separate opinion of Judge Vice-President Alfaro).
63. W. REISMAN, NULLITY AND REVISION 385–86 (1971).
64. *See generally supra* chapter 6.

By annexing the Bay, Britain showed that it was aware of its right. Later, however, the Union of South Africa, Britain's successor in interest, incorporated the Bay into its South West African mandate.[65]

From the passage of the 1922 South West Africa Affairs Act until Proclamation R202 transferred the administration of Walvis Bay to the Cape in 1977, administration of the Bay proceeded from Windhoek, the capital of the mandate, as if the Bay formed part of the mandated territory. The legal, political, social, and economic structures of Walvis Bay and South West Africa were thus unified. Public statements that Walvis Bay had been incorporated into South West Africa, such as those by the South African representative to the Permanent Mandates Commission,[66] created the expectation among residents of both territories that the integration would be permanent. Everything added to these expectations, from the kind of stamps used on mail to license plates on vehicles to the absence of border markings to maps of Namibia.

South Africa's willingness to incorporate Walvis Bay into the mandated territory is understood when one considers its designs on the mandated territory and its views of the mandate system. The Cape completed its annexation of Walvis Bay only after Germany had declared a protectorate over the rest of South West Africa.[67] While Germany dominated South West Africa, the Cape, believing that Germany's protectorate was not economically viable as long as that country did not possess the Bay, did little to develop the Bay.[68] Once the League of Nations granted the South West Africa mandate to South Africa, however, South Africa, determined to annex the mandated territory, incorporated Walvis Bay into the mandate. Although the mandate system did not allow annexation, in a colonialist world South Africa believed that the League would not enforce the nonannexation provision and thought that it could annex the mandated territory. Thus, for example, at the end of the Second World War, as other mandatory powers submitted their mandates to U.N. Trust Agreements, South Africa sought to annex South West Africa. By then, it had already integrated Walvis Bay into the mandated territory. The United Nations' refusal to permit annexation prompted South Africa to disregard the wishes of the organization, which it continued to do even though that conduct contravened international law.[69]

It can thus be concluded that in integrating the Bay into South West

65. *See generally supra* chapter 3.
66. *See supra* chapter 7 at 132.
67. *See supra* chapter 2 at 42–46.
68. *See generally supra* chapter 3 at 47–48, 61.
69. *See generally supra* chapter 1 at 4–11.

Africa, South Africa did not feel that its actions were threatening its title to the Bay. Rather, it regarded the integration as an intermediate step before it formally annexed South West Africa. South Africa's misimpressions do not negate its actions, however, which satisfy the first element of estoppel, and South Africa bears the responsibility for the consequences of these actions. Although South Africa knew of its right to incorporate Walvis Bay into itself, it chose not to assert its right and instead incorporated Walvis Bay into the mandated territory.

All that is necessary to meet the first element of estoppel is South Africa's failure to assert its right; its misimpressions about the consequences of its actions are irrelevant. Moreover, because of the information it gave to the Permanent Mandates Commission, South Africa knew that both the commission and the residents of Walvis Bay and Namibia would interpret its nonassertion or ineffective assertion of its right to the Bay as an abandonment of that right. Thus, the second criterion of international estoppel is satisfied. South Africa should have recognized that its acknowledgments by word and deed of the integration of the Bay into the mandated territory openly indicated to the world that the integration was permanent.[70] In this regard, the standard of proof in international law is not proof of actual knowledge, but proof that the facts were so notorious that South Africa should have known others would think it had abandoned the right.

An example of this is the 1951 *Fisheries Case (United Kingdom v. Norway)*, in which the ICJ imputed knowledge of facts on the basis of notoriety.[71] In that case, Britain contested Norway's delimitation of Norwegian territorial waters. Since about 1906, British fishermen had fished off the Norwegian coast. By a royal decree of 1812 not at issue in the case, Norway had established a four-mile limit for its territorial waters. Subsequent decrees of 1869, 1881, and 1889 and official pronouncements about them perpetuated the 1812 delimitation by a system of straight lines drawn from various outermost points of the *skjaergaard,* or rampart of rocks and islands along the Norwegian coast. Following a July 12, 1935, decree, Norway applied the system in a more detailed way than previously. Britain challenged this and after various incidents brought the case to the ICJ. In addition to holding that the Norwegian system was in accord with international law, the court main-

70. See statement by Walvis Bay mayor after 1977 proclamation ("I don't think anyone here had any idea Walvis Bay had a separate status"), *supra* chapter 4 at 68.
71. Fisheries Case (United Kingdom v. Norway) (1951) I.C.J. Reports 116 [hereinafter cited as Fisheries Case]. For discussions of the case, see Waldcock, *The Anglo-Norwegian Fisheries Case,* 28 BRIT. Y.B. INT'L L. 114 (1951); Evensen, *The Anglo-Norwegian Fisheries Case and Its Legal Consequences,* 46 AM. J. INT'L L. 609 (1952); Johnson, *The Anglo-Norwegian Fisheries Case,* INT'L & COMP. L.Q. 145 (1952).

tained that Norway had long applied the system of straight baselines. Other states, including Britain, had acquiesced in it, and Britain had not formally protested it until 1933 even though it knew of the long-standing practice.[72]

In the case of Walvis Bay, South Africa publicly announced its actions before the League. Such actions manifested themselves in the laws affecting the daily lives of residents of the Bay and the mandated territory; these actions were notorious and outweigh any contrary assertions that appeared in official reports in the 1960s and 1970s as the controversy over South Africa's continuing administration of South West Africa received ever-increasing international attention.[73] Furthermore, it would not have been reasonable for South Africa to expect residents of the Walvis Bay and mandated territories to rely on such statements when all legal and physical evidence (for example, the absence of boundary markers) indicated that Walvis Bay was part of South West Africa.[74]

Indeed, this reliance upon the facts of integration by the residents of the Walvis Bay and mandated territories satisfies the third condition of estoppel, that is, that a party must induce other parties to rely upon the nonassertion or ineffectiveness of its right sufficiently that belated enforcement would prejudice or harm them. Before 1977, the legal, political, educational, and economic system of Walvis Bay was the same as that of Namibia. The legal changes that followed the publication of Proclamation R202, including contradictory applications of Namibian and South African laws, caused great confusion and hardship among the residents of Walvis Bay, who had relied to their detriment on the impression created by South Africa that the Bay formed part of Namibia.[75] For example, the higher taxes of South Africa applied to Walvis Bay residents; certain South African apartheid laws that no longer existed in Namibia applied to Walvis Bay, resulting in loss of dignity and economic difficulties for residents. Residents' reliance on the integration of the Bay into Namibia and the hardship they experienced after the implementation of Proclamation R202 meet the third criterion of estoppel. Thus, South Africa is estopped from asserting claims to the Bay.[76]

72. Fisheries Case, *supra* note 71, at 138.

73. *See supra* chapter 3 at 59, chapter 4 at 81.

74. *See supra* note 70 and *supra* chapter 4 at 68, 76–77, 80 (statements by residents that Walvis Bay is not part of South Africa).

75. *See generally supra* chapter 4 at 68, 72–84, 86–87, 89.

76. South Africa's supporters have argued that the international community is estopped from invoking international estoppel because South Africa's impression that Walvis Bay was South African caused it to rely to its detriment by expending money on Walvis Bay. *See supra* chapter 5 at 100. Such expenditure cannot negate the consequences of South Africa's actions, namely, the integration of Walvis Bay into Namibia. Indeed, if South Africa's argument were

Additional Factors

Although South Africa's claim to Walvis Bay is unsustainable for reasons of international law, quasi-legal factors support Walvis Bay's being part of Namibia. The General Assembly should concern itself with creating a Namibia that is economically viable. This is not a new notion in international decision making. At the Berlin Conference of 1885, the colonial powers recognized the importance of access to trade in creating viable countries.[77] The states assembled at Versailles felt that Poland's access to the sea was economically and politically necessary for its independence.[78] Like Namibia today, Poland was economically dependent upon exports.[79] Without the corridor, it would have had to rely upon the goodwill of its neighbors for access to trade. Similarly, Namibia will not be a viable state without Walvis Bay, its only viable harbor. If it does not have access to the port, Namibia will be economically and perhaps politically dependent upon a South Africa already opposed to the notion of a SWAPO-dominated government.

Without Walvis Bay, Namibia has limited possibilities for transporting its exports. Its airports are of limited capacity, and transportation of large quantities of basic commodities by air is not cost-effective. Of Namibia's two harbors, only Walvis Bay is viable. The harbor at Lüderitz is undeveloped and undevelopable except at great cost.[80] Land routes are also problematic. Namibia's only tarred roads run from Walvis Bay to Swakopmund to Windhoek and from there north to Angola or south to South Africa. Its declining railway system runs from Walvis Bay to Windhoek to South Africa. With the exception of the road to the north, all overland routes go either to Walvis Bay or to South Africa. Even the good road to the north does not reach into Angola to its ports.[81] The cost of extending the roads or railways will presumably be prohibitive. Without the Bay, Namibia will be forced to rely upon South Africa.

South Africa may continue to use the Bay as a base for controlling shipping lanes off the Namibian coast. A newly independent Namibia without

---

taken to its logical conclusion, South Africa's expenditure on Namibia since it began to administer the mandated territory would estop the international community from maintaining that South Africa's occupation of Namibia was illegal. South Africa must bear the consequences of its actions. South Africa's expenditures on Walvis Bay do not work an estoppel against the international community, the Council for Namibia, or SWAPO.

77. S. Crowe, The Berlin West African Conference, 1884–1885, 167 (1942).

78. R. Donald, The Polish Corridor and the Consequences 9–10, 20–21, 141–42 (1929).

79. A. Tomas, The "Polish Corridor" and Peace 13–14 (1930).

80. *See infra* chapter 10 at 188–89.

81. *Id.*

a navy and without a harbor from which to launch one will be powerless to stop such activities. South Africa will retain control of Namibia's fishing industry as well.[82] Border closings or the imposition and stringent application of byzantine regulations governing imports and exports and immigration and emigration will, in such a situation, also be highly effective political weapons, as they have been in the case of Lesotho, a tiny landlocked state entirely surrounded by South Africa.[83] In addition, control of Walvis Bay will give South Africa military control of Namibia. Clearly, with Walvis Bay, South Africa will retain the key to the new government's survival.

The application of the concepts discussed here makes it apparent that under modern international law, South Africa's claims of sovereignty over Walvis Bay are untenable. Such a conclusion conflicts, however, with the realities of power in the modern world.

---

82. *Id.* An independent Namibia will also be helpless to stop South African interference in its territorial waters. See *infra* Appendix.

83. *See generally* J. HANLON, BEGGAR YOUR NEIGHBOURS (1986).

CHAPTER TEN

Conclusion

When legal scholars address a problem like that of Walvis Bay, they tend to restrict their discussions to the application of modern rules of international law. Such limited studies frequently lack the historical depth that is necessary if one is to apply the law to the facts adequately. They see law as a hermetically sealed body of rules divorced from the realities of power rather than as the evolving, dynamic expression of policy and world view that it is.

Ahistoricity is a serious shortcoming of the legal profession in a world where its members are often called upon to assist in resolving issues with international implications. As a result, because of its limited scope, even the best modern international legal scholarship is frequently no more than a polemic. Such a narrow perspective does a disservice to the parties involved in a particular dispute and to the international community.

By applying the study of the evolution of the concepts of sovereignty in international law to the study of the history of Walvis Bay, this work places itself at the interface of law and history. It rejects the nineteenth-century notion of law as a science that applies a finite number of rules to the case at hand and yields predictable results. Unfortunately, in spite of the realist revolution of the twentieth century and the seemingly obligatory lip service paid to law as a social science, this notion still seems implicit in many lawyers' approach to law. Analyzing legal problems from a historical perspective does much to undermine such a view.

The interdisciplinary method employed here offers advantages over present-minded approaches. It keeps scholars from automatically associating contemporary terminology with its textbook meanings by confronting them with unfamiliar terminology. They can thus discover and comprehend obscured structural patterns and explain modes of behavior that were unarticulated and perhaps unperceived by actual participants in historical events. With new analytical tools for approaching law in our own age, scholars can transcend conventional maxims about jurisprudence to discover how law operates in its sociopolitical nexus.

Applying this historical approach to the question of Walvis Bay reveals much about the politico-legal system. The emergence of the modern law of decolonization has been a long and tortuous process. Its absorption into the jus cogens has been marked by a shift in the realities of global power. The international community now includes all the world's peoples and is no longer the special domain of an exclusivist white, Western club of states. This study has explored the transition from an exclusivist club to an all-inclusive one. The transition involved three legal orders.

First, the colonialist legal order, which reached its zenith at the end of the nineteenth century and the beginning of the twentieth, which ignored the cultures of non-Western peoples. Second, there was a transitional legal order that espoused a rhetoric of self-determination of peoples but also flouted this through sometimes heinous discriminatory practices. Third, there is the modern international legal order of the second half of the twentieth century, in which decolonization based upon self-determination and equal rights has an important place. Considering the gradual movement from the first to the third legal order, the study has examined the problem of Walvis Bay on a microlevel, traced the historical development of the right of self-determination on the macrolevel, and applied the latter to the former to illuminate the nature of the dispute and suggest its possible resolution.

Two opposing visions of the international legal order underlie the arguments of the parties in the dispute over Walvis Bay. The South African view relies upon theories of law that, though once the norm, have gradually been modified as the nature of power in the world has changed until they have now been almost universally discredited. SWAPO's view is informed by modern international law as it has evolved since the end of World War II. That SWAPO's claim is preferable becomes clear once the legal discourse of the South African government is revealed to be no longer persuasive in light of recent developments.

Since medieval times, the question of sovereignty for indigenous peoples was a much debated topic in the Western legal tradition. The naturalists believed that lands inhabited by non-Christian and, later, uncivilized peoples were not terra nullius as long as those peoples had some form of political organization. The ideas of the positivists, who took the opposite view, held sway in state practice, however. Civilization in Western terms thus became the criterion for membership in the international community, and the lands of uncivilized peoples were the object of Western colonialism. In this legal order, an elaborate set of rules was developed to regulate relations among the Western powers with regard to the lands they sought to acquire. British practice concerning Walvis Bay was in accord with these rules.

As the doctrine of sovereignty developed, Western nations adopted a posture of encouraging and defending the exercise of self-determination by peoples rather than denying them such freedom. However, their motivation was born of economic and strategic concerns rather than humanitarian ones. Woodrow Wilson in particular employed an embryonic rhetoric of self-determination, and the League of Nations provided the framework within which the ideas of self-determination and anticolonialism were later articulated. Although the international community was expanded in this time to include, for example, the independent African states of Liberia and Ethiopia, most of the world remained under colonial domination. Cries for equal rights from educated black elites in Pan-Africanist organizations fell mostly on deaf ears.

The gap between the rhetoric of self-determination and its implementation as the norm became apparent during the Italian conquest of Ethiopia, when the League of Nations used rhetoric to disguise the conflict between the theory of self-determination and the actual operation of international law. In such an environment, the international community did not question South Africa's title to Walvis Bay.

Since World War II, the modern international legal order has evolved. The law of decolonization, of which self-determination and equal rights have been important aspects, is a cornerstone of that order. Viewed from a historical perspective, the triumph of the law of decolonization was not mere happenstance but was the product of many factors, including Allied wartime propaganda and its influence on colonized peoples; colonized peoples' participation in the war; the civil rights movement in the United States; the rejection of racism by scientists;[1] the expanded lobbying efforts of Western-educated elites from the colonies, culminating in independence for a great

1. On scientific racism, see L. THOMPSON, THE POLITICAL MYTHOLOGY OF APARTHEID 13–17 (1985); see also S. GOULD, THE MISMEASURE OF MAN (1981); N. STEPAN, THE IDEA OF RACE IN SCIENCE: GREAT BRITAIN, 1800–1960 (1982).

number of new states and the end of empire in most parts of the world in the late 1950s and the 1960s; and the swelling of the ranks of the United Nations by these new states.

After it had been an issue before the ICJ for more than twenty years, South Africa's occupation of Namibia was declared illegal. When the court first confronted the South West Africa issue, it had not yet shed its Western orientation. In its 1971 *Namibia (Advisory) Opinion,* the court finally recognized humanitarian concerns in its approach to the fundamental questions presented in the case: "One of the fundamental principles governing the international relationship thus established is that a party which disowns or does not fulfill its own obligations cannot be recognized as retaining the rights which it claims to derive from the relationship."[2] This new attitude was due to the altered composition of the court, which by then included more justices from so-called Third World countries, as well as to a shift in the tenor of international legal discourse with regard to the problem of self-determination. At least in theory, modern international law no longer recognizes colonialist claims like that of South Africa to Walvis Bay.

Indeed, the tremendous changes in international relations since the First and Second World Wars have created an international community of organized states from what was previously a somewhat anarchical collection of individual ones. New international law has developed to promote cooperation, harmonize the rights of states, and give ample room for common interests, thus bringing about what Judge Alvarez of Chile, in his dissenting opinion in the ICJ's 1950 advisory opinion on South West Africa, termed "international social justice."[3] The Walvis Bay dispute arose in the context of this legal transition.

South Africa has based its claim to Walvis Bay upon a seemingly straightforward chain of title. In doing so, however, it has transmuted the morality and conventions of a previous age into a claim that, if vindicated, will leave as a practical result a country with an eight-hundred-mile coastline, landlocked and politically and economically dependent upon South Africa. Most notably, the South African case fails to mention the development of legal doctrines since the time of the British annexation and is premised in large part upon an extensive and anachronistic discussion of the notion that Walvis Bay was terra nullius at the time of the annexation. Indeed, Walvis Bay was terra nullius within the meaning of that term as used by jurists of the late nineteenth century; yet, this argument does not recognize that ideas of sovereignty which once held sway have been gradually nudged out of the jurisprudential corpus.

2. (1971) I.C.J. Reports 34.
3. (1950) I.C.J. Reports 128, 176.

In South Africa's argument, the entire body of international law is not considered, but only those rules that formerly supported a claim of sovereignty. SWAPO, on the other hand, argues that the chain of title, even if valid at the time the events occurred, is no longer so because international law has evolved to the point where it will no longer support a colonialist claim such as South Africa's. This places SWAPO's argument squarely within the modern international legal tradition while recognizing the possibility that the chain of title was once valid.

South Africa's vision of the international legal system is a static one in which titles that were valid when acquired must never be disturbed. SWAPO's vision is a human rights vision. Two alternative theories of legality shape these visions—one predicated on outdated principles, the other on a changed and always evolving legal system.

The legal order accepted by the founders of the two world courts was based on legal principles that evolved over several centuries to govern the relations of the nations of Western Europe. This body of law focused on the international problems of a largely European and Christian political and social order. The structure and content of classical international law was developed by the states of Western Europe to regulate their relations with one another. As modified by state practice over time, the principles formed a coherent body of rules for centuries. These rules reflected the nation-state system of Western Europe and its economic values, focusing primarily on recognition, the mutual respect for national territory, and noninterference in internal affairs. It is this legal order that South Africa seeks to uphold when it insists that its title to Walvis Bay was recognized by an international treaty and confirmed by an international organization—that is, that the Berlin Conference sanctioned British sovereignty over Walvis Bay and that the mandate agreement excluded Walvis Bay from its scope.

Two major developments have undermined this theory of law. The first was the rise of Communist states—the Soviet Union, China, and the Eastern European countries—and the spread of Marxist ideology. The second was the emergence of the newly independent states of Asia, Africa, and the Caribbean, which along with those of Latin America form the so-called Third World. These states now constitute a majority in the United Nations, their citizens comprise a majority of people on the globe, and their jurists propound views that challenge traditional Western jurisprudential assumptions.

SWAPO's view of law may be seen to fit what some have termed Third World theory.[4] This theory maintains that many of the norms of the classical

---

4. On Third World theory regarding succession of states, see, e.g., Y. MAKONNEN, INTERNATIONAL LAW AND THE NEW STATES OF AFRICA (1983) (dealing with states in eastern Africa).

system evolved before the majority of states existed and were designed to meet the needs of the nation-states of a largely homogeneous Christian, Western Europe. Third World theorists also point out that these rules recognized a right of dominion for "civilized nations" and formed a justification for European colonialism in Africa and Asia. As a result, Third World theorists argue, states that played no role in the development of such norms should not be bound by them except to the extent that these states specifically choose, by treaty or conscious state practice, to be so bound. This explains SWAPO's insistence that South Africa's title, which had no consensual element, is no longer valid, as well as the OAU's acceptance of colonial boundaries because they suited the new states by creating order.

Even if it is agreed, however, that under modern international law SWAPO's claim to Walvis Bay is valid and that South Africa should relinquish control of it, the rhetoric of power versus right transposes the discourse to another plane, namely, the realities of the international system. When seen from this perspective, the operation of law in the international system furnishes little hope for equitable resolution of the dispute.

United States Chief Justice John Marshall once wrote of international law what might aptly have described it in our own time: "Like all laws of nations, it rests upon the common consent [of states]" and "is of force, not because it was prescribed by any superior power but because it has been generally accepted as a rule of conduct."[5] Put another way, even if international law derives from humanitarian concerns, it is of no consequence until those concerns become normative rules of behavior. Today the mix of self-determination and equal rights in the law of decolonization makes for a curious interplay of positivism and notions of natural rights. Self-determination and equal rights, though deriving from notions of natural law, have been transformed into positive law; this transformation has occurred through the adoption of Security Council and General Assembly resolutions and declarations, the signing of international instruments, and the incorporation of the ideas contained in such documents into the domestic law of many states. Expressions of humanitarian concern, grounded in notions of natural rights implicit in the human condition, have theoretically become transformed into rules of law.

In light of the changing standards of international law, including the shift from natural law to positive law regarding self-determination and equal rights, it is appropriate for idealists and others who place their faith in the bright hope that international law furnishes for humanity to argue that an

5. The Paquete Habana, 175 U.S. 677, 711 (1900).

independent Namibia has a right to Walvis Bay. Examination reveals, however, that even though there are many examples of successful application of the law of decolonization since World War II, these rights are merely rhetorical. When faced with the dynamics of power in a world where there are no positive law rights unless there are remedies for breach of them, the government of an independent Namibia has no hope of gaining Walvis Bay if the will of the international community to bring that about is lacking. The larger question of Namibian independence is a case in point.

Until 1988, Namibia was no closer to independence than when it was still the South West Africa mandate and the modern law of decolonization had not yet evolved to its present state. Although the rhetoric about the illegality and immorality of South Africa's occupation filled countless volumes, for decades the international community stood by helplessly, and perhaps in the case of some states with silent approval, as South Africa tightened its control over Namibia. The gap between the articulated norms of the international legal order and its success in implementing these in the Namibian case and many others was immense. Time after time, the contradiction between natural and positive law produced a vicious cycle of raised hopes and unfulfilled expectations, representing a fundamental and sometimes unbreachable division that those with humanitarian concerns ever struggled to cross. This contradiction bodes ill for the equitable resolution of the Walvis Bay dispute.

To suggest that the dispute be submitted to international adjudication would be facile in a world where the most powerful nations simply refuse to recognize the jurisdiction of the ICJ when it does not suit them. The United States and Nicaragua provide a case in point.[6] Unfortunately, the hope of a just world order based on compulsory jurisdiction has long deceived statesmen, diplomats, and the world public into thinking that a world governed by law is presently possible. Even at the conference of April 1945 at which the United Nations was organized, the United States, the United Kingdom, and the Soviet Union raised forceful opposition to automatic compulsory jurisdiction for the ICJ.[7] That opposition resulted in the adoption of the "optional

6. Although Article 94 of the U.N. Charter obligates each member of the United Nations "to comply with the decision of the International Court of Justice in any case to which it is a party," the same article assigns enforcement of a judgment against a recalcitrant party to the Security Council's discretion. The United States announced that it did not plan to comply with the court's judgment and vetoed a July 31, 1986, Security Council resolution that Nicaragua sought urging compliance with the court's decisions. New York Times, Aug. 1, 1986, at A3, col. 1. On the case itself, see generally Moore, *The Secret War in Central America and the Future of World Order*, 80 Am. J. Int'l L. 43 (1986); Rostow, *Nicaragua and the Law of Self-Defense Revisited*, 11 Yale J. Int'l L. 437 (1986).

7. Summary Report of the Fourteenth Meeting of Committee IV/1, Doc. 661, IV/1/50, 13 U.N.C.I.O. Docs. 226–27 (1945).

clause" of the statute of the ICJ.[8] The clause allowed each state to declare whether it would accept compulsory jurisdiction.

Today many states do not recognize compulsory jurisdiction. Although the number of states in the United Nations has grown tremendously since the 1950s, the number accepting compulsory jurisdiction has increased only gradually. Whereas by 1953, thirty-seven states, then a majority of the United Nations, had submitted to compulsory jurisdiction,[9] the record high of forty-eight optional jurisdiction clause adherents in 1985 represented only 30 percent of the United Nations' membership.[10] Perhaps more important than the declining percentage of U.N. members participating in the system has been the drop in participation by permanent members of the Security Council. Once the United States' termination became effective on April 7, 1986,[11] only one member of the Security Council, the United Kingdom, remained bound by the optional clause,[12] though it had by then developed another technique for avoiding adjudication that threatened its interests.[13]

Since 1972, the respondents in eight contentious cases before the ICJ have chosen either not to appear or not to participate at some stage in the proceedings.[14] In the case of Walvis Bay, it would surely be more attractive to the South African government simply to refuse to submit to the court's jurisdiction, to decline to appear, or not to comply if the court asserts jurisdiction. South Africa does not recognize the court's jurisdiction. Further, there is fundamental disagreement between South Africa and SWAPO on broad substantive areas, about the governing principles of international law and their appropriate application. South Africa would not commit itself to a judgment based upon any principles it regarded as incorrect. South Africa's response to decisions of the ICJ in the South West Africa cases is instructive; it rejoiced in the rule of law when the decisions favored its interests and ignored it entirely when the decisions did not.

Whereas some states reject international adjudication because of its

8. I.C.J. STATUTE ART. 36(2).

9. 1952–1953 I.C.J. Y.B. 171–82 (1953).

10. 1984–1985 I.C.J. Y.B. 66–101 (1985).

11. 86 DEP'T ST. BULL. 67 (Jan. 1986).

12. *See* 1984–1985 I.C.J. Y.B. 98–99 (1985).

13. Britain terminates its declaration and substitutes a new one excluding the specific matter in dispute. *See* Waldcock, *Decline of the Optional Clause,* 32 BRIT. Y.B. INT'L L. 269 (1956).

14. These cases include the two Fisheries Jurisdiction cases, (1972) I.C.J. Reports 12, (1972) I.C.J. Reports 30; the two Nuclear Test Cases, (1973) I.C.J. Reports 99; (1973) I.C.J. Reports 135; Pakistani Prisoners of War, (1973) I.C.J. Reports 347; Aegean Sea Continental Shelf, (1978) I.C.J. Reports 4; Iran Hostages Case, (1980) I.C.J. Reports 3; and Nicaragua, Jurisdiction, (1984) I.C.J. Reports 392. For an analysis of the performance of the ICJ, see R. FALK, REVIVING THE WORLD COURT (1986).

inflexible, zero-sum nature and prefer instead to take part in face-saving negotiations or to temporize, the 1987 pronouncement of the South African deputy minister of defence on Walvis Bay indicated the contempt with which South Africa would treat any move by the United Nations to arrange such negotiations.[15] Indeed, until 1988, the whole process of U.N. negotiations over Namibian independence had collapsed.

When South African President Botha announced a willingness to negotiate on Namibian issues at the opening of Parliament in January 1986, he offered an August date for South Africa's withdrawal from Namibia.[16] This withdrawal was conditioned upon the exit of some thirty thousand Cuban troops from Angola. The troops were there at the invitation of the Angolan government and assisted it in its struggle against the South African- and U.S.-backed guerrilla forces of UNITA. Known as linkage, this condition for South Africa's departure from Namibia was first insisted upon by U.S. Assistant Secretary of State for African Affairs Chester Crocker in 1981 and was adopted immediately by South Africa.[17]

The South African initiative appears to have been disingenuous, however, for at the time Botha's speech was made, the Reagan administration was courting Savimbi, the UNITA leader, as an anti-Communist hero and offering to assist him in overthrowing the Angolan government. Such circumstances made it impossible for the Angolans to entertain any thought of removing the Cubans and precluded the possibility that negotiations regarding Namibian independence would occur.

Meanwhile, the international press and the international community, perhaps tired of the failure of so many attempts in the past, merely yawned. The deadline for South Africa's withdrawal came and went without any developments. By that time, the world was preoccupied with ending white minority rule in South Africa. The Namibia issue disappeared from public attention. It seemed unlikely, given ever-increasing South African military spending on Namibia and the failure of negotiations, that Namibia would achieve independence before there was a new, nonracial government in Pretoria. The most likely candidate for forming such a government, the African National Congress (ANC), the major resistance movement in South Africa, maintained that Walvis Bay belonged to Namibia.[18] Yet no one could predict

15. *See supra* chapter 5 at 93.

16. Cape Times, Jan. 28, 1986.

17. *See* W. MINTER, KING SOLOMON'S MINES REVISITED: WESTERN INTERESTS AND THE BURDENED HISTORY OF SOUTHERN AFRICA 311 (1986).

18. Oliver Tambo, Speech at International Conference on Sanctions Against South Africa Organized by the United Nations in Cooperation with the Organization of African Unity, Paris, May 1981. The ANC position on the Penguin Islands is the same. Conversation with "Reg," September, A.N.C. Observer Mission to the United Nations, July 1987.

how or when or with what outcome a transition in South Africa would occur, and the government appeared to have dug itself in for the long haul. This left the people of Walvis Bay and the rest of Namibia in an unenviable position.

By 1988, however, South Africa had entered a quieter phase. A nation-wide state of emergency declared in June 1986 and renewed annually had, at least temporarily, quashed black protest. Stringent censorship laws and the expulsion of many foreign journalists had succeeded in removing news of violent confrontation from the world's newspapers, radio broadcasts, and television screens. Nevertheless, by then the South African economy was in a shambles. Its military presence in Namibia and Angola was proving extremely costly in both human and monetary terms, and a disastrous battle at Cuito Cuanavale in Angola, at which a large number of white South Africans died, had put South African military superiority in doubt. At home, continued military involvement was particularly unpopular with young white men, who by law are bound to serve for two years in the South African armed forces.[19] At the same time, with the ailing South African economy, the cost of running Namibia became a drain on the South African budget.

In the international sphere, the superpowers were keen to reach some accord in southern Africa. In the age of *glasnost* and *perestroika,* Soviet President Mikhail Gorbachev was bent on ending his country's involvement in various regional conflicts around the world. Chester Crocker of the United States was particularly keen to win a major policy victory in the area, his only one in over seven years. Angola, devastated by years of civil war, wished to normalize relations with the United States and have a measure of stability. Cuba, too, had been sending signals to Washington indicating a desire for at least some thaw in relations.

The coalescence of these factors resulted in U.S.–brokered talks beginning in July 1988 among Cuba, Angola, and South Africa that eventually resulted in a timetable for withdrawal of Cuban troops from Angola acceptable to South Africa and paved the way for the implementation of Security Council Resolution 435 of 1978, the U.N. plan for Namibian independence. Not formally included in the talks was the Soviet Union, which had observer status but which, represented by the senior diplomat Deputy Foreign Minister Anatoly Adamishin, no doubt brought much pressure to bear on its Cuban and Angolan clients. Also absent was SWAPO, which South Africa continued to refuse to recognize as having any special claim to represent the Namibian people.

---

19. An increasing number of white males refused to perform military service. *See generally* Berat, *Conscientious Objection in South Africa: Governmental Paranoia and the Law of Conscription,* 22 VAND. J. TRANSNT'L L. 127 (1989).

Finally, on December 22, 1988, an agreement was signed in New York providing for the implementation of the U.N. plan for U.N.-supervised elections leading to Namibian independence.[20] Under the agreement, the process was to begin on April 1, 1989, with the arrival of the United Nations Transitional Assistance Group in Namibia. Elections for a Constituent Assembly, which would draft a constitution, were scheduled for November, with independence to follow early in 1990. As had been established in 1978, the question of Walvis Bay was not raised. Already, a November 1988 press release from the Permanent Mission of South Africa to the United Nations had emphasized this point, briefly reiterating South Africa's chain of title argument, and concluded that "the question of Walvis Bay and the terms of [Security Council] Resolution 432 demanding that it be integrated into South West Africa/Namibia are therefore irrelevant to the process of implementation of Security Council Resolution 435 (1978)."[21]

South Africa has proposed that Walvis Bay be a free port under South African control. This idea is not new; it circulated in government circles at the beginning of the century. In the mid-1970s, local business interests became its proponents. In 1976, the Walvis Bay town council commissioned a study by the Department of Transportation of the University of Stellenbosch to investigate development possibilities for Walvis Bay.[22] The study suggested that as a free port Walvis Bay would provide various economic advantages. The main advantage would be the opportunity for merchants and manufacturers to import, store, and process goods for reexport free of customs duties and import controls. Local industries would then have an advantage in exporting products, as Hong Kong does today. Further, although the study did not mention this, South Africa might use a Walvis Bay with free-port status to avoid international economic sanctions.

The private sector in Walvis Bay formed the Free Port Action Committee in February 1980.[23] Composed of representatives of the Property Owners' Association, the chamber of commerce, and the Sakekamer, the committee advocated free-port status for Walvis Bay and publicized the need for governmental assistance to implement the recommendation of the Stellenbosch report. The committee argued that free-port status would be the ideal of economic and human freedom for Walvis Bay and the new Namibia. The chairman of the Walvis Bay Publicity Association said, for example, that

20. New York Times, Dec. 23, 1988.
21. Republic of South Africa, Permanent Mission to the United Nations, Question of Walvis Bay, Press Release 29/88, Nov. 18, 1988.
22. University of Stellenbosch, Transport Research Centre, Report of an Investigation into the Potential Development at Walvis Bay (1977) [hereinafter cited as Stellenbosch Report].
23. Windhoek Advertiser, Mar. 14, 1980; Windhoek Observer, Mar. 15, 1980.

Walvis Bay would have a great future if it were declared a free port.[24] The South African authorities could do away with certain legislation, such as the Group Areas Act and antigambling laws, allowing Walvis Bay to compete with Swakopmund, where the Group Areas Act had been abolished and gambling brought much revenue. Income was especially needed in Walvis Bay because of its dying fishing industry and declining population, decreased from twenty-seven thousand in 1976 to eighteen thousand in 1980.[25] In 1981, the prime minister's economic planning branch indicated that it would ask the Stellenbosch Department of Transportation to further investigate the free-port option.[26] Nothing more occurred.

The Advisory Committee for Transport Services in South West Africa/Namibia issued a report in July 1986 arguing that if Walvis Bay were to become a free port, it would have a negative effect on the transport system and industries of South West Africa.[27] The parties in Namibia's South African–installed Transitional Government of National Unity meanwhile proposed a condominium arrangement by which Namibia and South Africa would share the economic management of Walvis Bay equally.[28] The scheme was introduced by the Government of National Unity's minister of manpower and national health, who also suggested that two other possibilities be investigated with the South African government. These were the declaration of Walvis Bay as a free port and the abolition of income tax in the area to encourage offshore banking operations. In March 1987, the Government of National Unity announced that it would send a team to South Africa to come to an interim arrangement about Namibia's use of Walvis Bay. According to the minister of mining and tourism, this was to be "a condominium arrangement for the sharing of Walvis Bay's social, economic, and fishing resources on an equal footing."[29] Although by the end of 1987 there were no further developments, an agreement with any such puppet government would have been meaningless, as it would not have disturbed South African sovereignty over Walvis Bay. The parties of the Government of National Unity naturally did not dispute the South African claim to Walvis Bay, though they recognized that Walvis Bay is economically and socially an integral part of Namibia.

Even if Walvis Bay becomes a free port and an independent Namibia has access to its facilities, the failure of a Namibian government to adopt a pro–South African position could result in closure of the port. In addition, with its

24. Rand Daily Mail, Apr. 22, 1980.
25. *See supra* chapter 4 at 85.
26. Namib Times, Apr. 7, 1981; Namib Times, May 5, 1981.
27. Namib Times, July 11, 1986.
28. Windhoek Observer, Feb. 22, 1986.
29. Windhoek Observer, Mar. 7, 1987.

immense military facilities at Walvis Bay, South Africa will have an easy base for incursions into Namibia if Namibia should oppose that government's policies. South Africa has often conducted raids on neighboring states. Moreover, South Africa has frequently expressed the intent to intervene in Namibian affairs if the "red flag" of a supposedly Communist-inspired SWAPO government should fly over Windhoek.[30]

Although a Namibian government without Walvis Bay could theoretically use the southern Angolan ports of Porto Alexandre or Namibe (formerly Moçamedes) or the Namibian port of Lüderitz, none of these is practical. There is no direct rail link between the Angolan ports and Namibia. Porto Alexandre is only a minor port incapable of handling large volumes of traffic. Namibe, to its north, although a major Angolan port, is 250 miles by road from the border and an additional 250 miles from the nearest Namibian railhead, Tsumeb. Tsumeb might eventually be linked to the Angolan railway system, but the cost of such an undertaking would be prohibitive for a new nation with little foreign exchange.

It was rumored in 1983 that Angola, anxious for a rapprochement with the United States, had suggested to SWAPO that it leave Walvis Bay to South Africa and use Namibe instead.[31] SWAPO's leaders at first opposed the idea on the grounds that it would detract from their claim to Walvis Bay. The Angolans then pointed out that using Namibe could shift the strength of Namibia's farming economy away from white-owned lands in the south to northern areas where the majority of the black population lives. It would also deprive South Africa of an important bargaining advantage, namely, Namibian dependence on Walvis Bay. The South Africans registered their displeasure with such a plan by attacking Namibe and its railway line. Meanwhile, SWAPO's Central Committee was reportedly split between supporters and opponents of the Namibe alternative, but at a meeting in Luanda it did not endorse this option.

The port of Lüderitz is an equally unattractive possibility. Ever since issuing Proclamation R202, the South African government has promoted Lüderitz as South West Africa's only port. In April 1983, for example, the *Pretoria News* reported that "SWA/Namibia's only port begins its centenary celebrations this week. Lüderitz is the one sea outlet which an independent Namibia could develop to avoid dependence on Walvis Bay."[32] Using Lüderitz is not practical, however. Shipments from the port are confined to local needs, such as those of the small rock lobster industry. The port can

30. *See supra* chapter 5, note 14 and accompanying text.
31. EFR, Oct. 20, 1983.
32. Pretoria News, Apr. 15, 1983.

handle only relatively small vessels. It has a narrow, rocky inlet that could be enlarged only with great difficulty and an enormous capital investment. In 1987, the port had just 492 feet of wharf and small storage and cargo handling facilities. The water at the wharf is just twenty feet deep. Oceangoing freighters thus cannot be accommodated but must be loaded and unloaded by small flat-bottomed boats known as lighters.[33]

The geographical location of the port is also undesirable. A study in 1979 indicated that it is too far south of the main sources and destinations of cargo in central and northern Namibia that now use Walvis Bay as their port of exit.[34] The study also indicated that the rail link from Lüderitz to the interior had a low carrying capacity.[35] Two of the Penguin Islands are located at the entrance to Lüderitz Bay, and the South African navy could make access to the port difficult.[36]

With the Bay and the Penguin Islands, South Africa will control Namibia's richest fishing grounds, which, though now severely depleted, could be replenished with careful conservation and international efforts to prevent overfishing. Namibia will thus be deprived of a major source of revenue. In addition, it will have no facilities for processing fish. At the moment, the fishing industry, centered in Walvis Bay, is almost exclusively in the hands of white South Africans.[37] South African disruption of Namibia's fishing industry will affect not only the resources of the shore-based industry, such as pilchard, anchovy, lobster, sole, snoek, seals, and guano, which are mostly within the twelve-nautical-mile territorial limit claimed and controlled by South Africa, but also deep-water fishing.[38] Almost all deep-sea fishing occurs outside that limit in waters that South Africa claims as a two-hundred-nautical-mile fishery zone.[39]

South Africa has indicated that after Namibian independence it will apply its own two-hundred-mile zone to the Bay and each of the Penguin Islands. This will leave as much as 20 percent of the waters off the Namibian coast under South African control,[40] including the harbor, with its industrial

33. R. Green, Namibia: A Political Economic Survey, Discussion Paper No. 144, Institute of Development Studies, University of Sussex 47–50 (1979) (unpublished paper).

34. *Id.* at 48.

35. *Id.*

36. *See infra* Appendix.

37. *See generally* R. MOORSOM, EXPLOITING THE SEA 51–61 (London: Catholic Institute for International Relations 1984); Pieters, *Restructuring Namibia's Fisheries,* 1 IN FORMATION 69–80 (1987–88).

38. *See infra* Appendix, at 203, 208.

39. *Id.*

40. *Id.*

base, and important parts of the fishing grounds. Such a separation will also have the awkward effect of dividing the waters from Walvis Bay south into alternating sections of South African and Namibian territorial waters and fishery zones. There the naval superiority of South Africa will be a major factor if South Africa chooses to disregard Namibian efforts to limit the exploitation of resources in Namibian waters.

The 1982 Convention on the Law of the Sea recognized the concept of the exclusive economic zone, which accords every coastal state exclusive jurisdiction over the natural resources of the seabed, subsoil, and superjacent waters adjacent to its coast to a maximum of two hundred nautical miles.[41] Although the U.N. Council for Namibia signed the convention, its signature had no effect in the prevailing international climate. In its Algiers Declaration of June 1980, the council criticized "the illegal exploitation of Namibia's marine resources in its territorial waters" and decided "to counter South Africa's acts to extend illegally, in its own name, the territorial sea of Namibia and proclaim an exclusive economic zone for Namibia. The Council intends to use its own authority to extend the territorial sea of Namibia and to proclaim an exclusive economic zone for Namibia."[42] This declaration was in accord with the council's 1974 Decree on Natural Resources, which posited that "no person or entity . . . may search for . . . take . . . process . . .export . . . distribute any natural resource, whether animal or mineral, situated . . . within the territorial limits of Namibia, without the consent . . . of the United Nations Council for Namibia."[43] The declaration has been ineffective because the council was incapable of enforcing its decisions. Only the government of an independent Namibia will have a chance of stopping the exploitation of its fish and other resources.

In line with a worldwide trend, the South African government has legislated for a two-hundred-mile fishery zone, first in its 1977 proclamation extending the South African zone to Walvis Bay[44] and again in a 1979 proclamation of the administrator-general that applied to all Namibian waters.[45] By 1987, however, South Africa had refrained from imposing unilateral controls outside the twelve-mile territorial limit. Continued South African claims to territorial waters and a two-hundred-mile fishery zone off

41. *See* United Nations, The Law of the Sea. Official Text of the United Nations Conference on the Law of the Sea. U.N. Doc. E.83.v.5; *see generally* D. O'CONNELL, THE INTERNATIONAL LAW OF THE SEA (2 vols. 1982, 1984).

42. Council for Namibia, Algiers Declaration, June 1980.

43. Council for Namibia, Decree No. 1 (1974). The U.N. General Assembly subsequently adopted the decree.

44. *See infra* Appendix, note 41 and accompanying text.

45. *See infra* Appendix, note 42 and accompanying text.

both Walvis Bay and the Penguin Islands will, if strictly enforced, seriously impede Namibian fishing operations. Again, the South African navy will continue to be a major presence in South African waters. Such economic dependence will surely encourage political dependence. Even pro–South African officials in Namibia readily admitted that a Namibian government without Walvis Bay would be in a precarious position. The South West African secretary of finance put it best when he said, "Either Namibia gains control over Walvis Bay or this country will have to remain on very friendly terms with South Africa."[46]

Control of the Bay has regional implications as well. If Walvis Bay were part of an independent Namibia, the port might become more important than it already is because the pattern of trade would be likely to shift away from South Africa to independent Africa and elsewhere. This decreased reliance upon South Africa is precisely the goal of the nine southern African states comprising SADCC, the Southern African Development Coordination Conference.[47] Should this transformation occur, the tonnage of bulk imports, principally manufactured consumer and industrial goods, building materials, mining equipment, and foodstuffs sent via Walvis Bay would probably increase sharply. To a lesser extent this would also apply to exports, mainly frozen and processed beef.

Estimates suggest that more than two-thirds by weight of both exports and imports are transported by rail to and from South Africa.[48] If the major part of these were to be redirected, Walvis Bay could be expected to increase its yearly tonnage from about two million in 1980/81 to over five million within a few years, probably accounting for more than 80 percent of Namibian exports.[49] As most of Namibia's existing export markets and its cheapest potential import suppliers are outside South Africa, control of Walvis Bay would allow an independent Namibia to disengage itself quickly from its former ruler. In this context, the notion of a rail link to Botswana and Zambia, connecting Walvis Bay with the central African rail network, becomes impor-

46. Windhoek Advertiser, June 19, 1985.
47. Economist Bethuel Setai notes that SADCC "was formed in 1980 by nine African countries in the Southern African subregion. The objective was to reduce economic dependence on South Africa through coordinated regional projects in the sectors of transportation, communications, energy, food production and industry. SADCC was conceived neither as a free trade region nor as a customs union. It viewed its role simply as coordinating development infrastructure by creating an environment in which all the elements that favor the free exchange of commodities would exist." Setai, *The Migrant Labour Dependency Link,* INT'L FORUM AT YALE 24 (Spring 1988).
48. Stellenbosch Report, *supra* note 22, at 52; P. WALLER, SEKTORSTUDIE MATERIELLE INFRASTRUKTUR 21–22 (Berlin: German Development Institute 1979).
49. R. MOORSOM, WALVIS BAY: NAMIBIA'S PORT 59 (1984). Text accompanying *infra* notes 50–58 draws heavily on *id.* at 69–70.

tant, because Walvis Bay could become a major terminus of trade with central Africa.[50]

Plans for a trans-Kalahari railway to an Atlantic port have been mentioned periodically since the turn of the century, first for the Rand gold mines or for the Tsumeb mine under development at that time, then for an east-west link between Rhodesia and Walvis Bay.[51] Interest in such a plan grew again in the late 1970s because of two factors. First, the mining sector in Botswana grew rapidly once vast reserves of coal were discovered. Second, the independent black-ruled frontline states of southern Africa wished to minimize their economic dependence upon South Africa. The founding declaration of SADCC, which was signed by the heads of state in Lusaka on April 1, 1980, emphasized the necessity of improving transportation to Mozambican ports and mentioned "a possible railway from Botswana through Namibia to the Atlantic Ocean, thereby creating an alternative route to the sea for Botswana, Zambia and Zimbabwe."[52]

Already in 1979, the governments of Botswana and Zambia had expressed interest in such a railway. A SADCC study of Nambia stressed the railway's significance for developing mineral deposits and agriculture in central, western, and northern Botswana.[53] A heavy-duty line through Gobabis to Walvis Bay would also permit mining of the large coal reserves that were being prospected in the early 1980s in the central part of eastern Namibia.[54] According to the SADCC study, "the link of course is dependent on Namibia's recovering Walvis Bay or building a new deepwater port."[55] As the latter alternative would be very costly and take many years to complete, Walvis Bay could become an increasingly important bargaining weapon in South Africa's attempt to retain its economic stranglehold over neighboring states to the north.

Early in 1979, Prime Minister P. W. Botha of South Africa endorsed the concept of a "constellation of independent southern African states."[56] His statement came at a time when South African–sponsored rebel groups were interfering with the main alternatives to South African harbors by preventing the reopening of the Benguela railway through Angola and making the operation of the railway and oil pipeline between Zimbabwe and the port of Beira in

50. Green, *supra* note 33, at 51.
51. *Id.* at 51; Namib Times, Sept. 3, 1975; Windhoek Advertiser, Dec. 3, 1980.
52. SADCC, SOUTHERN AFRICA: TOWARD ECONOMIC LIBERATION 5 (Lusaka 1980).
53. Windhoek Advertiser, Feb. 5, 1979; Windhoek Advertiser, May 4, 1979; Windhoek Advertiser, Nov. 30, 1979; Green, *supra* note 33 at 51.
54. Namib Times, Oct. 28, 1980; Windhoek Advertiser, Feb. 13, 1981.
55. SADCC, Namibia, background paper, Conference at Arusha, Tanzania (July 2–4, 1979), at 36–37.
56. On the notion of a constellation of states, see J. HANLON, BEGGAR YOUR NEIGHBOURS 14–15 (1986).

Mozambique difficult. On November 18, 1981, ministers from the SADCC countries meeting in Malawi "condemned South Africa's aggressive actions, in pursuance of a policy of economic destabilization directed against SADCC member states."[57] They also "directly blamed Pretoria for the destruction of bridges near Beira and of navigation aids in Beira port, saying that the latter attack had been timed to coincide with the meeting."[58] In this context, SADCC and South African interests in a trans-Kalahari railway are at odds.

A consulting firm prepared a feasibility study for a trans-Kalahari line in 1979–80, and press reports suggested that South Africa might attempt to promote Walvis Bay as a terminus.[59] Although South African government and railway administration sources discounted the idea,[60] the use of Walvis Bay would be in keeping with the South African government's strategy to remain the economic lynchpin of the southern African region.

A spokesman for South Africa's Botswana desk at the Department of Foreign Affairs said at the time that he had no knowledge of the rumored negotiations between the two governments on the proposed railway. Nevertheless, he recognized that it was "quite possible" that the frontline states were attempting to secure the proposed project to develop a transport system that was independent of South Africa, as indicated in the SADCC agreement.[61]

In an address to foreign pressmen in Gaborone in 1981 President Quett Masire of Botswana said that the railway line to link Botswana to Walvis Bay was closer to realization than in the past, as negotiations were proceeding.[62] Johannesburg radio reported that several international organizations, including the World Bank, had agreed to lend Botswana an estimated R100 million to finance construction of the railway.[63] Not only would the building of the railway create hundreds of jobs, but a planned new ore terminal at the Bay costing about $90 million would reduce the port's dependence upon the ailing fishing industry.[64]

57. Guardian, Nov. 19, 1981.

58. *Id.*

59. Windhoek Observer, Nov. 18, 1978; Windhoek Advertiser, Oct. 24, 1980; Windhoek Advertiser, Oct. 31, 1980. According to the mayor of Swakopmund, when the feasibility study was done, the firm was to establish which harbor on the Namibian coast would be most suitable. Lüderitz was never considered because of the twelve miles of sand dunes around it. The study found that Henties Bay, north of Swakopmund, had a deep enough harbor but the bay was too exposed. Swakopmund was ruled out because of its shallow harbor. The mayor added that Swakopmund would never have been suitable because of the "cost factor involved in deepening the harbour." Windhoek Advertiser, June 27, 1984.

60. Windhoek Advertiser, Oct. 30, 1979; Windhoek Advertiser, Oct. 24, 1980; Namib Times, Oct. 28, 1980.

61. Windhoek Advertiser, Dec. 24, 1980.

62. Windhoek Advertiser, Dec. 24, 1981.

63. BBC, Dec. 30, 1981.

64. New African, Oct. 1981.

In August 1984, Masire said again that his government was considering building the line.[65] A final decision about whether work on the link would begin was to be taken in July 1985.[66] Nothing occurred. In July 1986 the Advisory Committee for Transport Services in South West Africa/Namibia issued a report indicating that the construction of a trans-Kalahari railway was far in the future and questioning whether such a line would ever be built.[67] All this leaves the people of Walvis Bay and the rest of Namibia in the same state of uncertainty in which they have found themselves for decades. The consequences of this situation may be dire for the future of the international legal order.

In the modern international system, structures of power and authority continue to be weighted against change, in spite of such developments since World War II as the globalization of participation in the international community and the collapse of the earlier consensus among active participants. Whether the world community should shift to new methods of resolving disputes or whether the ICJ should adopt a novel approach to international adjudication is beyond the scope of this book. Instead, it has sought to take into account not only the narrow legal issues but also the underlying political context and historical framework of disputes. There remains the question of the appropriate legal response to the issues, however. This response should be formulated in accordance with policy needs, which may well be more acutely appreciated by those who understand the history of international law and are sympathetic to its progressive development. Jurists and international decision-makers must recognize that it is the gradual transformation of the old into the new and the competition between them that shape the development of the law.

How the international community deals with issues of import to the Third World such as that of Walvis Bay will determine the course of international law and the role of international organizations like the United Nations and the ICJ. It is hoped that through a greater understanding of the evolution of international law, positive international law will become flexible and strong enough to accommodate the development of those values espoused by the majority of states. Otherwise the disillusionment experienced by people such as those of Walvis Bay and the rest of Namibia may cause them to lose all faith in the notion of a world governed by law. The cost of such an occurrence may be catastrophic.

65. Namib Times, Aug. 14, 1984.
66. Windhoek Advertiser, June 27, 1984.
67. Namib Times, July 11, 1986.

The Penguin Islands

L ike the question of sovereignty over Walvis Bay, that of sovereignty over the Penguin Islands has become an international issue. The islands have unexploited guano deposits and offshore diamond fields. More important, control of them means control of a portion of the waters off the Namibian coast. Whereas South Africa claims that it has title to the islands, SWAPO argues that they are integral parts of Namibia and should be under Namibian sovereignty.

The History of the Penguin Islands

Although the annexation of Namaland and Damaraland was an important issue in the Cape Colony in the 1870s and 1880s, the Colony's official involvement with southwestern Africa had begun already in the 1860s with the guano islands that became known as the Penguin Islands. Tiny, uninhabited, and lacking in fresh water, these rocky islands are situated off the coast of Namibia, most of them near Lüderitz. The largest island, Possession, measures only 222 acres, and others are nothing more than rocks. All except two are within a mile of the coast, and many are within sight of shore.[1]

1. From north to south, the islands and their distances from the shore in nautical miles are Hollandsbird, or Hollamsbird (5.8751 nautical miles), Mercury (.6468), Ichaboe (.72765), Seal (.848925), Penguin (.444675), Halifax (.202125),

Western sealers first frequented the islands at the end of the eighteenth century. In the early 1840s, a sea captain from the United States discovered guano there in vast quantities.[2] Thereafter, because of the value of guano as a fertilizer, guano collectors from France, Britain, the United States, and many other countries, as well as from the Cape, converged upon the islands. By 1844, several hundred vessels had gathered in the waters around Ichaboe Island. Almost immediately, all the guano was removed and the birds were driven away.[3]

In the late 1840s, various Cape Town firms sent caretakers to the islands to ensure that no one disturbed the birds during the mating and breeding seasons. By 1861, the amount of guano deposited annually had reached a value of £20 thousand.[4] The increasing supply brought many new collectors at sweeping season. Intent on maintaining their monopoly, the Cape Town firms that had been cultivating the guano claimed the area, and their representatives armed themselves with revolvers. Newcomers believed that since the islands belonged to no state, all collectors should have equal rights.[5] They, too, armed themselves, and various violent incidents occurred.

Rear Admiral Sir Henry Keppel, the naval commander in chief at the Cape, who was under much pressure from the Cape Town firms, feared that the lure of profits would prompt France to annex the islands, thereby giving it a permanent presence in the waters just beyond the borders of the Cape Colony. He urged the Cape to annex the islands.[6] In part to prevent French intervention and end the violence among collectors but mainly to gain control of this valuable resource, the captain of a British frigate took possession of Ichaboe Island on June 21, 1861.[7] Thirteen years elapsed before all twelve islands were formally annexed to the Cape.

Once the frigate captain's actions became known, a number of Cape Town guano collectors pressured Cape Governor Sir George Grey to annex "certain small Islands adjacent to Ichaboe."[8] On August 12, Grey issued a

Long (North .1617 and South .202125), Possession (1.334025), Albatross (.6468), Pomona (.08085), Plumpudding (.282975), and Sinclair's (.121275). Figures furnished by Michael Dulka, U.N. Map Librarian.

2. *See* B. MORRELL, MORRELL'S NARRATIVE OF A VOYAGE TO THE SOUTH AND WEST COAST OF AFRICA (London 1844); *see also* T. EDEN, THE SEARCH FOR NITRE, AND THE TRUE NATURE OF GUANO, BEING AN ACCOUNT OF A VOYAGE TO THE SOUTH-WEST COAST OF AFRICA (London 1846).

3. G.H. 1/282, Letter from Rear Admiral Sir H. Keppel to Captain Eden, Jan. 1, 1861 (KAB).

4. *Id.*

5. *Id.*

6. *Id.*

7. Act No. 4 of 1874, Cape of Good Hope.

8. Proc. 53 of 1861. G.H. 31/9, No. 156 of Dec. 18, 1863 (KAB).

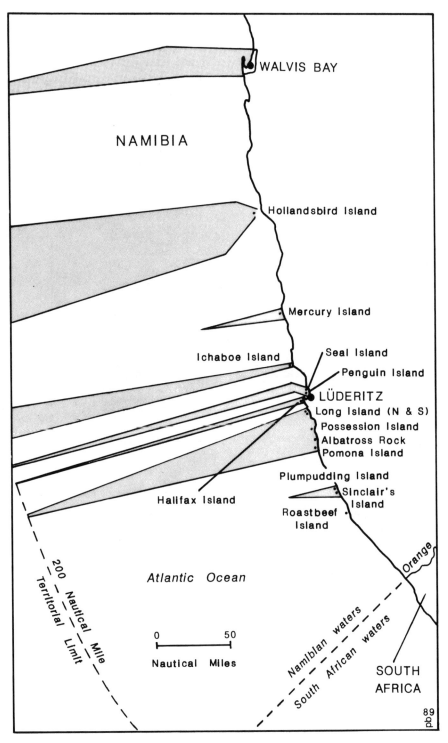

WALVIS BAY

NAMIBIA

Hollandsbird Island

Mercury Island

Ichaboe Island

Seal Island

Penguin Island

LÜDERITZ

Long Island (N & S)

Possession Island

Albatross Rock

Pomona Island

Plumpudding Island

Sinclair's Island

Halifax Island

Roastbeef Island

200 Nautical Mile Territorial Limit

Atlantic Ocean

Orange

Namibian waters

South African waters

SOUTH AFRICA

0   50

Nautical Miles

89 pb

Map 6. The Penguin Islands and fishery zones claimed by South Africa. (Roastbeef Island is not one of the Penguin Islands.)

proclamation declaring British sovereignty over Ichaboe and "certain Islands, Islets or Rocks on the coast of Africa, adjacent to the said Island of Ichaboe, that is: Hollandsbird, Mercury, Long Island, Sea Island, Penguin Island, Halifax, Possession, Albatross Rock, Pomona, Plum-pudding and Roast-beef or Sinclair's Island, and that such Proclamation should be subject to Her Majesty's gracious confirmation or disallowance."[9] Immediately thereafter, Grey left for New Zealand. The Cape authorities never reported the proclamation to the home government, and the sovereign never confirmed the annexation.

That the annexation had not been reported or confirmed escaped the attention of the Cape government until 1863, when a U.S. vessel took possession of a quantity of coal from Penguin Island and one of its officers murdered the unarmed chief officer of a Cape Town vessel.[10]

Sir Philip Wodehouse, Grey's successor, believed at first that a direct infringement of British rights had occurred. Upon discovering, however, that Grey's proclamation of 1861 had been neither reported nor confirmed, he consulted the home government, which repudiated Grey's annexation and maintained that because the islands were not British possessions, there had been no violation of British territory.[11] Although Britain demanded compensation from the United States, it was concerned not to become embroiled in a serious dispute on that account. Acting on instructions from London, Wodehouse issued a proclamation on May 9, 1864, indicating that Grey's proclamation of 1861, "having been recently brought to the notice of Her Majesty's Government, Her Majesty has disallowed the same, and that the several Islands, Islets and Rocks referred to in it, are not to be viewed as British Territory."[12]

The Cape guano merchants were still determined to have Britain annex the islands and made this known to the Cape authorities. Hence, in the same despatch in which Wodehouse reported the publication of his May 9 proclamation, he called upon the British government to reconsider its decision.[13] He reported that his government had leased the islands to some of the guano merchants and that they would undoubtedly demand compensation if he rescinded the leases in light of the proclamation.

9. G.70–'84 at 4. Native Affairs Blue Book, 1884–87, Papers and Correspondence Respecting Angra Pequina and Walwich Bay Territory.

10. The altercation is described in detail in G.H. 31/9, No. 156 of Dec. 18, 1863, and G.H. 1/11, No. 743 of Mar. 1, 1864.

11. Proc. 27 of 1864.

12. G.H. 1/11, No. 743 of Mar. 1, 1864.

13. G.H. 31/9, No. 31 of May 16, 1864.

The reply from London rejected any idea of annexation and indicated that, as for claims by the Cape guano merchants, the duty of compensation would "devolve on the Colonial government which annexed the Islands without either previous authority or subsequent report."[14] In December 1864, Wodehouse again called for annexation in a despatch to London.[15] He wrote that he had settled the compensation question by extending the lease of Ichaboe but that the merchants were unhappy because they claimed that guano from that island was fit for sale only when mixed with guano from the other islands. The merchants were thus determined to maintain their establishments on the islands and repel the intrusion of others. Wodehouse concluded his despatch by calling upon the home government yet again to reconsider its decision.

Since problems with the United States had been averted, the British government this time considered Wodehouse's petition. Believing that defense of the islands would not overburden the naval squadron at the Cape and that the islands' lessees were willing to protect them in peacetime as long as they could obtain valid leases, the home government sanctioned the annexation of the Penguin Islands to the Cape. Accordingly, on May 5, 1866, the captain of HMS *Valorous* took possession in the name of Queen Victoria of "Hollandsbird, Mercury, Long Island, Seal Island, Penguin Island, Halifax, Possession, Albatross Rock, Pomona, Plum-pudding and Roast-beef or Sinclair's Island, as well as the harbour commonly known as the Angra Pequina."[16] The Cape governor issued a proclamation on July 16, 1866, annexing the islands, including Ichaboe, but not the harbor to the Cape.[17] On February 27, 1867, letters patent issued in London after the law officers of the Crown determined that the annexation by proclamation alone was not valid.[18]

The Cape legislature attempted in 1873 to annex the islands through Act No. 1 of 1873.[19] This act was, however, incorrectly based upon the questionable proclamation of 1866 instead of upon the letters patent of 1867. Consequently, the British government objected to the act because it did not mention the letters patent.[20] The Cape Parliament, acting in accordance with the letters patent, then passed an enabling act on July 6, 1874.[21] Four days later, the

14. G.H. 1/11, No. 775 of July 5, 1864.
15. G.H. 31/9, No. 122 of Dec. 9, 1864.
16. G.70–'84 at 4. Native Affairs Blue Book, 1884–87. Papers and Correspondence Respecting Angra Pequina and Walwich Bay Territory.
17. Proc. 66 of 1866.
18. Act No. 4 of 1867 (Cape of Good Hope).
19. Act No. 1 of 1873 (Cape of Good Hope).
20. G.H. 1/20, No. 410 of Sept. 30, 1873; G.H. 1/20, No. 435 of Dec. 20, 1873.
21. Act No. 4 of 1874 (Cape of Good Hope).

governor proclaimed the annexation of the twelve islands to the Cape,[22] which administered them from that time.

By the end of the nineteenth century, years of collecting had greatly reduced the guano to be retrieved. By then, however, in the midst of Britain's dispute with Germany over the delimitation of the southern boundary of Walvis Bay, three questions had arisen about control of the Penguin Islands. First, Seal Island and Penguin Island sit right at the entrance to the Lüderitz harbor. As Britain controlled Walvis Bay, Germany was keen to develop an alternate harbor.[23] Swakopmund had not been a great success, so Germany turned its attention to Lüderitz, even though it recognized that a developed Lüderitz could never rival Walvis Bay. The German authorities hoped that the two islands and the harbor could be linked in a harbor development scheme.[24] Fearing that such a scheme would undermine British economic control of South West Africa, Britain refused to relinquish control of the two islands.[25]

Second, because Germany was determined to obtain as much of South West Africa's territorial waters as it could, it questioned the wording of the various proclamations that referred to Roastbeef or Sinclair's Island.[26] The German government noted that these were in fact two separate islands and demanded to know which Britain claimed. Britain decided that it had title to Sinclair's Island and relinquished any claim to Roastbeef.[27]

Third, and most important, Germany demanded that the territorial waters around the islands be delimited so that the extent of British rights in the area could be determined precisely. Both sides made proposals for the apportionment of the territorial waters.[28] The question was still unresolved in 1915, when South African forces invaded South West Africa during the First World War.

After 1896, the islands fell first under the jurisdiction of the state guano department in Cape Town and later under the Department of Sea Fisheries in Cape Town, which from 1976 leased the islands to private concerns. Administrators were present on some of the larger islands at best intermittently, and

22. Proc. of 1874.

23. *See supra* chapter 3 at 61.

24. LDE 3667 (5403), Letter from British Consul for German South West Africa, Lüderitzbucht, July 21, 1911 (Central Archives, Pretoria) [hereinafter referred to as SAB].

25. *Id.*; GG 278 (4/123), Acting Governor-General to Vice-Admiral P. W. Bush, Oct. 21, 1912 (SAB).

26. GG 278 (4/164), German Ambassador, Feb. 24, 1913 (SAB).

27. GG 278 (4/175), Minute 229, Nov. 27, 1914 (SAB); GG 278 (4/164), Confidential Dispatch from Secretary of State, Sept. 30, 1913 (SAB).

28. SWAA A.I.b.9, Abschrift K.A. II 2492/08, Auswärtiges Amt, No. II.S.4357.59510; Abschrift II.S.4357 (WA).

guano collectors' annual visits lasted only a few months. The smaller islands ceased to be used. By 1987, only Mercury and Ichaboe were still being exploited for guano by a private firm.[29]

The Penguin Islands were never mentioned in any of the laws applied to Walvis Bay or to Namibia. Official South West African publications did not refer to them until the mid-1970s, when the issue of Namibian independence occupied international attention. The *South West Africa Survey,* for example, made no mention of the islands in 1967. In 1974 it pointed out only that "certain islands along the coast of SWA are also part of the Republic of South Africa."[30] In South Africa, Union yearbooks never mentioned the islands.[31] Even after South Africa became a republic, there was no difference. By 1987, the Penguin Islands had never been mentioned in the physical description of the Republic, though Prince Edward Island and the Marion Islands, twelve hundred miles southeast of Cape Town, were.[32] The chapter on marine fisheries indicated only that guano "is collected from a number of islands and artificial platforms along the coast."[33] Presumably, this referred only to the guano islands in the waters off the coast of the Republic. Maps in South West African and South African official publications never indicated the Penguin Islands.[34] Other official and quasi-official publications also omitted them. For example, none of the maps in the *Atlas of the Union of South Africa* of 1959, published by the University of Cape Town geography department in conjunction with the South African Council for Educational, Sociological, and Humanistic Research, portrayed the islands.[35]

Only two islands were being exploited for guano by 1987, and the economic benefits accruing to South Africa from them were small. There was

29. Financial Gazette, July 1, 1977; Windhoek Advertiser, Aug. 13, 1982; Windhoek Advertiser, June 1, 1983; Interviews with staff members, Department of Sea Fisheries, Cape Town, July 1986.

30. *Compare* REPUBLIC OF SOUTH AFRICA, DEPARTMENT OF INFORMATION, SOUTH WEST AFRICA SURVEY 1967 *with* REPUBLIC OF SOUTH AFRICA, DEPARTMENT OF INFORMATION, SOUTH WEST AFRICA SURVEY 1974 at 3.

31. *See, e.g.,* UNION OF SOUTH AFRICA, UNION OFFICE OF CENSUS AND STATISTICS, OFFICIAL YEAR BOOKS OF THE UNION AND OF BASUTOLAND, BECHUANALAND PROTECTORATE, AND SWAZILAND 1922–60 [hereinafter cited as UNION YEARBOOKS].

32. *See, e.g.,* REPUBLIC OF SOUTH AFRICA, DEPARTMENT OF FOREIGN AFFAIRS, SOUTH AFRICA 1988. OFFICIAL YEARBOOK OF THE REPUBLIC OF SOUTH AFRICA 1987–88.

33. *See, e.g., id.* at 646.

34. *See, e.g.,* UNION YEARBOOKS, 1922–60, *supra* note 30; REPUBLIC OF SOUTH AFRICA, DEPARTMENT OF FOREIGN AFFAIRS, OFFICIAL YEARBOOKS, 1973–87; REPUBLIC OF SOUTH AFRICA, DEPARTMENT OF INFORMATION, SOUTH WEST AFRICA SURVEYS, 1967–87.

35. UNIVERSITY OF CAPE TOWN, DEPARTMENT OF GEOGRAPHY, & SOUTH AFRICAN COUNCIL FOR EDUCATIONAL, SOCIOLOGICAL, AND HUMANISTIC RESEARCH, ATLAS OF THE UNION OF SOUTH AFRICA (1959).

apparently some diamond prospecting. Island Diamonds, a subsidiary of the South African corporate giant De Beers, reportedly conducted these operations, but the extent of its activities remained unknown.[36] The real value of the islands appeared to lie, just as it had for Britain against Germany, in the stake they gave South Africa in the waters off the Namibian coast.

Territorial Waters

In the late nineteenth century and well into the twentieth, the Cape Colony and later the Union and Republic of South Africa adhered to the British view that their territorial waters extended for three nautical miles from the low-water mark on the coast.[37] After its invasion of German South West Africa in 1915, South Africa made no distinction between South African and South West African waters. Then, following a worldwide trend, the South African Territorial Waters Act of 1963 made provision for a territorial sea of six nautical miles and a fishery zone of twelve nautical miles.[38] The act defined the Republic to include "the territory of South-West Africa."[39]

Again in line with an international trend, the South African government amended the act in July 1977 to extend South African territorial waters to twelve nautical miles and the fishery zone to two hundred nautical miles.[40] The new act, which omitted the definition of the Republic, specifically indicated that it would leave Namibian waters as they had been under the act of 1963. Proclamation 234 of 1977, promulgated some three weeks after Proclamation R202 transferred the administration of Walvis Bay to Cape Town, set a date of November 30 for the act of 1977 to become effective. A press report from the South African government indicated that the new limits would apply to Walvis Bay but not to South West Africa.[41] It made no mention of the Penguin Islands. In 1979, a proclamation of the South West African administrator applied the new South African limits to Namibian territorial waters.[42] Thus, the preexisting unity was reestablished de jure.

Although the South African government did not mention the Penguin

36. Financial Gazette, July 1, 1977; Sunday Express, Aug. 15, 1982.

37. Stassen, *South Africa's Jurisdictional Claims to Areas of the Sea*, 3 S. AFR. Y.B. INT'L L. 149 (1977). On the law of the sea, see generally D. O'CONNELL, THE INTERNATIONAL LAW OF THE SEA (2 vols. 1982, 1984).

38. Act 87 of 1963.

39. *Id.*

40. Territorial Waters Amendment Act, No. 98 of 1977. On 200-mile zones, see generally Hollick, *The Origins of 200-Mile Offshore Zones*, 71 AM. J. INT'L L. 494 (1977).

41. South Africa: In Brief, Territorial Waters, Johannesburg in English for Abroad, 2100 GMT, Sept. 23, 1977; BBC, Sept. 26, 1977; *see* Stassen, *supra* note 37, at 152–53.

42. Windhoek Advertiser, Nov. 6, 1979; Namib Times, Nov. 6, 1979.

Islands at the time of the 1977 act, in 1980 it stated that because the islands were South African, the South African limits applied;[43] these were restricted only by the rules of international law concerning the regime of islands and the apportionment of the waters surrounding such islands. In 1982, a South African fisheries spokesman said, "There can be no doubt that the islands belong to South Africa, and that each has its own claims to territorial and fishing rights."[44] According to Piet Kruger, the South West African secretary for economic affairs, however, even though South Africa had charts tracing the precise boundaries of the claimed offshore zones, it was not enforcing the distinction between South African and Namibian zones for practical reasons.[45] Instead, until Namibian independence, South Africa would regard them as Namibia's territorial and fishing waters. Various South African officials confirmed Kruger's statement and agreed with him that after Namibia gained independence, the situation would have to change.[46] By 1987, the delimitation of these boundaries had been much studied in South African government circles. Information about the precise delimitation as envisioned by the South African authorities remained classified, but it was reported to be 20 percent, including the waters off Walvis Bay.[47] This meant dividing the territorial waters and fishery zones from Walvis Bay south into alternating sections of South African and Namibian waters.

By then, however, South Africa's claims to the Penguin Islands and a percentage of the waters off the Namibian coast were the subject of international controversy.

The Dispute

Prime Minister Vorster of South Africa first raised the issue of the Penguin Islands in June 1977 when he spoke in the South African Parliament during the debate on the South West Africa Constitution Amendment Bill.[48] The

43. Windhoek Advertiser, May 30, 1980.
44. Windhoek Advertiser, Aug. 13, 1982.
45. *Id.*
46. *Id.*
47. Windhoek Advertiser, Aug. 13, 1982; Interview with Albert Hoffmann, Legal Division, South African Department of Foreign Affairs, Pretoria, Aug. 1986.
48. Republic of South Africa, House of Assembly Debates, June 14, 1977, cols. 10126–27. Vorster stated: "Nor was it Walvis Bay that was never part of the mandated territory. There are islands along the coast of South West Africa as well, which belong to South Africa, and similarly, they, too, were never part of the mandated territory. In 1861 they were partially and in 1866 finally annexed by the British as such. The territories were de-annexed and, as in the case of Walvis Bay, the British transferred them to the Cape. There are many such territories. I shall mention the following: Mercury, Bird, Long Island, Soal [*sic*], Penguin [*sic*], Halifax, Possession, Albatross,

following month, South Africa passed the amendment to the Territorial Waters Act, which took effect in November that year, a month and a half after the publication of Proclamation R202 regarding the administration of Walvis Bay.

In early May 1980, a Council for Namibia Mission of Consultation visited Barbados to discuss with that country's officials the recent developments in Namibia. A joint communiqué issued by the government of Barbados and the council reaffirmed support for Security Council Resolution 432 on Walvis Bay and insisted that Namibia become independent with its territorial integrity preserved. It then condemned South African "bantustanization policies, its practice of *apartheid,* its declaration of an economic zone for Namibia, and its claim to sovereignty over several islands including the Penguin Islands, which are an integral part of the Territory of Namibia."[49] The communiqué also deplored the plundering of Namibia's resources by South Africa and its allies in defiance of Council for Namibia Decree No. 1 of 1974. Later that month, another Council for Namibia Mission of Consultation visited Guyana. A joint communiqué issued by the council and the Guyanese government adhered to the views contained in the earlier communiqué.[50]

In response, on May 29 the South African representative to the United Nations sent a letter to the U.N. secretary-general outlining South Africa's position, which was based entirely upon the chain of title events. The document maintained that the Penguin Islands "are South African territory and South Africa exercises full sovereignty over these islands."[51]

The following month, the Council for Namibia criticized South Africa's interference in Namibia's territorial waters. The U.N. General Assembly responded to the South African claim on March 16, 1981, by passing Resolution 35/227, "*strongly condemning* as an act of colonial expansion the decision of South Africa to annex Walvis Bay and to claim sovereignty over the Penguin and other offshore islands, thereby undermining the unity and territorial integrity of Namibia."[52] The resolution also reaffirmed the Namibian people's right to self-determination in a "united Namibia, including Walvis Bay and the Penguin and other off-shore islands" and indicated that since the islands "are an integral part of Namibia . . . any decision by South Africa to

Pomona, Plum Pudding and Roast Beef. . . . [Interjections.] I want to make it very clear that 'Plum Pudding,' 'Roast Beef' and all those territories are South African property. There should be no doubt whatsoever about this. I am mentioning this specifically because there are signs—at this stage I am putting it no higher than this—that certain circles will dispute South Africa's ownership of Walvis Bay and, if need be, the islands as well. South Africa will not and cannot accept this under any circumstances."

49. Council for Namibia, NAM/502, May 12, 1980.

50. Council for Namibia, NAM/508, May 21, 1980.

51. South African Permanent Representative to the United Nations to United Nations Secretary-General, May 29, 1980, S/13968 [hereinafter cited as South African Letter].

52. U.N. GAOR Res. 35/227 (1981) [emphasis in original].

claim sovereignty over those islands is illegal, null and void." SWAPO also condemned South African assertions of sovereignty over the islands. On November 4, 1981, for example, SWAPO's secretary-general stated that "SWAPO would not accept a Namibia without Walvis Bay and the Penguin Islands."[53]

As in the controversy over Walvis Bay, South Africa and SWAPO and their respective supporters framed their arguments in legal terms.

The Arguments of the Parties

The South African government restricted its position, articulated in the letter to the U.N. secretary-general, to a recitation of the chain of title events and stressed that Germany had recognized British sovereignty over the Penguin Islands at the end of the nineteenth century.[54] Implied in the argument of its supporters was that because South Africa had valid title to Walvis Bay and the islands, only the extent of South Africa's waters remained to be determined.[55]

SWAPO confined its position to broad legal principles, as did the Council for Namibia.[56] In 1987, no writers sympathetic to SWAPO had yet examined the question.[57] As in the case of Walvis Bay, the shift in theory and practice from a colonialist legal order to the modern legal order has had various consequences for the Penguin Islands and for the delimitation of the waters off the Namibian coast.

Changing Concepts of Sovereignty

The Colonialist Heritage
International law has long held that islands within the territorial waters of a state belong to that state.[58] Therefore, prior to their annexation, all of the

53. BBC, Nov. 6, 1981.

54. South African Letter, *supra* note 51, Annexure. The letter fell prey to the nineteenth-century confusion and incorrectly referred to Sinclair's and Roastbeef as one island. Roastbeef, which is not claimed by South Africa, is some 48 miles south of Sinclair's Island. *See supra* notes 26–27 and accompanying text. The November 1988 press release from the Permanent Mission of South Africa to the United Nations about Walvis Bay reiterated South Africa's chain of title argument regarding the islands but contained inaccuracies. It claimed that "Ichaboe, the Penguin Islands and eleven others were also annexed by Britain in 1861 and 1866 respectively. Sovereignty over this entire group was transferred to the Cape Colony in 1874. In 1910 . . . the islands became part of South Africa and remain so to this day." Republic of South Africa, Permanent Mission to the United Nations, Question of Walvis Bay, Press Release 29/88, Nov. 18, 1988. *See also supra* chapter 10, note 21 and accompanying text.

55. Stassen, *supra* note 37, at 152–53.

56. *See, e.g., supra* note 53 and accompanying text.

57. Although not addressing the islands, one article on Walvis Bay indicated that some of its arguments regarding the Bay might apply to them. Goeckner & Gunning, *Namibia, South Africa, and the Walvis Bay Dispute,* 89 YALE L.J. 903, n.2 (1980).

58. K. JAYARAMAN, LEGAL REGIME OF ISLANDS (1982).

Penguin Islands except for one, which was within the three-mile limit existing then, would automatically have fallen within the jurisdiction of a Namibian state. At that time, however, there existed no coastal state recognized under the prevailing standards of international law. Britain and the Cape had, in the case of all the islands, valid annexation of terra nullius. Lüderitz's initial claim to the islands notwithstanding, Germany ultimately recognized them as British.

The Modern International Legal Order
As the right of self-determination of peoples has become part of the jus cogens under modern international law,[59] the U.N. General Assembly must safeguard this right as it oversees Namibian independence. The question is whether the Namibian unit of decolonization includes the Penguin Islands and the waters surrounding them. In the case of the islands, the concepts of both intertemporal law and international estoppel defeat South Africa's claim. Hence, the unit of decolonization includes the Penguin Islands.

Intertemporal Law
According to the concept of intertemporal law, the original title to territory may lapse or become invalid through the operation of new applicable law, such as the law of decolonization. In the case of the Penguin Islands, the new law of decolonization that arises from the right of self-determination displaces South Africa's claim to the Penguin Islands, which is based upon nineteenth-century colonialist rules governing the acquisition of territories. By 1980, when the dispute arose, the right to self-determination was a basic right of customary international law and formed part of the jus cogens. Since any right, transaction, or benefit that violates the jus cogens is null and void, the new law of decolonization and SWAPO's claim based upon it supersede South Africa's claims of sovereignty to the Penguin Islands. As in the case of Walvis Bay, the doctrine of uti possidetis, which allows colonial boundaries to stand after the end of colonialism, does not negate the doctrine of intertemporal law. A secondary colonial state like South Africa cannot rely upon uti possidetis to mask its breach of the jus cogens through its disregard for the right of self-determination.

Estoppel
The three elements necessary to satisfy estoppel are that (1) a state party, aware of a right that could be enforced, must choose not to assert it or must assert it ineffectively; (2) the party must know that its nonassertion or ineffec-

59. *See supra* chapter 8 at 146–50.

tive assertion may be interpreted as an abandonment of the right; and (3) the party must induce other parties to rely on the nonassertion or ineffective assertion of the right sufficiently so that belated enforcement would prejudice or harm them.

Once South Africa invaded South West Africa, although it collected guano from the Penguin Islands, it did not attempt to distinguish between the territorial waters of South Africa and South West Africa. In keeping with its designs on incorporating the mandated territory into South Africa, it interpreted the definition of South Africa's territorial waters to include South West Africa. Meanwhile, quotas for fishing in the waters off the Namibian coast were set by the authorities in Windhoek, with no distinction made for South African waters off Walvis Bay or the islands. With the exception of occasional guano collectors, who by 1987 were visiting only two islands, Namibian fishermen depended on the islands and the waters around them for fish and other marine resources. South African authorities made no attempt at that time to interfere with their activities or to assert claims to the islands. Indeed, Namibian fishermen centered at Lüderitz reported in 1986 that they "knew nothing" about South Africa's claims to any of the islands and that they "always used them as part of South West."[60]

South Africa did not feel that its actions were threatening its title to the islands and its access to the surrounding waters. Rather, it believed that treating the islands and their territorial waters as part of Namibia was but a preliminary step to eventually incorporating all of Namibia into South Africa. Since misimpressions do not negate actions that satisfy the first condition of estoppel, South Africa must bear responsibility for the consequences of its actions.

The first condition of estoppel is thus satisfied by South Africa's failure to assert its rights to the islands and the surrounding waters. In addition, because it failed to establish firm claims to the islands and the waters, South Africa knew that Namibian residents would interpret its nonassertion or ineffective assertion of its rights to the Bay as an abandonment of that right. Hence, the second criterion of estoppel is satisfied. South Africa should have recognized that its acknowledgments by deed of the integration into Namibia of the islands and the waters surrounding them indicated to the world openly and obviously that the integration was permanent. In this regard, the standard of proof in international law is notoriety. Here South Africa's failure to stop Namibians from exploiting the resources was so notorious that it should have known others would think it had abandoned the right. The failure to attempt to

60. Interviews with fishermen, Lüderitz, Mar. 1986.

stop the Namibian fishermen who were exploiting what they believed were Namibia's resources constitutes notorious action and outweighs contrary assertions of sovereignty that appeared in the late 1970s and 1980s as the controversy over South Africa's continuing administration of Namibia received increasing international attention.

The Namibian fishermen's reliance to their detriment upon the apparent integration satisfies the third element of estoppel, namely, that a party must induce other parties to rely upon the nonassertion or ineffectiveness of its right sufficiently that belated enforcement would prejudice or harm them. In this case, if there is belated enforcement, Namibian fishermen, who are already suffering, would be forced to curtail their operations even further. Thus, South Africa is estopped from asserting claims to the Penguin Islands.

Additional Factors

As with Walvis Bay, quasi-legal factors also support the notion that the Penguin Islands and the surrounding waters are part of Namibia. The U.N. General Assembly should concern itself with creating an economically viable Namibia. The prospects for doing so are diminished as long as South Africa retains control of the islands and the surrounding waters, because that will leave a portion of the waters off the Namibian coast in South African hands and will divide Namibia's southern waters into alternating South African and Namibian zones. South African naval superiority will then be a major factor. South Africa may disregard Namibian efforts to limit exploitation of resources in Namibian waters. It may also disrupt the Namibian fishing industry and interfere with all Namibia's efforts to control its southern waters. In addition, with two of the Penguin Islands at the entrance to Lüderitz harbor, South Africa can easily interfere with any Namibian fishing interests or naval operations centered there.

As in the case of the Bay, the application of the legal and quasi-legal concepts discussed here indicates that South Africa's claims to sovereignty over the Penguin Islands fail under modern international law.

Chronology

Millennia B.C. Nama-speaking people living in Namibia

Before A.D. 300 Herero-speaking people living in Namibia

1652 Dutch East India Company founds a refreshment station at the Cape of Good Hope

1793 Duminy attempts to annex Walvis Bay for the Dutch

1795 Britain takes the Cape Colony from the Dutch

1796 Alexander attempts to annex Walvis Bay for Britain

1803 Batavian Republic (Dutch) regains the Cape

1806 Britain reconquers the Cape

1840s Guano collectors converge upon the Penguin Islands

1852–54 Britain recognizes the South African Republic (Transvaal) and the Orange Free State as independent Boer states

1863–70 The war of the Missionaries and Traders in Damaraland and Namaland

1870 Peace Treaty of Okahandja

1872 Kamaherero sends a request for protection to the Cape governor

1874 Kamaherero sends a second request for protection to the Cape governor

Penguin Islands annexed to the Cape

1876 Palgrave's journey to Namaland and Damaraland as special commissioner

Palgrave-Herero Agreement (treaty establishing a protectorate)

1877 Britain annexes the Transvaal

1878 Dyer issues a proclamation at Walvis Bay, taking possession of the Walvis Bay territory in the name of Queen Victoria (Walvis Bay annexed to Her Majesty's dominions)

British letters patent issued (permitting the annexation of Walvis Bay to the Cape Colony)

1880–81 Transvaal Afrikaners regain independence in the First Boer War

1884 Germany declares a protectorate over South West Africa
Governor of the Cape, acting under authority of the letters patent, annexes Walvis Bay to the Cape Colony

1899–1902 Britain conquers the Boer republics in the Second Boer War

1910 Cape Colony, the Transvaal, Natal, and the Orange Free State form the Union of South Africa, a white-ruled, self-governing British dominion

1912 Founding of the African National Congress (ANC)

1914 South Africa enters the First World War as a member of the British Empire

1915 South Africa invades German South West Africa
Proclamation of martial law treats Walvis Bay as part of South West Africa

1919 Treaty of Versailles strips Germany of South West Africa
First Pan-African Congress

1920 South West Africa entrusted to South Africa as League of Nations C mandate

1921 Second Pan-African Congress

1922 Three related laws link Walvis Bay to South West Africa
Bondelswart massacre

1923 Third Pan-African Congress

1925 Rehoboth affair

1927 Fourth Pan-African Congress

1935 Italy invades Ethiopia

1939 South Africa enters World War II on the side of the Allies

1945 Founding of the United Nations
Fifth Pan-African Congress

1948 National Party comes to power in South Africa

1949 South Africa refuses to submit further reports on South West Africa to the United Nations

1950 *South West Africa (International Status)* case before the International Court of Justice (ICJ)

1955 *South West Africa (Voting Procedure)* case before the ICJ

1956 *South West Africa (Hearing of Petitioners)* case before the ICJ

1960 South West Africa People's Organization (SWAPO) founded
United Nations General Assembly Resolution 1514, the Declaration on the Granting of Independence to Colonial Countries and Peoples

1961 South Africa becomes a republic and leaves the Commonwealth

1962 *Ethiopia and Liberia v. South Africa (First Phase)* before the ICJ

1963 South African Territorial Waters Act

1964 Publication of the Odendaal Report
1966 *Ethiopia and Liberia v. South Africa (Second Phase)* before the ICJ
SWAPO begins armed struggle
U.N. General Assembly Resolution 2145 terminates mandate over
South West Africa
General Assembly issues the Covenant on Civil and Political Rights
and the Covenant on Economic and Social Rights
1967 U.N. Council for Namibia established
1968 General Assembly changes name of South West Africa to Namibia at
SWAPO's request
1969 U.N. Security Council endorses termination of the mandate
1970 Security Council Resolution 276 declares South African occupation
of Namibia illegal
General Assembly issues the Programme of Action for the Full
Implementation of the Declaration on the Granting of Independence
to Colonial Countries and Peoples
General Assembly issues the Declaration on Principles of International Law Concerning Friendly Relations and Cooperation Among
States in Accordance with the Charter of the United Nations
1971 *Namibia (Advisory) Opinion* rendered by the ICJ (Security Council
resolution binding and states must not recognize South African
occupation)
1973 General Assembly recognizes SWAPO as the authentic representative
of the Namibian people

1975–76 Angola and Mozambique become independent states and join the
United Nations
1976 Security Council Resolution 385 on United Nations–supervised
elections in Namibia
1977 South African amends the Territorial Waters Act of 1963
Proclamation R202 transfers the administration of Walvis Bay from
Windhoek to the Cape
South African–appointed administrator of South West Africa takes
office
Proclamation 234 puts the Territorial Waters Act as amended into
force
General Assembly Resolution 32/9 condemns South African actions
regarding Walvis Bay
Certain discriminatory legislation repealed in Namibia
1978 Security Council Resolution 432 supports the "reintegration of
Walvis Bay within its territory"
Security Council Resolution 435 on independence plan for Namibia
South African–controlled internal elections in Namibia; Democratic

Turnhalle Alliance wins 41 of 50 seats
1980 Zimbabwe becomes independent and joins the United Nations
South African letter to U.N. secretary-general regarding South
Africa's claims to the Penguin Islands
Council for Namibia issues the Algiers Declaration, condemning
South African interference in Namibian territorial waters
1981 General Assembly Resolution 35/227 condemns South Africa's
claims of sovereignty over the Penguin Islands
1983 South West African National Assembly dissolved; South African–
appointed administrator becomes sole ruler of South West Africa
1984 New constitution in South Africa gives Coloureds and Asians but not
Africans limited participation in South African political system
1985 Transitional Government of National Unity takes power in Windhoek
1986 Nationwide state of emergency declared in South Africa
1987 South Africa renews nationwide state of emergency
1988 South Africa renews nationwide state of emergency
Accord reached on Namibian independence
1989 Namibian independence process begins
South Africa renews nationwide state of emergency
Namibian elections occur

Index